STIGMA REVISITED

ST/GMA REVISITED

IMPLICATIONS OF THE MARK

edited by

Stacey Hannem and Chris Bruckert

University of Ottawa Press
Ottawa

University of Ottawa Press
542 King Edward Avenue
Ottawa, ON K1N 6N5
www.press.uottawa.ca

The University of Ottawa Press acknowledges with gratitude the support extended to its publishing list by Heritage Canada through the Canada Book Fund, by the Canada Council for the Arts, by the Federation for the Humanities and Social Sciences through the Awards to Scholarly Publications Program, by the Social Sciences and Humanities Research Council, and by the University of Ottawa.

We also gratefuly acknowledge the Department of Social Sciences at the University of Ottawa and the Research Services at Wilfrid Laurier University, whose financial support has contributed to the publication of this book.

Library and Archives Canada Cataloguing in Publication

Stigma revisited : implications of the mark / edited by Stacey Hannem and Chris Bruckert.

Includes bibliographical references and index.
Issued also in electronic formats.
ISBN 978-0-7766-0783-2

1. Stigma (Social psychology) 2. Stereotypes (Social psychology). 3. Marginality, Social. I. Bruckert, Chris, 1960- II. Hannem, Stacey, 1979-

HM1096.S75 2012 303.3'85 C2012-904326-5

This book is dedicated to our sons:

Jonathan and *Samuel*; *Benjamin* and *Simon*

With your very existence, you affirm the need to fight for social justice.

Contents

Acknowledgements

We would like to thank the people who have contributed to the creation of this volume:

- First, and foremost, we thank the participants in the various research projects presented in this book who took the time and gave of themselves to share their stories with us. We hope that we have done justice to your experiences and that your voices ring true in these pages.
- Bob Gaucher for your enthusiasm and support for this project and, more broadly, for the role you have played as an inspirational teacher and mentor to each of us.
- The contributors, who shared our vision to attend to the voices of the subjects, and each brought unique insights to this collection.
- The two anonymous reviewers who painstakingly took the time to comment on this manuscript. Your insights were invaluable.
- The editors and staff at the University of Ottawa Press for their hard work and assistance.
- Wendy and Tom Greenlaw, who opened their home to us, allowing us the time to edit the final draft of the manuscript.
- Wilfrid Laurier University and the Faculty of Social Sciences at the University of Ottawa for providing grants that make the publication of this volume possible.

Stacey would like to thank:

- My PhD committee at Carleton University: Aaron Doyle, Flo Kellner, and Catherine Kelly, for their comments on early versions of the material presented in this book. You have each in your own way pushed me to be a better scholar, and I am grateful.

- Michael Petrunik, who grounded me in the Chicago school, gave me a passion for sociological theory, and taught me to make good coffee. All of your lessons have been invaluable to this project.
- My parents, John and Merri-Sue Hannem, for teaching me at a young age to have compassion for the challenges that others face, and for their unconditional love and encouragement.
- My partner, Christopher Greenlaw, for supporting me unconditionally and having faith that this book would actually get finished; and my children, Jonathan and Samuel, who bring joy to my life every day. I love you.
- Last, but certainly not least, Chris Bruckert. You have taught me so much as a teacher, a mentor, and a friend. Thank you for seeing the potential in this project and for your hard work; it could never have happened without you!

Chris would like to thank:

- My collaborators in the sex worker rights movement for their wisdom, perseverance, and fierce commitment to bettering the world. In particular Jenn Clamen, Fred Chabot, and Nicholas Little for being inspiring and encouraging and always supportive.
- My colleagues and friends in the Department of Criminology with a special call out to Robert Gaucher for opening my eyes to so much and for starting me on the journey.
- My partner and friend Brent Ward. For all our differences, you were there when it counted.
- I end with a huge thank you to Stacey Hannem for being an amazing collaborator and friend and inspiration. Thank you for sharing your ideas, your time, and your spirit. Thank you too for the vision and the countless hours of work.

Introduction

Chris Bruckert and Stacey Hannem

Ervin Goffman's seminal book *Stigma* (1963), published almost half a century ago, has inspired generations of students, researchers, and scholars (including the editors and contributors to this volume) who draw on the conceptual tools as they seek to "make sense" of the social world. In the last decade, we have seen an exciting body of work emerge. Authors build on the insights of those who came before them but strive to overcome the astructural bias of Goffman's work through nuanced integrated theory, drawing on, for example gender theory (Whiteford and Gonzalez 1995; Gray 2002), Marxism (Bruckert 2002), and Foucault (Hacking 2004). Of course, the significance of Goffman's slim volume extends well beyond the realm of the academy precisely because stigma is not merely conceptual, theoretical, and analytic in nature. It is deeply *personal*, and the language of stigma provides an expressive vehicle to speak of dynamic "everyday" experiences that resonate in and through our lives as we (often simultaneously) live and negotiate, challenge and embrace, perpetuate and resist, stigma. In this collection, we aspire to a holistic approach that builds on academic representations and everyday experiences.

The organization and content of *Stigma Revisited: Implications of the Mark* speaks to the tensions in our commitment: our obligation as academics and activists to honour everyday lived experiences; our recognition that all social actors (including stigma researchers) are personally implicated as the recipients and perpetuators of stigma; our appreciation that stigma is not only interpersonally realized but also *structurally* embedded; and our commitment to the academic enterprise characterized by solid research and rigorous analysis. It also speaks to another tension, our desire to pay homage to the traditions of the Chicago school and the early sociologists of "deviance" who first questioned the nature and definitions of deviance, problematized dominant social constructions, and validated experiential authority (see Becker 1963; Polsky 1967). At the same time, while grounded in ethnographic and constructionist roots, we also engage with more contemporary debates around epistemology to recognize that academic knowledges are themselves the product of the interaction between the researcher and the researched, each of whom brings a unique life history and perspective to the encounter.

Throughout the volume, the narratives of marginalized persons, those who are experts in their own lives, are central. First, the book contains three first person accounts of the everyday realities of stigma by Nicholas Little, "Crazzy" Dave Dessler and Charles Huckelbury. The inclusion of these accounts speaks to our commitment to greater epistemological openness and to exposing the reader to voices that might otherwise not be heard. Stigmatized individuals may not scatter their texts with the words of Foucault and Goffman, but that does not mean they do not have a profound and deeply insightful understanding of stigma. Nor does it mean they cannot speak the truth to power. Indeed, we believe these "raw" narratives, which have not been carefully sliced and diced and served up sandwiched between academic analyses, shed much needed light into the world of the "other." This brings us to the second distinctive component of the volume. Just who is the other? Researchers who poke and prod are also social actors who judge and are judged. In the prologues that begin each chapter, the authors speak in their own voices and take the reader "behind the facade." In the process, they invite the reader to see academics as conflicted social actors who struggle to negotiate their own and others' stigmatic assumptions. The final characteristic of the book is also the heart of the text—careful qualitative research that respectfully attends to the voices of experience, while using the conceptual tools of sociology to make sense of their worlds.

We begin with Nicholas Little's piece "Down, Out, Crazy!" which speaks powerfully not only to stigma but also to the tensions and dialogue that permeate the collection. We then move on to Stacey Hannem's theoretical discussion of stigma, which draws on the work of Erving Goffman, Michel Foucault, and governmentality theorists to develop an integrated theoretical framework that positions us to think through the often-intersecting nature of interpersonal and structural stigmas. This chapter explores the structure/agency debate and the implications of structural limitations for the actions of marginalized persons, and provides a conceptual point of departure from which to understand and position the substantive chapters that follow. The remainder of the volume intersperses "speaking out" narratives and first-person "prologues" by the research contributors with the results of original ethnographic research examining different stigmatic "marks"—sexual deviance, "disreputable" labour, mental illness, racialization, criminality and association, and the cluster of stigmatic assumptions that cling to each of these discredited identities.[1]

While the populations discussed in this collection are quite diverse, we will return to a number of themes that emerge across the chapters in our concluding reflections. The first is both banal and highly significant: interpersonal stigma resonates through the lives of social actors and conditions their experience of the social world. In fact, the narrative prologues to the chapters are sometimes disconcertingly revealing—Chris Bruckert was advocating for sex worker rights at the same time as she was protecting herself from the repercussions of her "disreputable" past; Stacey Hannem engaged in a defensive and distancing internal dialogue upon finding herself identified as a member of the stigmatized population she was researching.

Clearly we are implicated in the realization of stigma. However, as we will see throughout this volume, the "marked" *live* stigmatic assumptions in profound ways—the avoidance of former friends of which Hannem's participants speak, the racial profiling evident in the narratives of the Afghan-Canadian men who took part in Vajmeh Tabibi's research, and the physical attack on a street-based sex worker that Nicholas Little describes are just a few examples. Moreover, it is not only the experience of being marked but also the anticipation of stigma that is significant. The former long-term prisoners who talked to Melissa Munn anticipated rejection and, although they were ultimately surprised to encounter "amazing reversals," this trepidation conditioned their experience of release. Indeed, the narratives throughout this volume reveal that anticipated stigma and a deeply felt realization of "otherness" have a profound effect on how "marked" social actors interact with others in their daily lives. "Stigma consciousness" (Pinel 2004) results in the expectation that stigma will be encountered so that any negative incident is interpreted as the result of one's stigmatized identity. We see this when one of the Afghan men that Tabibi interviewed asserted that the rude treatment and bad service he experienced at a restaurant was *because* he was an Afghan man, *not* because the waiter was having a bad day or was a generally unpleasant person or any

1 For example, in Kevin Walby's chapter we see that although there is a stigma attached to male with male sex and "gayness," it is highly problematic that gay men are often (mistakenly) assumed to be pedophiles, involved in luring and seducing young boys into sexual acts. We see that this secondary stereotype of men who have sex with men has even become structurally embedded into regulatory policies where police and peace officers are made responsible to "crack down" on male with male sex in public places (washrooms and parks) in order to protect vulnerable young boys who might become victims of sexual luring.

of a host of other possible explanations. Anticipated stigma also leads marked individuals to manage their identities through non-disclosure or selective disclosure, to withdraw from social engagement or avoid potentially embarrassing situations. Even in the absence of evident discrimination, stigma has significant consequences for one's life—wives of prisoners withdraw from social interaction (Hannem), and Afghan men fruitlessly attempt to "pass" as Canadian-born at the American border (Tabibi). In short, stigma consciousness is stigma's "hidden" cost in that it colours individuals' interpretations of their daily interactions and effects their way of being in the world.

Similarly, even "non-deviants" are not immune to the effects of stigma. The reality of *courtesy stigma* (or what Hannem calls "transferred stigma") is that individuals may be marked by association with stigmatized others, even if they are not themselves the bearer of a discredited mark. The families of prisoners and ex-prisoners and the families of sex workers, and the friends and partners of HIV-positive persons, exemplify the contagious nature of stigma that Goffman noted. Narratives reveal that this transferred stigma becomes a mark in its own right and has its own costs, in addition to the collateral punishments of association with a criminalized or marginalized person.

While marginalized individuals experience interpersonal stigma, this does not mean that they are passive victims of the process. Throughout this volume, the agency of the "marked" is evident in highly variable resistance strategies as social actors seek to protect and reclaim a spoiled identity. Some, like the self-injuring women in Jennifer Kilty's chapter, seek to manage stigmatization by rendering the "evidence" invisible. Others like "Crazzy" Dave draw on their ability to deconstruct the discourse to insulate their "selves" from judgement; still others, like the sex workers in Bruckert's piece, do careful identity work to distance themselves from the stereotypes associated with sex work.

Repeatedly we see that marginalized persons often seek to protect themselves by discursively conjuring up a "straw deviant" that conforms to the dominant stereotype and against whom they position themselves as moral. For example, the intra-group stigmatization of prisoner's families who critique others as drug "mules" powerfully legitimates the official correctional discourse, even while individual family members attempt to demonstrate that they are different from the stereotype. Of course we must be careful to acknowledge this process and its implications but reserve judgement. Marginalized individuals, like all social actors, use the tools at hand to their advantage and it is precisely the readily available nature of stigmatizing discourses that is problematic. Moreover we need to appreciate, as Charles Huckleberry's reflections on the disenfranchisement of prisoners poignantly remind us, that the commonality of stigma across (and within) populations does not eliminate the significance of stratification and the uneven distribution of cultural, social, and fiscal resources.

The final theme is also the point of departure for the book—structural stigma. Structural stigma occurs when stigmatic assumptions become embedded in social policies and practices. Through the language of risk, particular groups are identified as "dangerous" (to health, to moral order, to security etc.), which in turn legitimizes myriad forms of surveillance and intervention. Structural stigma is evident, for example, in the elevated age of consent for anal sex that criminalizes young men who have sex with men (Walby), the licensing process of body-rub parlours (Bruckert), the institutional response that both penalizes and psychologizes incarcerated women who self-injure (Kilty), the post-September 11 identification of Afghan men as "risky" (Tabibi), the arbitrary regulation of former long-term prisoners (Munn), and the continued focus on prisoners' families as the primary source of drug trafficking in prisons (Hannem, Chapter Six). We also see that resistance to structural stigma is constrained, for reasons that range from lack of access to resources, to invisibility, to a lack of collective will. Specifically, the intra-group stigmatization engaged in as a form of identity management by stigmatized individuals is counterproductive to collectively challenging structural forms of stigma. This finding inspired us to conclude the collection with a call to action and academic activism that would engage with the structural realities of stigma and work to deconstruct hegemonic representations of marginalized populations.

Chapter One

Speaking Out

Down, Out, Crazy!

Nicholas Little

"*I'm not crazy*," she says in a crazed sort of way. "*I'm not. I'm not crazy. Do you believe I'm not crazy?*"

She's not speaking to me. She's speaking to a guy standing beside her at the bus stop. I'm a few feet away from them on the corner, listening while waiting to cross. I'm still trying to decide if she's crazy and, if so, what sort of crazy she is, but his mind is evidently already made up. His two steps toward me, and away from her, tell both of us that, yes, she's crazy. And that crazy was not in his evening plans.

I cross the road. I'm headed to the *ByTowne Cinema*. Not for a movie but for their movie guide, which has a 15 percent off coupon for the *Horn of Africa* restaurant. That's where my two roommates and their two girlfriends are waiting for me. The queers are gonna share two vegetarian platters and some curried lamb before heading a block down, where there's a dance party put on by Agitate, the local queer women of colour collective.

I grab the guide and find the coupon, ripping it out right there as cars whiz by on one of Ottawa's busiest streets, smack in the middle of Lowertown, a neighbourhood formerly characterized by the down-and-out, who are now being replaced by the up-and-coming. The up-and-coming don't like the down-and-out, and especially don't like it when the down-and-out circle the block endlessly, around and around, looking for game. So the up-and-coming altered the down-and-out's streets to create a maze of one-ways that make it hard to circle and harder yet to eke out a living, slowly pushing the down-and-out altogether under.

I look up to see how it's going across the street. Two guys in their twenties are headed towards her and I can tell she's asking them how their night's going, where they're headed, if they're looking for fun. They pass by and she looks down the street and then back up the other way where she spots a cop car coming. She steps back from the curb and into the bushes at the side of the sidewalk. I can hear her cursing as the cop car passes. I zip through traffic to get back to the other side, coupon in hand.

Stuck at the meridian, I see her retreat through the bushes and into the coffee shop parking lot behind, but I can't tell why. One eye on four lanes of traffic and the other on the darkness she disappeared into, I see something sail through the air in her direction. What was that? I weave through and make it to the sidewalk to see three young bodies emerge from the parking lot, looking back over their shoulders, laughing, fearful. Something sails through the air again. What was that? And a fourth body emerges from the lot: running, laughing, defiant, proud, and afraid. He stoops beside an iced-up snow bank to pack a third snowball hard and tight, looks back into the dark lot and launches. She's in there somewhere, getting nailed by ice in the dark.

What do I do? Who am I right now? In Ottawa, in 2009, both rich yet somehow tied to these streets by a shared occupation; both queer yet somehow tied to the hyper-hetero world of street sex and married-with-children johns; both a wanted man and a hated man—feminine, queer, bottom, submissive; both her brother and a total stranger; both under attack when she is and also detached, not responsible, out with lesbian pals for beer and dancing. What do I do?

What if that was my boyfriend, if it was an HIV+ lover, if it was one of the teens who come to me for fresh crack pipes and to shoot the shit, if it was my buddy with cancer of the mouth and quickly expiring hope, if it was my mother in her wheelchair, if it was my two-spirit cranky-ass crush.

I choose quickly and I choose quickly on purpose. I do nothing. I figure she'd brush me off. I figure this sense of solidarity is all in my head. I figure she's already hardened enough by life on the streets that this is small potatoes in her world. I figure this is every day for her and she'd laugh at me. I figure she'll look at me with blank eyes and ask how my night's going, where I'm headed, if I'm looking for fun. I figure she'll think I'm crazy.

Small scars. Daily confusion. Tiny traumas unacknowledged by the up-and-comers as they drive the down-and-outers clear over the edge. As I walk toward the Horn of Africa restaurant, I hear one of the teenagers, a girl, say to her friends, "*But she's awful! She's a walking disease!*"

Even as she says it, I know that when I tell non-believers they will doubt whether she used those exact words. They will quietly doubt if I've not lost my rational objectivity because I associate too much as a peer. They won't say it but they'll start to question my judgment because I so often tell tales like this and yet they never see it in their own lives. Or they'll claim that this teenage girl is an anomaly. They'll claim she's young now but will later learn and I am overreacting and anyway, "*Nicholas, do you ever worry your reactions are becoming too passionate, too emotion based?*"

This is what I carry with me as I walk down Rideau Street and tomorrow it will be repeated in a new way, almost imperceptible. Almost. Same tiny trauma repeated anew and I wonder where all those tiny traumas go. They don't just disappear. So where and when do they come out of me? This is what I carry with me as I walk down Rideau Street and I remind myself that I am not crazy. I'm not. I am not crazy. Do you believe I'm not crazy?

Chapter Two

Theorizing Stigma and the Politics of Resistance

Symbolic and Structural Stigma in Everyday Life

Stacey Hannem

The goal of this book is to examine the social phenomenon of stigma as a substantive, everyday experience, and to contextualize the lived realities of stigmatized and marginalized persons theoretically. We need to appreciate that stigma is both symbolically realized in individual interactions and structurally embedded in the cultural values, practices, and institutions of society. To realize this objective we need a new theoretical perspective. While the work of Erving Goffman (1963a) has justifiably been the authority on stigma for several generations of academics, his focus on understanding stigma as a function of interaction at the individual level is not conducive to exploring the institutional and societal regulation of "discredited" individuals. Building on the work of others, such as Brian Castellani (1999) and Ian Hacking (2004),[1] I would suggest that Michel Foucault's broader perspective on the production of truth, knowledge, and power provides a useful conceptual point of entry for thinking about the construction of stigma and its effects on individuals and groups. At the same time, however, Foucault's work is itself lacking in its consideration of the individual subject and agency. As Castellani (1999) states,

> While [Foucault] wonderfully illustrated over and over again how practice, as an interaction, structures the rules of formation involved in the construction of subjectivity and "truth," [he] refused to acknowledge the important role interacting

1 While Castellani (1999) and Hacking's (2004) work is most notably developed, others have also proposed using Foucauldian theory in combination with interactionist thought; see for example Cahill 1998, Bruckert 2000.

> individuals have on this process, and was therefore unable to fully appreciate the importance of agency. (260)

In 2004, Ian Hacking identified the work of Foucault (1961) and Goffman (1961) as presenting complementary accounts of "making up people" and explored how the two theorists could contribute to his own efforts at understanding how "the actual and possible lives of individuals are constituted" (288). In his brilliant article, Hacking demonstrates how both Foucault and Goffman may be seen as grounded in the existentialist thought of Jean Paul Sartre. He argues that in his quest to comprehend how classifications of people interact with the people so classified he has come to realize that labels, like institutions, artefacts, and interaction, may both limit individuals' possible understandings of themselves and constitute possibility. As Sartre (1959) emphasized, the boundaries of one's knowledge and experience present limitations to how one might understand one's self and on the consequent choices that one may make. Hacking (2004) goes on to explain that "the choices that are open to use are made possible by the intersection of the immediate social settings, target of the sociologist, [Goffman] and the history of that present, target of the archaeologist [Foucault]" (288). Hacking uses Goffman's book, *Asylums* (1961), and Foucault's *Folie et Déraison: Histoire de la folie à l'âge classique* (1961) (published in English as *Madness and Civilization* in 1965) to demonstrate how their studies of mental illness and the mentally ill might be used in concert to produce a more holistic understanding of how the mentally ill are "made up" as people.

Hacking insists from the outset that, as a philosopher "steeped in Foucault," he is "not concerned with completing Goffman, but rather with filling out Foucault" (278). He states,

> Foucault gave us ways in which to understand what is said, can be said, what is possible, what is meaningful—as well as how it lies apart from the unthinkable and indecipherable. He gave us no idea of how, in everyday life, one comes to incorporate those possibilities and impossibilities as part of oneself. We have to go to Goffman to begin to think about that. (300)

My goal here is the opposite of Hacking's; as a sociologist, schooled in the traditions of the Chicago school and concerned with the everyday, lived realities of my subjects, I wish to explore what Foucault—and an understanding of the archaeology of divisive stereotypes and discriminatory institutions—might contribute to an understanding of how lived realities are constituted and shaped by the limits of social structure, and what insights that might have for a more activist political agenda. By incorporating Goffman's work (and symbolic interactionism, more generally) with Michel Foucault's post-structural perspective, I offer here a point of entry to articulate a more holistic picture of the phenomenon of stigma and the complex relationship between interaction, knowledge construction, and power. In short, this discussion is aimed at using Foucauldian insights to expand on Goffman's analysis of stigma. This creates a new space for sociological theory that integrates the individual experience into the larger macro-structures of power, government, and social institutions and opens up avenues for deconstructing previously taken-for-granted knowledges that are experienced as limiting and oppressive.

In this chapter, I build on Hacking by examining the complementary offerings of these two traditions and demonstrating how each can inform our understanding of stigma; first laying out the key ideas of Goffman and Foucault, respectively, and then bringing these perspectives together to explore the symbolic and structural aspects of stigma. Specifically, what is added to Hacking's analysis concerns how modern notions of risk are used by institutions to constitute structurally stigmatized populations, thereby creating and/or reinforcing symbolic, interpersonal stigma and discrimination.

Goffman Revisited: Situating the Structure/Agency Debate

The work of Erving Goffman is generally presented as being based in the tradition of George Herbert Mead and is labelled as symbolic interactionist (Scheff 2005), drawing on the notion that reality is constituted through interaction and the use of symbols to define objects and roles. According to interactionists, the individual is imbued with a subjectivity and agency that allows him or her to be an active participant in the creation of social situations and in the definition of his or her identity and role in those interactions. All individuals, however, enter into an interaction with a relatively static set of characteristics that define, in whole or in part, the identity of the person and limit the identity that he or she may portray to others. Gender, age, ethnicity, sexuality, occupation, and social status are examples of some characteristics that may play a role in identity formation and in the presentation of the self to others. However, Goffman never explicitly laid out his intellectual heritage in his writing, and therefore the claims of symbolic interactionists to Goffman's work are suspect.

Randall Collins (1986; 2004) has argued that Goffman was in fact not an interactionist[2] but a follower of Durkheim and the British social anthropologist

2 In fact, in his earliest writings, it would have been impossible for Goffman to identify himself as a "symbolic interactionist," as Blumer did not coin the term until the 1969 publication of his book, *Symbolic Interactionism: Perspective and Method,* more than a decade after the publication of Goffman's first books and articles. However, Goffman would certainly have been aware of the work of George Herbert Mead, which forms the foundation for the perspective.

Radcliffe-Brown, particularly concerning his understanding of social ritual (or interaction ritual) as the key to maintaining the normative social order. Where Durkheim analyzed ritualized responses to sacred (religious) objects in pre-industrial societies as a means of preserving and reproducing the shared social order and beliefs (collective conscious), Goffman picks up on Durkheim's later assertion that "the individual had become the principal "sacred object" in modern secular society" (Collins 1986, 107). Collins therefore argued that "unlike Mead, Thomas and Blumer, the self in Goffman is not something that individuals negotiate out of social interactions: it is, rather, the archetypal modern myth... we are *compelled* to have an individual self not because we actually have one but because social interaction requires us to act as if we do" (Collins 1986, 107). In other words, our modern preoccupation with individuality requires that we behave *as though we were concerned with how others view our selves,* because to fail to do so would bring into question the true importance of identity and cause a breakdown in the shared social order.

Collins' analysis of Goffman's functionalist roots suggests then that Goffman's understanding of the role of self and identity was as a means of preserving the larger social order through interaction ritual and presentation of self, a position that clearly emphasizes the importance of structure as shaping possibilities for individual action. This is echoed in Hacking's (2004) links to the existentialist philosophy of Sartre, which emphasises that human choices are always made within the confines of structural limitations. This structural-functionalist position, however, does not preclude a thorough examination of the situational actions of individuals. While this may seem counterintuitive to narrow, stereotyped representations of Durkheim's functionalist theory, foregrounding structure does not prevent one from recognizing that individuals must still enact their everyday lives within the confines of those boundaries and, in some sense, construct and perpetuate that social reality—or may at least be charged with failing to challenge it.[3] In fact, Goffman (1983) argued in his posthumously presented presidential address to the 1982 American Sociological Association meetings that the interaction order (everyday face-to-face interactions) must be treated as useful

3 Durkheim's own theorizing on the functional aspects of deviance suggests that individual acts of deviance are sometimes responsible for introducing change to social understandings (definitions) of deviant behaviour—altering the social order. He argued that sometimes the actions of an individual would be punished and that punishment would appear unjust to others, calling into question the definition of the law. He went on to argue that "we must not say that an action shocks the conscience collective because it is criminal, but rather that it is criminal because it shocks the conscience collective. We do not condemn it because it is a crime, but it is a crime because we condemn it" (1933, 81). In this sense, even Durkheim himself appears to have had some interactionist/constructivist leanings.

social data in its own right, and not merely as the visible effects of social structure. Even if one were to accept the functionalist supposition that face-to-face interaction ritual is enacted purely in the interests of the social order, this leads one down a slippery dialectical slope: where does social order (structure) originate? The interactionist position suggests, in fact, that social order is negotiated in interaction and cannot be assumed to have an *a priori* existence. Later adherents to Blumer's exposition of symbolic interactionism have clarified this position to emphasize the fundamental inseparability of self and structure: "Neither individual or society nor self or other are ontologically prior but exist only in relation to each other; thus one can fully understand them only through their interaction, whether actual, virtual or imagined" (Snow 2001, 369).[4]

While Goffman may have been theoretically concerned with issues of structure, it is embedded and is rarely substantively addressed in his writings, which, *on the surface*, paint colourful and nuanced portraits of human interaction and ritual. His book *Asylums* (1961), which examines the nature of total institutions, is the one notable exception. Perhaps Ann Branaman (1997) best described Goffman when she wrote,

> Erving Goffman is the quintessential sociologist of everyday social life. The self, social interaction, social order, deviance, social inequality, calculation and morality—all are taken up in Goffman's writings. Goffman's major contribution is to portray the interdependence of these phenomena by painting them into a complex portrait (xlv).

Our project in this volume is to pick up the threads of social structure that are cleverly woven into Goffman's work and to bring them to light in the same way that he so brilliantly exposed the minutiae of everyday life; to examine laws, institutional practices and policies as the visible evidence of structure and social

4 Howard Becker's writings on labelling theory and the interactionist perspective on deviance were published in 1963, notably the same year that Goffman's *Stigma* went to press. Although Becker is an interactionist, his analyses clearly demonstrate his awareness of issues of power and structure insofar as groups in society with disparate points of view are acknowledged to have varied ability to have these concerns recognized and addressed by society as a whole. In short, those with the most power, resources, and social capital are seen as able to have their beliefs and concerns enshrined in law and social practice, while the actions and beliefs of those with less power are marginalized and defined as "deviant" or problematic. While Becker does not use the term "stigma," he does examine the experience of being an "outsider" who is labelled deviant and the implications that this label has for constraining identity and agency. Becker's analysis, however, is lacking in the detailed analysis of individual agency and interaction with "normals" in response to such labels that Goffman provides, and it does not examine personal resistance to, or negotiation of, the deviant label in any depth. His lack of attention to resistance reveals Becker's unidimensional understanding of power and suggests that a Foucauldian analysis of power has much to add to the interactionist tradition.

order just as ritual, demeanour and talk are analyzed as forms of symbol and interaction in the social world. Here we show how the importance of symbol and structure, micro and macro, social life and institution are irreversibly tied up in the phenomena of stigma in society.

Stigma in Interaction

Erving Goffman published his seminal book, *Stigma: Notes on the Management of Spoiled Identity*, in 1963. In it, he identifies stigma as "an attribute that is deeply discrediting" and that reduces a person, in the minds of others, "from a whole and usual person to a tainted, discounted one" (1963a, 3). However, stigma is more precisely defined by Goffman not as an attribute alone but as a "relationship between attribute and stereotype" (4). That is, an individual possesses a particular attribute (i.e., the quality of having a conviction for a criminal offence) defined by others, based on stereotypes, as an undesirable or negative characteristic. This attribute, then, and the perception of it, result in avoidance or discriminatory behaviour directed toward the stigmatized person.[5] This discriminatory behaviour is the observable evidence of stigma. Stigma is not inherent in the individual attribute but is realized in interaction with other non-stigmatized ("normal") persons. To be present, stigma need not be realized in overtly discriminatory action, but often operates on a sub-surface level, colouring interactions and creating tension or avoidance behaviour.

Goffman (1963a) also identified that some discrediting attributes appear to have the quality of being transferrable: the stigma that accompanies it is spread from the stigmatized individual to those close to him or her (30). He referred to this type of transferred stigma as a "courtesy stigma." For Goffman, the transferrable nature of stigma is directly related to our social interpretation of the "*with*" relationship (47). There is an implicit assumption that the character and characteristics of an individual's companions may be used as a source of information about the person. Those who are with discredited or stigmatized persons are then marked by association with the discredited individual and may, in turn, pass the stigma to other close connections, "twice-removed" (30). For Goffman, "the problems faced by stigmatized persons spread out in waves, but of diminishing intensity" (30).

Some characteristics carry with them a perception of discredit or stigma that can have an impact on one's interaction with others; the marks of criminality, of "deviant" sexuality, of racial "otherness," and of mental illness examined in

---

5 See Link and Phelan (2001) for a detailed analysis of the process of stigmatization and refer to Walby (this volume) for a discussion of Link and Phelan's model.

this book are just some examples of the types of inherent or acquired traits that may affect understanding of, or reactions to, an individual. In some cases, the stigmatic characteristic is not obvious to others—the individual, in fact, is not immediately discredited but is *discreditable*. The individual is then faced with the choice of whether to reveal this discrediting information and how and when to do so. Goffman suggests that discreditability, while enabling individuals to avoid immediate and overt discrimination, becomes particularly problematic if the discreditable individual is unwittingly accepted as "normal" by someone prejudiced against the "type of person" that he or she may be revealed to be (42). *Passing*—the concealment of discrediting information—is one means for stigmatized persons to manage their social interactions with others and to define themselves positively in the context of the interaction (Goffman 1963a). The phenomenon of passing is generally considered to be directly related to the visibility of the stigmatic attribute. For example, a physical abnormality is readily evident, and it would be very difficult for a person so afflicted to pass as "normal," whereas a "moral" failure, such as a criminal record, is not immediately discernible and may be concealed in many circumstances.

The concept of visibility is crude, however, and Goffman cautions that we should be cognizant instead of the "evidentness" or "known-about-ness" of a stigmatic attribute. In many situations, stigma in interaction and the ability to pass are more related to the context and history of the interaction than the visibility of the attribute itself. For instance, a stigma need not be "visible" to be known about in a small town or social circle where gossip is prevalent, and the individual need not have firsthand knowledge of the stigma to "know about" it (49). There are also situational contexts in which there is an expectation or a requirement to reveal a discrediting characteristic that might otherwise remain hidden. For example, ex-convicts may be asked about a previous criminal record in the context of a job application, men who have sex with men may find themselves disclosing this information to a health professional or in the context of donating blood. Thus, even if the stigmatic attribute is not a *visible* one, it may become known about or revealed in social and professional interactions, making passing a challenge.

In other cases, situations may arise in which passing is not only possible but is the only viable option that does not presume upon the relationship a kind of forced intimacy. Particularly with a sensitive, invisible stigma,[6] many social situations and temporary or superficial relationships do not warrant or allow for

6 Such as the relation to an imprisoned offender, a previous criminal conviction, infection with the AIDS virus or other STIs, etc.

disclosure of such a personal confession (Goffman 1963a, 74–75). This everyday form of passing through nondisclosure is generally unproblematic and allows surface-level interactions to occur without concern for prejudice or discriminatory behaviour. It makes sense, then, that a discreditable person is not saddled with a perpetual or static label, or subject to stigma in every interaction. Most persons who possess an invisible stigmatizing attribute also have a "normal" identity that they present in many social contexts, carefully managing the impressions that they give to others. However, the act of passing also creates a situation in which a person may be discredited if the stigmatic attribute should become known in an unforeseen or embarrassing incident (75). The potential for discredit looms large in the consciousness of the individual and may condition his or her social interactions, lest the secret be inadvertently revealed through words or mannerisms.

The presence of a stigmatic attribute can have the effect of creating a power imbalance within an interaction between the stigmatized and the "normal," even if the "normal" in the interaction is unaware of the threat that they pose to the identity of the discreditable individual. The discreditable individual, being aware of the possibility of discredit and stigma, is placed in a position of discomfort and thus may become guarded or tense in anticipation of a negative reaction. As May (1999) suggested, an individual's perception of stigma may also be shaped by their own sense of shame and the "suspicion of toxicity." Because stigma is rooted in cultural understandings and definitions, individuals who carry discreditable characteristics are aware that others may react negatively to them. Indeed, being a part of the larger society, were they not themselves afflicted, they might have a similar negative perception. Therefore, discreditable persons find that the possibility of negative reactions have a profound effect on their interactions with others, colouring them with caution and constant vigilance.

In considering the potential outcome(s) of an inadvertent "outing," it is necessary to consider the perceived focus or sphere of influence and disqualification that the particular stigmatic attribute exerts (Goffman 1963a, 49–50). In other words, what kind of discredit does the stigma create? There appear to be three types of discredit that result from stigma—social, physical, and moral discredit. Goffman initially distinguishes between three types of stigma: deformations of the physical body, "tribal stigmas" of race, nation, and religion, and weakness of character, as exemplified by mental illness or involvement in criminal activity (4). Each of these types of stigma meets with a different response and level of comfort from "normals." A physical disfigurement, for example, may render an individual less attractive and he or she may be perceived as less capable in social situations, such as in service work, but this disfigurement would not affect perceptions of his or her morality. Other attributes, such as the stigma of a criminal conviction, may have a broader and more general impact on perceptions of the individual's respectability, trustworthiness, and/or abilities.[7]

Stigma related to character and morality appears to have the greatest impact in terms of levels of discrimination and acceptance from "normals" in the larger society. Goffman (1963a) documents that physical stigmatic attributes are generally perceived as being beyond the scope of individual control and therefore elicit varying degrees of sympathy and acceptance in social contexts—not that these individuals are necessarily treated as "normals," but that they are afforded a certain deference and leniency for their deficits (114–23). A blemish of character, on the other hand, is seen as a personal failure of the will and responsibility for this failing lies squarely within the individual. A stigma attached to character, then, while perhaps easier to conceal, is potentially far more socially debilitating for those who are "outed" or who choose to disclose their discreditable attribute. The revelation of a previously hidden "character flaw," such as involvement in criminal activity, brings into question the forthrightness of the individual as well as his or her moral standing and is likely to have a negative impact on relationships with those who were previously unaware.

Goffman's focus was on uncovering the experience of stigmatization in interpersonal interaction—he documents examples of individuals' techniques and adaptive strategies for the management of a social stigma and includes a limited discussion of the impact of social stigma on the individual psyche. What is conspicuously absent (and, I would argue, lacking) in Goffman's analysis is a more profound discussion of the genesis and nature of stigma that would illuminate questions such as: Where does it come from? How and why do some attributes come to be defined as stigmatic or discrediting in certain social contexts, while perhaps not in others? Who is responsible for defining stigma and what is its relationship to power, stereotype, and discrimination? What are the roles of stereotype and stigma as organizing structures in our complex society? It is to these questions that I now turn and demonstrate how Michel Foucault's post-structural theorizing provides valuable insight into the macro-structural, cultural, and institutional aspects of this complex phenomenon.

---

7 Having a parent or spouse in prison seems to bring into question the personal morality and "riskiness" of the individual. It is often assumed by educators and social workers that the children of convicted criminals are, themselves, more likely to be delinquent and involved in activities of questionable moral status. In fact, there is no concrete evidence to this effect, but the questionable moral standing of the parent is assumed to be an inherited characteristic, whether through genetics or socialization.

Michel Foucault: Power/Knowledge and Structures of Inequality

The root of Michel Foucault's intellectual project was systematically to uncover the history of thought and the structures that shaped and constrained human understanding of our world over time—the "archaeology of knowledge." Over the course of his career, he applied this framework to various topics of social and political concern: mental illness, sexuality, crime and punishment, and the government of populations. In considering each of these epistemologies, Foucault recognized that at any given point in history, there are substantial constraints on what and how individuals are able to *think*. Knowledge is constrained, not only by language and by terms of expression but by historical context and social structures that limit the ability to conceptualize and imagine (Gutting 2005). For Foucault, the structures that form the context for thought in a given period are, in and of themselves, a useful object of analysis and can help us to understand how social meanings and social actions evolve over time.

Foucault has been criticized for focusing on systems of thought and social contexts and in the process rendering the individual—as an active, engaged subject—invisible[8] (Gutting 2005, 33). Even in his examination of forms of knowledge applied at an individual level, Foucault maintains his concern with larger structural implications rather than the impact on the individual. For example, in speaking of his work on psychiatry and madness, Foucault (1994) states, "I have tried to see how the formation of psychiatry as a science, the limitation of its field and the definition of its object implicated a political structure and a moral practice…" (116). However, Foucault does not examine (as a primary source of knowledge) the personal experiences and resistances of those labelled mentally ill and thus regulated by this political structure and moral practice. Individual thought and experience is limited to the confines of what the historical and social structures of the time will allow, and was interesting to Foucault only in terms of what light it could shed on the larger structural context of the system or society in which it was created. Foucault (1977) appears to eschew phenomenological and existential conceptions of human thought and agency in favour of a positivistic conception of structure:

> I would say that if now I am interested, in fact, in the way in which the subject constitutes himself in an active fashion, by the practices of self, these practices are

8 Of course, this criticism must be understood in light of the reality that Foucault's inattention to the individual was quite deliberate, believing as he did that studying the actions of individual subjects would only obscure the wider practices and discourse that he felt were more important to an accurate understanding of power.

> nevertheless not something that the individual invents by himself. They are patterns that he finds in his culture and which are proposed, suggested and imposed on him by his culture, his society and his social group. (11)

If the archaeology of knowledge is concerned with considering what structures of language and ontology impact on understanding, thought, and agency, Foucault's genealogical project worked alongside to uncover the origins of these structures and the "history of the present." Foucault argued that in order to understand and evaluate the present situation, one must unearth the past and trace discourse and policies from their origins (Gutting 2005, 50). His project was, in essence, to trace back and to render visible the implications of authoritative claims. There is a tendency to argue the functionality of current thought and policies—that is, that they evolved out of necessity to address certain deficits in our society. However, careful analysis of these policies in retrospect, and with the benefit of historical perspective, often reveals their arbitrary nature, integrally linked to the preservation of systems of power rather than to the improvement of society as a whole. Foucault's genealogy of systems of punishment and rule in *Discipline and Punish* is an excellent example of how benevolent "improvements" in a social structure (the judicial system) are directly linked to the maintenance of power and government. Foucauldian scholars demonstrate that while the neoliberal system of "government at a distance" has the appearance of a retraction of control, in actuality it is merely a change in the form of regulation that disperses control into the structures of everyday life and the psyches of individuals, thereby enabling the state to "walk softly and carry a big stick" (Braithwaite 1995).

Equally essential to the Foucauldian project was his conception of the intimate link between power and knowledge. Structures of power are able to shape possibilities of knowledge, and those in positions of power have a certain amount of control over what is defined as "truth." In this sense, when truth or knowledge is redefined, the redefinition is not the product of thought, but of power: "When thoughts change the causes are social forces that control the behaviour of individuals… power transforms the fundamental archaeological frameworks (epistemes or discursive formations) that underlie our knowledge" (Gutting 2005, 50). In this way, power both creates and constrains knowledge within a society.

Linking Goffman and Foucault: Stigma in Interaction and in Structure

Foucault's work can be greatly augmented by the grounded ethnographic and existential examination of the lived realities and agency of these social actors.

Further, an application of Foucault's genealogical framework to the concept of stigma would allow us to provide a structural analysis that Goffman does not approach—the "origin" of stigma, generally, and a historical understanding of the specific contexts in which particular attributes were defined as discrediting. In the following sections, we will examine the complementary aspects of these two traditions and explore the possibilities offered by drawing on ideas from each.

A characteristic shared by both Foucault and Goffman was the tendency to discount notions of objective truth. For Foucault, truth was necessarily relative to the structures of power that created it (Gutting 2005). That is, what is true for individuals in one space and time may not necessarily be so for individuals in a different social and historical context. In the tradition of symbolic interactionism, Goffman takes an even more relative and micro-structural approach to the concepts of knowledge and truth. For Goffman, truth is negotiated within interaction. And yet, even two individuals engaged in a social relationship need not have the same truth or experience of that interaction. While Foucault's analysis neglects the experiential aspect of truth, Goffman appears to ignore the larger implications of power differentials that exist in some interactions, while at the same time failing to address the role of power and domination in shaping one's experience and definition of a situation.

For Foucault, power is not absolute and only exists relationally—thus, where there is power there is always resistance (Foucault 1982). Somewhat surprisingly, Foucault acknowledged the potential for individuals to question knowledge and truth, and the human capacity for agency and imagination to work beyond the confines of knowledge/power, yet did not attend to resistance, the very thing for which he had created theoretical space. He placed far greater importance on institutional knowledge and looked at individual knowledge as merely reflective of larger structures rather than attending to the contested nature of truth and knowledge. A point of entry for such a reflection would be to consider the difference between "knowledge" and "truth." Individual experiences may constitute a form of truth without becoming knowledge and being integrated into the larger social structure of understanding, while power may create knowledge that is not in fact "true." A common example of this phenomenon is the stereotype. A stereotype is a collective knowledge of a particular type or group of persons that, in many cases, is not an accurate (true) reflection of particular individuals within that category. The individual experiences of marginalized persons may not be incorporated into the body of accepted knowledge, particularly if such experiences challenge existing structures of power and social policies. However, this lack of recognition does not negate the importance of individual truths for social action.

On the other hand, Goffman's near total focus on interaction in everyday life does not adequately address the aspect of power and its impact on knowledge. Although, like Blumer (1969), he acknowledges that truth is negotiated and arrived at through interaction (Goffman 1967), he fails to set out the impact of power on interaction explicitly, beyond the face-to-face experience. Goffman (1967) refers only to the "asymmetrical rule," which creates an expectation that "leads others to treat and be treated by an individual differently from the way that he treats and is treated by them" (52–53). Unlike Foucault, Goffman concerns himself only with this visible result of power differential and not with the origins of the asymmetrical rule or the knowledges attached to it. The structural origins of power become particularly relevant when one begins to consider situations not in which individuals have *gained* power or deference by virtue of merit, but in which individuals have been *disempowered* because of some stigmatic attribute. Again, we see a space where these two perspectives can inform and complement one another. This allows us not only to trace the historical genesis of stigma and marginality, but also to examine the contemporary dynamics and experiences of those who live within the confines of a stigmatized identity. In the following section, we will look at the politics of marginality and the function of stigma in the government of risky populations.

Stigma, Discrimination, and the Government of the Margins

Foucault's (1978) concept of the marginal is a useful place to begin consideration of the situation of stigmatized populations. Foucault theoretically differentiates the situation of the marginalized in our society from that of the abnormal or "other." For Foucault, the marginalized are still a part of the larger society; they speak the same language and share many of the same values as mainstream society. They also often play essential social and economic roles. Yet marginalized people inhabit a liminal social space either because 1) their identity and life is significantly defined by values that are counter to the mainstream, or 2) they belong to a group whose welfare is systematically subordinated in order to further the interests of the larger, mainstream group (Gutting 2005). This description of the "marginal" speaks to the locations of many stigmatized populations, including those addressed in this volume.

> The marginalized have values that can meaningfully challenge our own and needs that could be plausibly satisfied within our society … the claims of the marginal are based on critiques of specific features of our society that can be modified without total overthrow. (Gutting 2005, 89)

The experience of individualized, symbolic stigma is a common one for many people who belong to marginalized groups. While it may be experienced as hurtful, most often individuals are able to negotiate symbolic stigma successfully.[9] For the most part, symbolic stigma remains primarily a psychological or emotional concern limited to the individual person; at least until such time as there is collective resistance that names the problem, generates social consciousness, and allows people to see themselves as members of a stigmatized population. The issue of symbolic stigma becomes one of sociological concern when it is symptomatic of stigma at a structural level: when stigma is systematically applied by agencies, institutions and individuals to a particular group of people or population as a whole—moving beyond stigma as a perception of an *individual* attribute, to a wider, stereotypical concept of stigma that taints an entire group and pushes them to the margins of society. Increasingly we find that these structural-level identifications of stigmatic attributes are related to the notion of risk, and interventions are justified by the rhetoric of risk-management.

Individuals whose way of being runs counter to mainstream mores and standards of behaviour are often considered to be risky or to somehow threaten the social order and thus may be subject to intervention or surveillance designed to minimize their risk to the general population. For example, the children of prisoners may be subject to interventions designed to reduce the risk of future offending,[10] and Afghan-Canadian men post-9/11 may be the targets of enhanced security measures at airports and border crossings. While these types of regulation, at times, may be necessary to prevent a legitimate threat, and the difficulties experienced may be necessary for the maintenance of social order and the protection of the public, the welfare of marginalized individuals is presumably sacrificed for the well-being of the majority. Although interventions and the subsequent distress they may cause individuals are not always avoidable in our society, I would argue that measures might be taken to understand and address the difficulties encountered by marginalized persons. As suggested by Foucault, a critical characteristic of marginalized populations is that they are already a part of our social order. Efforts to be more inclusive do not require an overthrow of existing structures, but merely

9 Many studies discuss negotiations of stigma and stigma management in interactions. See for example, Bruckert 2002; Corrigan and Lundin 2001; Goffman 1963a and others.

10 Children with an incarcerated parent often exhibit acting out behaviour and difficulties in school and may find themselves involved with child welfare services, mentoring programs, and other social development programs designed to reduce the risk of future offending (see, for example, Virginia Commission on Youth 2002; Withers 2003; House of Hope 2003). While these interventions are meant to improve the child's current and future welfare, there is no doubt that there is a stigma attached to being the "problem child" in a classroom or group of children and interventions may exacerbate the acting out behaviour by causing the child to internalize a negative label.

an awareness of the problems and an adaptation of reactions to combat the effects of structural stigma.

Link and Phelan (2001) use the concept of *structural discrimination* to define a situation in which policy makers and administrators are unaware of the negative consequences that certain policies may have for a particular group of people. This lack of awareness leads to systematic discrimination and hardship for those negatively affected. *Structural stigma* is the inverse of this notion, with similar consequences. As I define it, and as it is used throughout this volume, structural stigma arises out of an *awareness* of the problematic attributes of a particular group of people and is based on an intent to manage a population that is perceived, on the basis of the stigmatic attribute, to be "risky" or morally bereft. Here the symbolic meets the structural in a way that causes an inherent disadvantage to a group of people. This stigma is *structural* because the difficulties that arise from it are not so much a product of the stigma itself, or any inherent problems that arise from the condition, but of the institutional and conceptual structures that surround it. Whether or not an individual experiences symbolic and individualized stigma in interactions, he or she is marked and may be subject to a myriad of interventions, regulations, and surveillance, not on the basis of *individual* factors, but on the recognition that he or she belongs to a statistically "risky" group. "Stigma has affected the structure around the person, leading the person to be exposed to a host of untoward circumstances" (Link and Phelan 2001, 373).

The concept of structural stigma is differentiated from discrimination and structural discrimination then by virtue of intent on the part of the intervener or "normal" in the interaction. Discrimination is the visible result of symbolic stigma and occurs without the intent to manage a particular person or population, but rather with the intent of separating that person or group from the "normal" and to impart shame or disgrace. Structural discrimination, as conceived by Link and Phelan (2001) has no aspect of intent to harm or disgrace, but results from a lack of careful forethought as to the consequences of bureaucratic policy or practice for a particular population.[11] Structural stigma, on the other hand, is the result of a carefully calculated decision at an institutional or bureaucratic level to manage the risk that a particular population is perceived to present, either to themselves, to

11 For example, in the United States, the federal Adoption and Safe Families Act of 1997 allows for the forced termination of parental rights after fifteen months in foster care. The average prison sentence in the United States is eighteen months, meaning that many incarcerated parents may lose their children completely while they are in custody, despite the non-voluntary nature of the situation (Travis et al. 2003; Virginia Commission on Youth 2002). Although this law was never intended to target incarcerated parents but to protect children and enable the state to find stable home environments, its unintended consequence is to unfairly disadvantage incarcerated parents who do not wish to relinquish their parental rights.

the institution, or to society. Unlike discrimination, there is no intent to *harm* the individual or the population and in fact, the stated goal of policy makers is often to help or improve the situation. However, when the need for assistance is justified by the inherently "different," "risky" or "tainted" characteristics of the population, stigma is created in the very agencies that are supposed to be providing help.

This conception of structural stigma clearly goes beyond Goffman's concern with individual interactions and moves toward the archaeology of stigma. Foucault's work would suggest that there is a need to uncover the roots of the stigma in order to understand and address the problem. Drawing on Mary Douglas' (1966) work on "pollution and taboo," the perception of risk or danger is commonly based on cultural understandings of purity and defilement. For example, in North America, criminality (particularly predatory or violent crime and street crime) is considered one of the most taboo or immoral types of behaviour and this cultural precept has resulted in the stigma of criminality being associated with a high level of risk or danger that is subject to a myriad of reactive and proactive interventions. The "risk" to be managed may or may not be a tangible risk, calculable in an actuarial sense.[12] What matters is that a risk of danger or defilement is perceived and reacted to in a way calculated to reduce or eliminate the possibility of the undesired consequence. Regardless of whether the risk of criminality is "real" (actuarially calculable) or symbolic,[13] I would argue that defining a group of persons as a collective risk in this manner serves to increase stigma at both symbolic and structural levels as individuals negotiate interactions with government and social agencies and other persons.

While Goffman's approach would dissect individual interactions for evidence of stigma and identity management, Foucault's genealogic approach would suggest that we examine the origins of these policies and practices and the power/knowledge that accompanies their implementation. These knowledges of risk become a part of our corporate understanding and stereotype of marginalized persons; structural stigma is applied to individuals in interaction in the guise of risk management, whether or not there is any evidence of discrimination. The natural response of persons to whom power/knowledges are applied in the form of intrusive or distressing interventions is to resist and challenge these problematic discourses. In the remainder of this chapter, we will engage with the theoretical relationship between stigma and resistance and examine the individual and collective forms of resistance that result from imbalances of power.

12 Ian Hacking (2003) differentiates between "real, figurative, metaphorical and symbolic" pollution. The same distinctions can be made between forms of risk.

13 See Douglas (1966).

Resistance

For Foucault, interaction is infused with power relations and therefore also, of course, with resistance (Foucault 1982). The power/knowledge that creates inequality is challenged by the marginalized discourses and understanding of those who live with stigma. At an individual level, resistance to stigma serves to balance inequities and help the individual to maintain a sense of himself or herself as a whole, undamaged person. At a structural level, resistance may be used to debunk stereotypes and undermine existing, top-down definitions and explanations of the experiences of marginalized individuals. Resistance, then, can be found in the individual and collective voices of those who are usually silenced.

According to Miller and Kaiser (2001), resistance to stigma has been documented in two primary forms: avoidance and engagement. The first, avoidance, involves "physical and/or social withdrawal or disengagement from stigma related stressors" (79). Individuals may opt not to reveal their discreditable attribute to others, or may avoid contact with those who discover and/or are aware of it.[14] Marginalized individuals may also choose to minimize experiences of stigma and discrimination as a means of denying the impact of stigma on their life; essentially, denying that there is a problem at all (80). Engagement coping, on the other hand, is aimed at gaining control over an event, factor, or interaction (Miller and Kaiser, 2001). Stigmatized individuals may challenge the beliefs and stereotypes that they are subjected to and they may attribute poor outcomes to prejudice.[15] This challenges not only demeaning stereotypes but also stigmatizing policies and practices. Individuals may also engage in *"disidentification,"* in which the stigmatic attribute is devalued and ceases to frame the identity of the individual, protecting self-esteem and self-worth (Miller and Kaiser, 2001). Finally, acceptance is a form of engagement

14 While Miller and Kaiser (2001) refer to this type of avoidance behaviour or passing as a form of individualized resistance, others have characterized it as a means of stigma and identity management (see Goffman 1963; Bruckert 2002; Corrigan and Lundin 2001; Kilty, this volume; Tabibi, this volume; Hannem, this volume; Bruckert, this volume). In fact, one might argue that stigma management and identity management encompass aspects of resistance as the discredited or discreditable individual endeavours to portray and protect a positive social identity and to prevent the discreditable status from becoming a master status that effectively limits their social mobility and opportunities. On the other hand, this type of individualized struggle must be differentiated from larger, political resistance movements and engagement aimed at destigmatization and the debunking of stereotypes. But certainly many forms of resistance exist on a spectrum from individual to mass political struggle.

15 For example, the child of a prisoner may argue that he/she is no more likely to become criminal than any other child and, when faced with examples of prisoners' children who became criminal, may suggest that structural discrimination and the stigma of labelling pushed those children into deviance.

in which the individual accepts the inevitability of stigma and discrimination and ceases to allow the stigma to be emotionally problematic (Miller and Kaiser, 2001). This is a less adaptive strategy because it is not conducive to movement for change. Resistance to stigma is most commonly engaged in at the individual level; a single person fights to maintain his or her personal identity in the face of social stereotypes that are seen as unjust or inaccurate representations. However, unpacking the notion of structural stigma requires that we also recognize the need for collective resistance that strikes at the root of our stigmatic assumptions about so-called risky people. Beyond Miller and Kaiser's (2001) "engagement coping," challenges to stigma must mobilize a new discourse that historically situates and debunks essentializing and limiting myths about marginal groups, replacing these ideas with an ethic that emphasizes the individuality and inherent human value of marked persons.

Theorizing the Politics of Stigma and Resistance

While Goffman's analysis of face work and identity management is ideal for uncovering sites of individual resistance, a Foucauldian approach can provide an understanding of the power/knowledge that accompanies structural stigma and that needs to be challenged to make way for change and the breaking down of stereotypes. It is clear that a holistic understanding of the phenomenon of stigma in interaction requires the explanation of both the structural and experiential aspects. To concentrate on micro-level interactions is to ignore the structures of power and knowledge that create the possibility of stigma and shape our interactions; to focus exclusively on the structures and institutions that create stigma is to silence the voices and lived experiences of those affected and marginalized by stigma. Goffman's qualitative descriptions of individual struggles of identity management and shame need to be augmented not only with the experiences of "normals" who come into interaction with the stigmatized, but also with a genealogy of the social structures of normalcy and difference that create generalized stigma and attitudes of prejudice. Only by uncovering the cultural and historical structures of thought that create and maintain stigma can we begin to break down false stereotypes and barriers that lead to discriminatory policies and marginalize entire groups of citizens.

This chapter has outlined the basis of an integration of Goffman and Foucault that will be useful for further study of stigma and other interactions of power. Detailed genealogies or histories of the various forms of stigma that surround marginalized groups would also be useful tools for challenging and breaking down stereotypes and power/knowledge that create inequalities and discrimination; but it is through the lives and interactions of individual people that these struggles are played out and competing knowledges are created. Ultimately, it is individuals who are most affected by stigma and whose lives will be most improved by its destruction. In this sense, like Foucault's studies of madness and sexuality, this book (and the studies it contains) is not only a theoretical project but a political one as well.

Chapter Three

The Mark of Racialization

Afghan-Canadian Men Negotiate Stigma Post-9/11

Vajmeh Tabibi (with Stacey Hannem)

Prologue

Prior to the events of September 11, 2001, I used to enjoy answering the question "Where are you from?" I was frequently asked this by co-workers or strangers, while waiting at bus stops, or working in a retail store. To me it was an enjoyable game and I would respond with another question: "Where do you think I am from?" They would guess several European, South American, or Middle Eastern countries and were never able to discern the country of my birth. When I would disclose that I was born in Afghanistan, I found that very few Canadians knew about its political and social history. In fact, the majority did not even know its geographical location. Nonetheless, some would express interest in knowing more about Afghanistan and I was happy to educate Canadians about my country of origin.

In the immediate aftermath of September 11, 2001, knowing the negative connotations attached to Afghan identity, I consciously decided to continue to disclose my country of origin to strangers and acquaintances in order to educate them about Afghans and the politics of the Middle East, and to correct the erroneous presentations of the media and politicians. I quickly found that in the post-9/11 world, people had automatically entrenched opinions about Afghans and did not want my knowledge and explanations about my people. On September 13, 2001, only two days after the attack, I faced differential treatment while having a conversation with my co-workers about why the nineteen hijackers flew planes into the Pentagon and the Twin Towers. My co-workers had assimilated and believed the media and dominant political discourse around the attacks, and they were hostile to my different interpretation. The conversation turned into an ugly argument and, as result, I spent the rest of the day in silence, ignored by my co-workers. However, I did not immediately cease my efforts to educate people, and continued to engage with customers in the retail shop where I worked, disclosing my country of origin to strangers if they asked. Very soon, I made the choice no longer to be forthcoming about my ethnic identity and to employ "passing" in order to avoid the annoying, simplistic, and careless comments that people made. For instance, one customer asked, "How come your husband allows you to work here?" Another, presumably in a misguided attempt to be empathetic, noted, "Oh, you poor thing! You must be glad to be living in Canada."

Later, when I obtained employment in the federal public service, I believed that hiding my ethnic identity would no longer be necessary. I reasoned that most of my co-workers were educated people who would not embrace the superficial dominant discourse. I was swiftly proven wrong. Not long after starting work, a male co-worker asked about my country of origin during lunch hour and I, eager to open a discussion about Afghanistan and to provide a true picture of who Afghans really are, told him. I was dumbfounded when he commented "Oh. I am sure whenever you tell people you are from Afghanistan, they reply, 'Do you have a bomb in your bag?'" I was even more distraught that the others at the table laughed or smiled or simply continued their conversations.

In the aftermath of 9/11, the pleasant guessing game of where was I born had turned into unpleasant confrontations. I also discovered that some members of my family and my Afghan friends had similar and even more troubling discriminatory experiences. The men in particular spoke about their experiences of racial profiling at the borders and the airports. In response, I decided to conduct a research project in order to understand better the impacts of the post-9/11 discourse on Afghan-Canadian males' day-to-day lives and to give them a voice in a world where dissenting opinions are increasingly silenced.

On September 11, 2001, a series of attacks occurred in the United States of America. Four commercial airliners were hijacked by a group[1] of Muslim men from the Middle East. Two of the planes were flown into the World Trade Center (known as the Twin Towers) in New York City, one struck the Pentagon in Washington, DC, and another crashed in a field in Pennsylvania. In response to these attacks that took the lives of approximately three thousand people, the government immediately enacted a wave of unprecedented anti-terrorism measures and security policies. These political changes were accompanied by widespread anti-Middle Eastern, anti-Arabian, and anti-Muslim sentiments among the public.

The "War on Terrorism," as declared by the Bush Administration, had profound implications for government policy through the implementation of extensive anti-terrorism laws and security measures; it also resulted in changes to the everyday lives of Middle Eastern, Arabian, and Muslim persons as they began to face racial profiling and government surveillance. Suddenly, Afghan-Canadians and Afghan-Americans found themselves defined as "risky" individuals in official discourse and in their everyday encounters with other social actors. This stigma category emerged in a historically unique context that allowed the notion of risk to be associated with the Arabian/Muslim identity within the public mindset in the span of literally a few hours. While other racially and culturally stigmatized groups have long histories associated with their "otherness," rarely can the creation of stigma be traced to a single event in history, as with the Afghan people and the events of 9/11.

As an Afghan-Canadian woman, I realized that life would not be the same after 9/11 for many Middle Eastern, Arabian, and Muslim individuals, including Afghans. My own experiences and those of my friends confirmed the reality of the newly ascribed status of being "risky." This chapter draws on ten semi-structured interviews conducted between December 2005 and July 2006 with Afghan-Canadian men residing in Canada.[2] Through their stories, the experiences and perceptions of Afghan-Canadian men who were suddenly defined as "risky" in government discourses, in state practices, and in social interactions are examined; and a framework presented through which to understand how they manage and/or resist this ascribed status. The structural modes of stigma that arise in interaction with government and regulatory authorities, and the men's responses to these discriminatory practices, renders visible individual technologies of resistance to stigma and the everyday effects of interpersonal stigma. The

1 It is believed that nineteen men were involved in the hijackings. Of these individuals, fifteen were from Saudi Arabia, two from United Arab Emirates, one from Lebanon, and one from Egypt.

2 This research was conducted for Tabibi's MA thesis in criminology at the University of Ottawa.

chapter concludes by framing the reclamation of ethnic identity as a collective form of resistance that can be used as a catalyst for destigmatization and large-scale change. This chapter begins by placing this research into historical context by sketching the political, social, and legislative consequences of the attacks that took place on 9/11, then frames the theoretical and methodological position of this research and analysis.

Contextualizing 9/11

In the immediate aftermath of 9/11, the stated purpose of the Bush administration's "War on Terrorism," was ostensibly to bring Osama bin Laden, the leader of al-Qaeda, to justice as well as to prevent future acts of terrorism and the emergence of terrorist networks. In order to achieve these goals, the administration levied economic and military sanctions against nations perceived to be harbouring terrorists, beginning with the United States-led NATO coalition attack on Afghanistan.

On the domestic front, the United States government immediately created the *USA PATRIOT Act* (Uniting and Strengthening America by Providing Appropriate Tools Required to Intercept and Obstruct Terrorism), which granted unprecedented powers of surveillance, search, and seizure to law enforcement officials and created the Department of Homeland Security (Thompson 2004). Furthermore, the Immigration and Naturalization Service (INS) implemented a "special registration" program, also known as the National Security Entry and Exit Registry System (NSEERS) on September 11, 2002 (Cainkar 2004). This program required particular categories of non-citizens[3] to register with the INS, to be fingerprinted and photographed, and to respond to questioning and adhere to routine reporting (Cainkar 2004). Another notable implication of the September 11 attacks was the detention of thousands of Muslim Arabians living in the United States. According to Cainkar (2004), eighty-thousand Middle Eastern, Arabian, and Muslim individuals, most of whom had immigrant status, were fingerprinted under the *Alien Registration Act* of 1940. Furthermore, the United States government extended its preventative detention of the alleged al-Qaeda and Taliban members by imprisoning 650 individuals from forty-two countries in Guantanamo Bay, Cuba (Ratner 2005; Steyn 2004; Vierucci 2003).

3 All males over the age of sixteen who had entered the United States (whether before or after September 11, 2001) from 25 designated countries were required to register with the NSEERS program. The list included Afghanistan, Algeria, Bahrain, Lebanon, Iran, Iraq, Libya, Syria, Sudan, Eritrea, Morocco, Oman, Qatar, Somalia, Tunisia, United Arab Emirates, Yemen, Pakistan, Saudi Arabia, Kuwait, Bangladesh, Egypt, Jordan, Indonesia, and North Korea.

Canada followed the United States' example and produced its first anti-terrorism legislation in October 2001. Proclaimed into law in December 2001, the *Anti-Terrorism Act* has been criticized for its incompatibility with the *Canadian Charter of Rights and Freedoms* due to the inclusion of a pre-emptive detention clause, expansion of surveillance powers, and the authorization of mere suspicion of terrorist involvement as a legitimate basis for investigation, warrants, and wiretaps (Choudhry 2001; Roach 2003). In addition, the Canadian government created the department of Public Safety and Emergency Preparedness (PSEP) to facilitate information sharing and collaboration within and between the government ministries (Bell 2006) and amalgamated several federal departments to create the Canada Border Service Agency in 2003.

While the September 11 attacks resulted in a myriad of government reactions to the new "risk" of terrorism, the citizens of Western nations also altered their interactions with those who might be perceived as "risky." Middle Eastern, Arabian, and Muslim people and even others who might (mistakenly) be perceived as Muslim (for example, Sikhs) in both Canada and the United States were the victims of defamatory remarks, physical assaults, vandalism, destruction of property, and even murder (Ahmed 2002; Brown 2003). While such hate crimes were presumably the acts of a few individuals, opinion polls conducted in the two countries revealed overall support for government security initiatives, including the racial profiling[4] of individuals of Middle-Eastern origin at the borders and in airports as a means of detecting and preventing future terrorist attacks (Cainkar 2004). We see then that the aftermath of September 11 fundamentally changed the relationship between North Americans and Middle Eastern and Muslim persons (whether immigrants or visitors) at both the structural and interpersonal levels. In the following section, this change is theoretically situated before examining how structural and symbolic stigmas have affected the lives of Afghan men living in Canada, post-September 11.

Theoretical Approach

This chapter draws on diverse theoretical traditions—Goffman's conceptualization of stigma, Foucault's governmentality and resistance, and the literature on

4 Racial profiling is defined as "separating a subsection of the population from the larger whole on the basis of specific criteria [markers of race/ethnicity] that purportedly correlates to risk and subjecting the subgroup to special scrutiny for the purposes of preventing violence, crime or some other undesirable activity. Racial profiling thus entails the use of race as a proxy for risk..." (Bahdi 2003, 295). While the Canadian Anti-Terrorism Act does not specifically mention or endorse the use of such measures, neither does it prohibit them. There is much evidence to demonstrate that racial profiling does, in fact, take place in Canada and legislators' failure to condemn the practice explicitly may implicate them as complicit, if not supportive, of this approach.

the emergent "risk" discourse. This integrated analytic approach allows us to situate participants' experiences within a broader social, regulatory, and discursive framework. Examining participants' experiences in their one-on-one interactions using Goffman's stigma theory provides a microanalytic framework by which to consider the nature and dimensions of stigma and how it is managed. However, this theory fails to provide a framework for macro-level analysis of structural stigma. It is therefore necessary to turn to theories of risk and Foucault's governmentality. These theoretical approaches enable us to make sense of structural stigma, its genesis, and its impact on the lives of these men. The application of "risk" discourse illustrates how this rhetoric has facilitated, necessitated, and legitimated the construction of a "risky" population and the subsequent treatment of this population in terms of policy and practice. Finally, in order to analyze participants' multifaceted everyday acts of contestation and the development of an alternate discourse by the oppressed (Scott 1990; Mullaly 2001) the concept of resistance, stemming from Foucault's bifurcated notion of power, is employed.

The Research Participants

All of the men who took part in this research were born in Afghanistan and at some point fled to neighbouring countries such as Iran, Pakistan, and India, either because of the Soviet invasion of 1979 or the 1989–1992 civil wars. Most of the men lived in these host countries for many years before seeking permanent residency in Canada. These commonalities notwithstanding, the men came from a variety of cultural,[5] religious,[6] linguistic,[7] and educational backgrounds. This is an important point to bear in mind, as it speaks to the difficulty in defining Afghans as a homogeneous population. Given the diversity of these individuals and their personal, social, and religious characteristics, there are many different experiences and perspectives in the post-9/11 world. In other words, Afghan men comprise a heterogeneous population.

---

5 The population of Afghanistan is divided into several ethnic groups. The CIA World Factbook provides the following main ethnic composition as such: Pashtun 42%, Tajik 27%, Hazara 9%, Uzbeck 9%, Aimak 4%, Turkmen 3%, Baloch 2% and other 4%.

6 There are two denominations in Islam: Shiite and Sunni. Generally, Shiites are the minority in the world comprising between 10–15% of all Muslims (Miller 2009). Shiites are also the minority in Afghanistan. Most Shiites speak Dari and generally live in the northern and western parts of the country; the Sunnis in Afghanistan mostly speak Pashto and live in the southern parts of the country (i.e., Kandahar). This is an important distinction, because being a Shiite and speaking Dari mark some Afghan people as a minority who have experienced stigmatization in their own homeland.

7 Afghanistan has two official languages, Pashto and Dari (Persian), which are spoken by 50% and 35% of the population respectively.

In the coming section, we see the interplay of structural and interpersonal stigma at airports and borders, which are regulatory sites where the participants were subject to surveillance practices and differential treatment. This analysis of structural level stigma concludes with a discussion of strategies of resistance. The analysis of interpersonal (symbolic) stigma focuses on the experiences and management techniques employed by the men in their interactions with the public, particularly at work, school, and social functions.

Challenges of Structural Stigma

Structural stigma is manifested in the rules, policies and procedures of government and public and private entities (see Hannem, this volume). In the wake of the September 11 terrorist attacks, the American and Canadian governments enacted and implemented anti-terrorism laws, security policies, and surveillance technologies in an effort to minimize and curtail the risk of future terrorist activities (Cainkar 2004). While the language of race and racial profiling are not specifically employed in the legislation, the Canadian *Anti-Terrorism Act*, by its very nature, implicitly directs the attention of authorities to those groups who have been associated with the act of terrorism and emphasises the risk that they pose (Bahdi 2003). Structural stigma meets symbolic stigma when government officials enact these security and surveillance policies (for example at the borders and at the airports) by focusing on persons of Middle-Eastern ethnicity in a targeted and biased way, and subjecting them to more intense scrutiny and less courteous behaviour than other (non-Middle-Eastern-looking) people receive. The stated intention of the intensified security policies was not to inflict harm and/or shame onto the targeted population (Middle Eastern, Arabian, and Muslim individuals) but rather to employ security policies to ensure public safety. Nonetheless, the participants in this study experienced racial profiling and differential treatment as result of these regulatory practices. The two attributes that would mark one as the intended subject to heightened surveillance at airports and national borders post September 11 were having a “Middle-Eastern look” and having Afghanistan as one’s country of birth.

First, possessing a “Middle-Eastern look” marks an individual as someone who may belong to a statistically “risky” population, and leads him or her to be subjected to a variety of interventions, regulations, and surveillance practices. This appearance imputes a *discredited* status (Goffman 1963a) as the physical characteristics that mark one’s ethnic heritage are not easily hidden and are open to interpretation by others, which in turn invites further investigation and surveillance. Second, the revelation of Afghanistan as one’s country of birth also legitimates increased scrutiny and suspicion; however, an individual's homeland is not immediately visible to others. Country of origin is a *discreditable* status (Goffman 1963a) that reveals itself at sites of official regulation, such as border crossings, when documentation of nationality is required. Thus, it would appear that Afghan males are both discredited, as persons who are visibly marked by their Middle-Eastern ethnicity, and discreditable through the revelation of their country of birth as the point of origin of the September 11 attacks.

Experiences of Structural Stigma at Official Regulatory Sites: Airports and Borders

Soon after the events of September 11, 2001, security measures were tightened at Canada–US border crossings and at airports and Middle Eastern, Arabian, and Muslim men[8] came under scrutiny by border and airport officials. All participants who travelled to the United States or Europe post-September 11 encountered differential treatment from border and security officials in the form of racial profiling. An examination of their narratives reveals that many of them believe they were targeted initially due to their "Middle-Eastern look"; when passports revealed "Afghanistan" as their place of birth, this resulted in further discrimination. Indeed, the discreditable status of an Afghan male must be disclosed to border and airport officials, and as such, "passing" is not possible. In other words, the men's identities within these regulatory sites become "spoiled" (Goffman 1963a).

Amir is a young man in his mid-twenties, who had travelled to the United States before and after September 11; his experience provides a rich example of the interplay between structural and symbolic stigma. Prior to September 11, Amir (a Canadian citizen) crossed the Canada–US border with ease and was only required to present his citizenship card. One week after the attacks, he was targeted by border officials because of his "Middle-Eastern look"[9]:

8 The public seems to have a gendered perception of the risk of "terrorism," likely because all of the 9/11 hijackers were men and there have been fewer highly publicized incidents of terrorism perpetrated by females. Thus, while Afghan women do experience discrimination and stigma, they are not generally targeted as potential terrorists in the same way that Afghan men are.

9 Amir's experience resonates with many research studies that found a positive correlation between having a "Middle-Eastern look" and being racially profiled in the post- 9/11 period (Ramirez et al. 2003; Cainker 2004; Fiala 2003). These authors conclude that if a person's physical features are interpreted as being "Middle Eastern," then they are more likely to be stopped and thoroughly searched than someone who has the physical features of a European person (Ramirez et al. 2003).

They stopped my car and the first thing they asked me was where I was born, and as soon I mentioned Afghanistan, they asked me to pull over and go inside. Soon I was inside they go over the same question. "Are you religious?" "Do you go to Mosque?" "Do you pray?" "Do you drink?" They asked if I fast. How much I believe in Islam? How much I read the Qur'an? And all those things … I was sitting about six hours at the border being questioned by guys… basically some personal questions as well… at the end of the sixth hour they fingerprinted me and took my picture and sent me on my way.

Flying to the United States, he experienced a similar process:

Couple times that I flew there [the USA] … waiting in line ready to check in, I was singled out of the line. And I was the single person taken into a room, just because you know, I looked Middle Eastern. And they took my shoes off and searched my bag and they had to register me and take my fingerprints and picture…

Other men reflect on similar experiences while travelling to the United States and Europe. They emphasise that their "Middle-Eastern look" and the subsequent passport checks, which indicated Afghanistan as their place of birth, appear to mark them as "risky." Hakim, a former medical doctor recounts:

I pass through the United States and then to Britain. In both times I sensed a difference in the officials' treatment of me as opposed to other travellers. Because I got Canadian passport but the place of birth is Kabul, Afghanistan. The first time in Ottawa airport when I was going through the security… I was kept in the booth much longer than others and the officials had to go and consult with someone and I saw them talking for a few minutes. And I was wondering what it was all about. The only thing that prompted this kind of reaction was that I had the place of birth Kabul, Afghanistan, in my passport and then they questioned me "when was last time you were in Afghanistan?" "Have you ever gone to Pakistan?" and when I said "Yes, I have" they were looking at me as if I was admitting to carrying something quite dangerous. And both times this happened…

The men's narratives speak to the impact that structural stigma (intensified security measures targeted towards Middle Eastern, Arabian, and Muslim individuals including Afghans) has on their lived experiences.

Structural stigma directed at the newly defined "risky" population of Middle Eastern persons and/or Afghans post September 11 can also manifest in surveillance. Habib, who is in his late forties, had pre-booked a flight to Europe for September 12, 2001, intending to travel on vacation. The 9/11 attacks resulted in his flight being postponed. Two RCMP officers contacted him a few days after

9/11 and questioned him about the purpose of his travel, about his personal life, and about his political views. Finally, the officers advised him not to take the trip because he would face rigorous security checks at the airports. Ultimately, he never flew to his vacation destination:

They [RCMP officers] ask me to go to their office and I went to their office. We had a very friendly conversation, ...they ask me very friendly "Do you want to go for pleasure or business?" [I said] "No, just for the pleasure" and they said "Well if you go only for pleasure then don't go... well I am telling you friendly because you will have some problems in the airport on the way to Holland and coming back, it's up to you."

Lyon (2001) points out that the purpose of surveillance is to identify and monitor persons who belong to a suspicious category; as such, it reinforces social distinctions, underscoring the us/them division. Habib's experience exemplifies the operation of surveillance techniques as a mode of regulating and managing a "risky" population (Afghans) in the post 9/11 period. The aforementioned experiences demonstrate that having a "Middle-Eastern look" and "being born in Afghanistan" goes beyond a symbolic form of stigma by marking a group of people as "risky" and subjecting them to many forms of intervention and regulation.

Responses to Structural Stigma

The men who participated in the research had anticipated differential treatment at governmental sites of regulation after September 11. Most complied out of fear of the consequences of resisting. Despite the utter unpleasantness and insulting experiences, informants most often exercised caution during their interactions with regulatory officials.

Reza, who has been living in Canada for twenty years, voiced his discomfort with the German officials when he was interrogated at the Hamburg airport but was silent about similar treatment while travelling to the United States. More tellingly, he was careful to appear calm and co-operative despite feeling angry and uncomfortable when the American officials subjected his then five-year-old daughter to extensive searches at every checkpoint. He clearly states that he followed the rules and stayed co-operative for his own protection because he perceived that any disagreement or dissent with the United States officials could have had a punitive outcome:

I did this in Germany [arguing about being questioned extensively by an officer] and I would have done it probably anywhere else except in US. You don't want to argue too much especially with these new laws and changes. They can put me in jail for few days and I'm the one who's gonna lose. So I accept those stupid new rules they have, so I follow that. When we were coming back from Los Angeles, after we did all of our checkups, they [airport officials] checked my daughter completely. Totally like checking her again before entering in the plane. At the gate before we enter they checked us, only us again, and mostly my daughter. She was five at that time and I didn't like that at all, not at all. I was angry.

Similarly, Amir, a Dari speaking Shiite Muslim, travelled to the United States through the Canada–US border on numerous occasions and every time he was stopped and interrogated for hours. He states that he endured and tolerated border officials' security practices because he feared the consequences of expressing his disagreement and felt "powerless" in the presence of authority. He communicates his inability to dissent at border crossings, where he had to comply with the new regulations:

I wasn't expecting crossing the border to be as easy as it was before September 11th. So I had to comply, what else could I have done? I was stopped and interrogated during eight trips to America. And believe me it was not fun and I got angry every time. I had to do what they asked me to do!

Amir once tried to "pass" as someone born in Canada in order to avoid questioning and the prolonged waiting period imposed by the officials at the border. His attempt was unsuccessful:

Well the first question has always been where I was born? I did not tell them [border officers] where I was born and I told them I was born in Canada, and the officer kept asking and I said Canada. Well after few times asking then the officer snapped at me that if I was born in Canada my citizenship card would have been, looked different than theirs…finally I told them I was born in Afghanistan and then I was told to pull my car over and to go inside for some questioning which lasted six hours…

His experience illustrates that "passing" as a method of stigma management by a discreditable individual in the presence of authority figures is challenging; this is especially so in the context of post-9/11 where Middle Eastern and Muslim individuals are not only symbolically marked as departing from the "ordinary and natural" as stigma theory predicts (Goffman 1963a, 3) but are also structurally marked as belonging to a "risky" population (Cainkar 2004).

The aforementioned stories of Afghan men speak to the authoritarianism[10] that permeates airports and borders in the aftermath of 9/11. Oppression is one of the key pillars of authoritarian practices in which "a person... does not have certain rights that the dominant group takes for granted, or is assigned a second class citizenship... because of his or her membership in a particular group or category of people" (Mullaly 2002, 28). Based on his analysis of post-9/11 security policies, Conason (2007) concluded that the United States government has exhibited authoritarian qualities by enacting laws that infringe on civil liberties, disregard due process, curtail dissent, and oppress Muslim and Middle-Eastern individuals. Certainly, the men in this study communicated experiences of authoritarianism at airports and borders. The potential punitive consequences associated with any opposition and/or disobedience to intrusive and invasive security checks seemingly left them no option but to comply. They were defined as members of a "risky" population that required surveillance and intervention. As Foucault (1982) argued, where there is power there is resistance as the oppressed strive to assert agency. The following section examines the phenomenon of resistance as it emerged amongst Afghan men in the post-9/11 context.

Resisting the Mark of the "Risky" Racialized Other

Resistance refers to the "tactics, strategies and practices" subordinate groups employ, either to contest the dominant discourse and/or to assert agency (Bruckert 2002; Pickett 1996). Creating an alternate discourse that dismisses and challenges the dominant discourse can be conceptualized as a covert act of resistance. The men's narratives reflect multifaceted and nuanced alternate discourses that challenge hegemonic presentations regarding the motivations behind the attacks, question the "true" objective(s) of the American "war on terrorism," and contest representations of Afghans as Taliban.

Challenging the Dominant Discourse about 9/11

One of the notable strategies of resistance the men adopt is to challenge the Bush administration's construction of 9/11 as disseminated and reiterated by the mainstream media. In a 2001 speech, then President Bush presented his government's view of the motivations of the 9/11 terrorists:

10 Authoritarianism can be described as "a form of social and state control characterized by strict obedience to the authority of a state or organization, often maintaining and enforcing control through the use of oppressive measures" (Nelson 1994, iiv).

> They hate ... a democratically elected government. ... They hate our freedoms—our freedom of religion, our freedom of speech, our freedom to vote and assemble and disagree with each other.[11]

Many participants categorically dismissed George W. Bush's assertion and a number provided an alternate perspective, shifting the focus onto American foreign policy. For instance, Ebi, a Shiite in his mid-thirties, argued that the United States government's Middle Eastern policies ignited these events and that ultimately the Americans were responsible for provoking the attacks:

> *I thought about the history and politics of the United States and what they've been doing so far and then I realized... it's them provoking the whole movement... maybe this was their [the terrorists] way of fighting back with the United States...*

Habib, like Ebi, also shifts responsibility for the attacks to the United States government, but presents a different position: he questions the tactical ability of al-Qaeda and the Taliban to carry out such a massive assault on American territory. He contends that the United States government was either complicit or deliberately ignored warnings by other countries in order to allow the terrorist incident to happen:

> *CIA and FBI have roots in every country and all around the world. How come this incident happened and they didn't know about it? And at the same time, the Indian, French, and German governments were warning the United States in summer of 2001 that there would be an attack on the United States but they didn't take it seriously. Why? It's not easy for al-Qaeda or Taliban to make this kind of plan.*

Participants' accounts demonstrate their critical assessment of the dominant discourse as well as their engagement in creating an alternate discourse that would explain the events of 9/11 and challenge North Americans' understanding of the attacks as sudden, unprovoked, and unwarranted. By seeking a political justification for these attacks, the men reconstruct the events within their historical, sociopolitical context. Unlike the Bush administration's singular presentation of the attacks as acts of hatred against the American way of life, devoid of historical or political significance, the participants in this study frame the actions of the Taliban as a rational response to political and historical oppression by the United

---

11 George W. Bush, September 20, 2001, Address to a Joint Session of Congress and the American People.

States.[12] By questioning the role of American officials and policies in the attacks, and suggesting the complicity and/or responsibility of the American government, they set the stage to examine the objectives and the implications of the resulting "war on terrorism" critically.

Challenging the Dominant Discourse about the "War on Terrorism"

Several participants present an alternate discourse that questioned the legitimacy of, and motivation behind, the American "war on terrorism," suggesting different reasons for the American invasion of Afghanistan. A few contend that the real objective of this war lay in accessing oil-rich countries such as Uzbekistan and Tajikistan. Amir, who is angry about the United States' military attack of Afghanistan, is emphatic:

> *But the Taliban regime was also the regime that Bush's Administration was trying to stretch an oil deal with them. So, it [the War on Terrorism] had as much to do with business, as it had to do with terrorism…*

Habib echoes Amir's discourse but adds his own reflections on the situation:

> *From [a] strategic point Afghanistan is key to connecting north to the south. Afghanistan was the only one key road to gas and oil in northern countries and the pipeline had to pass [through] Afghanistan. They [the US government] were waiting for something to happen… so September 11th was a good excuse for the United States to attack Afghanistan…*

Amir, who currently lives in the United States, expands on this alternate discourse that the "war" was motivated by access to oil to include a discussion of the potential economic benefits:

> *It is not about anti-terrorism, it's not about providing security for people. It's about keeping people in paranoia. Keeping people in paranoia is what these people feed on. What people fail to realize is who is benefiting from this whole thing. US army is benefiting. Dick Cheney does not have a kid in the army who has to go to war. So why not keep the war going so his pockets get bigger while some poor minority kid is fighting the war… No one is attacking the cause of problem, no one is going to the root of the problem…*

---

12 For a detailed discussion of Afghanistan's colonial past and the USA's historical involvement, see Gregory, 2004.

By imputing a capitalist motive to the "war on terrorism," these men are not only explicitly questioning the legitimacy of the war and Americans' understanding of their government's actions, they are also implicitly questioning the morality of those who would make war for personal profit and use fear to compel the political support of a nation. This type of resistance allows the stigmatized individuals, figuratively speaking, to turn the tables and depict their accusers as immoral and unjust, thereby inverting the dominant discourse about Afghanistan and Afghans.

Another alternate explanation for the "war on terrorism" focuses on the occupation of Afghan territory as a strategic boon for the American military, with long-term implications for American interests in the Middle East. Yunis, who supports the United States' military attack on Afghanistan, framing it as an "intervention" rather than an attack, explains that Afghanistan's strategic geographic position motivated the American government to build a military base from which they could more easily police the Middle-East region:

> *Afghanistan has a strategic position geographically. You can easily monitor all neighbouring countries like Russia, China, and Iran. Which right now the United States is calling evil. That's going to be very great for the United States to have a base in Afghanistan…*

This characterization of the war as a strategic military play again calls into question the claim that the Bush government's primary motivation was to "fight terrorism" and more broadly throws some doubt on the veracity of the discourses of human rights and anti-terrorism used to legitimize the invasion of Afghanistan (and later Iraq). As a form of resistance, this process closely resembles Sykes and Matza's (1957) neutralization strategy of "condemning the condemners." This technique portrays the condemners in a negative light by drawing attention to their hypocrisy in order to undermine the legitimacy of their authority. Similarly, the tendency of Afghan men to question the legitimacy of the "war on terrorism" and the American invasion of Afghanistan allows them to throw doubt onto the portrayals of Afghans as terrorists and the "risky" identity that was created for them. Another form of resistance to the dominant discourse was to challenge the portrayal of the Taliban and to construct alternate explanations for their actions. The next section attends to this.

Challenging the Dominant Discourse about the Taliban

There are clear differences between participants' narratives of the Taliban and their relationship to the people of Afghanistan. Some identify the Taliban as Afghans and rationalize their actions, while others deny that the Taliban are Afghans and maintain that they are Arabian. As such, this second group is creating an alternate discourse that dissociates Taliban identity from Afghans, at the same time as they are affirming the dominant discourse by labelling Arabian people as (potential) Taliban members. Nonetheless, at the heart of both dialogues is an opposition and resistance to mainstream portrayals of the Taliban.

Amir and Hamid, who present as proud young men and describe themselves as "*true believers of Islam*," draw attention to the cultural practices of the Afghan people in order to challenge the stereotypically negative views of the Taliban. They identify the Taliban as Afghans who uphold the Afghan tradition of "guest-loving." This is understood as an honourable tradition in which guests are deeply respected, sheltered, and protected, in a display of unconditional hospitality. The men speak about the weeks following 9/11 when the Taliban regime refused to surrender Osama bin Laden to the United States government. However, their interpretation of the situation is dialectically different from the American government's characterization of this act as one of hostility and defiance. In this alternate presentation, the Taliban's reaction is understood as rooted in Afghanistan's culture of hospitality. Because of the respect and safety afforded to guests, the Taliban could not honourably surrender or betray their guest, Osama bin Laden.

> *Like right after September 11th. they asked Taliban to give up Osama and the Taliban refused to give him up just because the Taliban are from a Pashton background, and it's in their culture that once you become their guest, they will not give you up.*

In sharp contrast to the discourse of Amir and Hamid, a number of participants strenuously denied that the Taliban are Afghan at all. Instead, they contend that the Taliban are predominantly Arabian or Pakistanis trained by either Pakistan or Saudi Arabia or the CIA in Afghanistan territory. These men create an alternate discourse that identifies the Taliban as Arabian, in effect, defending their Afghan identity by dissociating any identification of the Taliban as Afghans. This discourse adheres to a mainstream understanding that the Taliban are in fact engaged in dangerous or negative behaviour and does not challenge North Americans' characterization of the Taliban as terrorists. At the same time, they are attempting to preserve their own identity as positive and "non-terrorist" by identifying Arabians as the "real" Taliban. Hakim's comments provide an example:

> *These [Taliban] are mostly Arabs, mostly funded by Pakistan because they are the procreator of the Taliban who are doing such things...*

Yunis, while maintaining the same arguments about the Arabian identity of the Taliban members, allows that some Afghans might have joined the Taliban as a means of providing for themselves financially:

> *Taliban was a group of unorganized people, which was exported from the neighbouring country Pakistan to Afghanistan and these people were sent to do political missions in Afghanistan. It has nothing to do with Afghani people... Taliban were foreigner. We have some people who were involved with them because of the hardness of their lives...*

In order to bolster their argument these men suggest that suicide bombing is a characteristic Arabian tactic. Najib, a university student who supports US policies, states:

> *We [Afghans] did not have suicide bombers. It's an Arabic thing, I don't know because I personally never heard of Afghanis being suicide bomber, in 25 years of war. And those people who do that [suicide bombing], I am sure are Arabs.*

Alternate discourses about the Taliban can also be linked to earlier criticisms of American foreign policy and the complicity of the US government. While Habib identifies the Taliban to be Arabian and Pakistani, he also blames the governments of the United States and Saudi Arabia for financing and creating the fundamentalist movement that led to the development of the Taliban:

> *The reality is that the United States helped these fundamentalists, financed them, trained them. It was 1981 or '82 that the United States invested... and Saudi Arabia invested money. And the United States was just programming and giving money to Pakistan to create the Taliban. So Taliban is not something new. Saudi created 5000 religious schools in Afghanistan. Taliban were foreigners; 80 percent of Taliban soldiers [were] from out of the country. They were not Afghan, only 20 percent were Afghans, and the remaining ones were Arab or Pakistani or whatever.*

Individuals who attempt to separate the Taliban from Afghans are resisting "being mistaken for other co-cultural groups" (Chuang 2004, 352). This ethnic identity confusion is an experience common to many Middle Eastern people, including Afghans, who are often assumed to be Arabian. The men consistently affirm that they identify as Middle Eastern but not as Arabian. This distinction becomes increasingly important in the post-9/11 context, and in light of these alternate discourses that equate the Taliban with Arabian ethnicity.

The narratives presented above exemplify how stigmatized groups may covertly resist their discredited image by means of alternate discourses that challenge negative stereotypes and affirm positive characteristics (Hollander and Einwohner 2004). Through these alternate discourses, Afghan men attempt to dissociate the Afghan identity from the Taliban and terrorists, and to de-legitimatize the US government's "war on terrorism," calling into question the hegemonic representations of Afghanistan as a site of terrorism.

According to Hollander and Einwohner's (2004) classification, these types of alternate discourses may be characterized as either covert or attempted resistance. While the men themselves intend to challenge mainstream understandings of Afghans and the war on terror, their arguments may not be recognized as resistance by observers (the public) or by the targets of their resistance (the US government and mainstream media). Although this form of resistance has not been entirely successful in transforming others' opinions or reactions to Afghans, it is an effective means of identity preservation and serves to assist in managing stigma on a personal level. Two other covert means of resistance and identity preservation emerged from these interviews: embracing a Muslim identity and embracing an Afghan identity.

Embracing a Muslim Identity

Amir, formerly a non-practicing Muslim, suggests that his post-9/11 re-evaluation of his religion may have been linked to the attacks: as he sought answers, he explored Islam and subsequently came to embrace the religion and its practices. The religion has since become an integral part of his personal identity. Kundnani (2002) examined young Muslim British men's inclination towards Islam in the post-9/11 period and found that the majority embraced the religion by strengthening their practices and wearing Muslim "markers" (i.e., the beard). Amir's comments resonate with Kundnani's findings:

> *That [the September 11th events] brought me closer to my religion. I was sitting in Canada looking to America. So I am not gonna sit there and get extremely upset about what happened. It really made me research it [Islam]. I did a lot more research than in the past ten, fifteen years of my life in Canada. And I would say it brought me closer to my religion.*

In addition to reaffirming his religious beliefs in the days following the September 11 attacks, Amir also started to grow his beard in October 2001. In the context of his study of Muslim men in Britain, post-9/11, Kundnani (2002) classified such practices as overt acts of everyday resistance. However, Amir rejects the suggestion put to him that the annual growing of his beard could be understood as an act of resistance, and instead explains it as a "personal thing":

> *I can't say that I grow a beard because of September 11th and... because of religious reasons. I don't want to point to that. But I do grow my beard every year and it became a tradition since 2001. I mean I grow a beard at that time but it wasn't because of religious or political reasons. I grow a beard at the beginning of October and it's a yearly thing for me now and has became a tradition. But I am not gonna say it's because of Islam and this and that. It is just a personal thing for me.*

Abbass, a practicing Muslim in his late twenties, intensified his religious ties after the events of September 11. He notes that his religious identity and practices are the only available tools he can employ to resist:

> *I was attending my Friday prayer occasionally in the Mosque and after 9/11, I found out we didn't do anything wrong... I didn't do wrong. My faith is strong; I kept my Friday prayer in the Mosque. They get their planes and bomb it [Afghanistan] and I am going to keep my faith strong and I fight with my faith, nothing else...*

The events of September 11 prompted some participants to renegotiate their religious identities and practices. By reclaiming the traditions of their faith, they sought to reaffirm their religious identity in the face of widespread public misinterpretation and, sometimes, outright hatred of Islam. A closely related phenomenon is the tendency for Afghan-Canadian men to (re)claim their ethnic and cultural identity as a means of positively redefining what it means to be an Afghan male. In openly declaring their status as Afghans, they demonstrate that not all Afghan men are "terrorists" and attempt to reclaim pride in their homeland.

Claiming Ethnic Identity

In his recent travels to Afghanistan, Yunis noticed that Afghan customs officials sought to spare travellers the stigma associated with visiting their country by not stamping their passports. His fellow travellers' acceptance of this practice upset Yunis, and he deliberately asked the official to stamp his Canadian passport. Arguably, Yunis resisted the stigma attached to travelling to Afghanistan by openly "marking" his official document and asserting agency by claiming his ethnic identity and expressing pride in this identity.

> *I went [to Afghanistan] with my Canadian passport [and] I told them "I have nothing to hide just put the stamp." I don't want to hide my Afghan nationality. I'm proud to be Afghani.*

Such everyday resistance practices allow participants a measure of control where they can exert power and agency. Feelings of powerlessness are a hallmark of oppressed and stigmatized persons, and acts of resistance are a necessary part of maintaining personal identity and preserving a sense of self-efficacy. Although such practices do not challenge stigma and discrimination directly, they may be tactically necessary where open challenges are not always possible. These men found their lives irreparably altered by the sudden redefinition of their identity and the mainstream equation of "Middle-Eastern-ness" with terrorism. The situation faced by Afghans is unique because of the dramatic transformation of their ethnic identity in mere hours. The accounts below present some of the lived experiences that resulted from the creation of this new stigma category of "(potential) terrorist" and underscore the profound implications for those so marked.

Living with Stigma

Following September 11, many Middle Eastern, Arabian, and Muslim people, including the research participants, confronted negative reactions and derogatory comments in public. Hamid speaks to this:

> *I was in the cafeteria, I was getting food and a guy started talking to me and he is like "How are you?" "Where are you from?" I said "I am from Afghanistan" he is like "Oh one of those terrorists."*

Another account by Amir speaks to the stereotypical depiction of terrorists and the extent to which Afghan ethnicity/identity has become associated with risk. It also demonstrates that these scripts permit social actors to abandon normative patterns of social interaction. Upon learning that he was born in Afghanistan, one of Amir's clients interrogated him during a lengthy phone conversation and he felt compelled to respond to her increasingly inappropriate questions:

> *I was actually doing help desk support for an American company and had a customer who had called from America. And once I told her my name and where I was from, because she was asking me where I was from. As soon as I told her where I was initially from, her voice just turned and all of a sudden she sound scared. She asked me if I was in a "sleeper cell," um I thought it was funny. I laughed at it. I tried to make a joke about it but she was dead serious. She wanted to know if I was in a "sleeper cell." And she wanted my name, address, and all the information. And she wanted to speak to my manager just to, you know, make sure.*

In contrast to Amir's passive acceptance of his interrogation, Hamid took a much more assertive approach, challenging the assumptions that would stigmatize him:

Another Arab guy actually surprised me. He was Christian Lebanese. When I said my name is Hamid and I am from Afghanistan and while we were conversing he is like "You guys are like Osama bin Laden." I said "actually... Osama bin Laden is Arab and he is not Afghan, so he has more to do with you my friend." He is like, "I am Christian I have nothing to do with him." I say "What you mean you are Christian you have nothing to with him? You think I have something to do with him? Because we share the same religion doesn't mean I support his ideas."

Amir recounts another incident that occurred just two weeks after September 11 when he and his fiancé were at a restaurant:

I remember I walked into a restaurant about two weeks after 9/11. And the waiter... I asked him for a straw and he threw the straw at me at the table. I am sure it was because I looked Middle Eastern, I don't think he would do it to a white person.

There are many possible explanations for the waiter's behaviour, but what is significant here is that Amir's reading of this encounter is conditioned by stigma consciousness, defined by Pinel (2004) as "the extent to which targets believe that their stereotyped status pervades their interaction with members of the outgroup" (39). The pervasiveness of the "war on terrorism" rhetoric in North America and its association with Afghanistan has serious implications for the Afghan person's understanding of his interactions with others. The realization of his discredited/discreditable status conditions his expectations of others' behaviours and reactions, creating the possibility that any incident of perceived incivility will be interpreted as a response to the stigma category or stereotype. The stigmatized individual need not directly experience discriminatory or negative behaviour from others in order to feel subjectively that he is socially discredited. It is this stigma consciousness that leads individuals proactively to attempt to manage their spoiled identity through passing, avoidance, or selective disclosure, common stigma-management techniques that will be discussed below.

The association with terrorism and the risky status that has been attached to the Afghan identity opens these individuals to a myriad of negative social encounters. As the preceding accounts demonstrate, strangers will not hesitate to depart from the scripts of common courtesy in social interactions to inflict defamatory remarks, rude treatment, or interrogatory behaviour. These reactions to the Afghan identity shed light on the pervasiveness of the messages of "risk" and fear of terrorism that have permeated North American society in the wake of the 9/11 attacks. The effects of a spoiled identity can be devastating to interpersonal and professional relationships; however, Afghan men employ a range of strategies to manage interpersonal stigma and to deal with the tensions that arise in interactions with others. Two of the most common techniques, "passing" and avoidance, will be discussed in detail below.

Managing Interpersonal Stigma

This analysis has demonstrated that the men are often positioned as discreditable individuals, where the "spoiled" aspect of their identity is not immediately known to others. In these situations, they are able to exercise some degree of agency by using a diverse range of strategies to manage the information about themselves available to others. Two participants tried to "pass" during interactions with strangers in order to deflect and/or protect themselves, while others used different methods to reduce tension arising in interpersonal interactions; for example, withdrawal, strategic avoidance, and disclosing stigma to a selected group.

Abbass and Habib, whose occupations require contact with strangers, employ "passing" techniques and conceal their ethnic identity in order to protect themselves from potential hate-related incidents. Kanuha (1999) asserts that stigmatized individuals engage in passing as a mode of self-protection when the social sanction of the stigma is severe. Cognizant of hate-motivated discriminatory acts against Afghans, Abbass frequently employs silence as a method of stigma management:

> *People were toughening in Canada, I remember an Afghan man had a pizza store restaurant they tried to burn it. They started insulting people, so I thought it's better to shut my mouth a little. It's very hard to say I am one of those people over there [Afghanistan]. My religion, country, and society are under attack. You are either with the people [Canadians] or against them. So no, I didn't tell those who didn't know that I was Afghani, I just said nothing. But when asked a lot I said in Canada we are all Canadian, and I was not a Canadian citizen at that time…*

Similarly, Habib sought to pass as a Canadian and in the year following September 11 consciously steered conversations to avoid having to reveal his Afghan identity:

> *I was talking to a lot of customers in the beginning after September 11th. It was hard for me when anybody asked me "Where are you from?" I couldn't say I am from Afghanistan. Instead, I would say "We are all Canadians" and changed the subject. I was just wondering if I say I am from Afghanistan maybe they would react because I was feeling that being from Afghanistan meant finger pointing. Because there was a lot of hatred*

among the people. Maybe a year after 9/11 then I could say "Yeah I am from Afghanistan," and if they had any question, I would clearly explain to them.

When one's biography is well known, it is difficult to pass. When Abbass's identity became "spoiled" at work and his co-workers made derogatory remarks on a regular basis, he avoided confrontation and distanced himself from potential tension by seeking work elsewhere:

I was working at a couple of places at that time, I remember because my boss knew everything and as a joke, they would point the finger like "Yeah you guys tough, you are Afghani." Such things mean bad horrible things. They were joking and finger pointing. I left two, three jobs.

Though not as dramatic as Abbass's abandonment of his work, a number of the men in this study avoided travelling to, or through, the United States in order to evade the intrusive surveillance practices that have become the norm for Afghans post-9/11.

I decided not to go because I do not want somebody like border and airport agents or American people to look at me like a stranger, no. I wouldn't allow that, no. (Abbass)

[To] be honest with you, if I have something not serious I am not going [to the USA]. But I was going before September 11th often. (Yunis)

The desire to manage stigma or to avoid potential conflict can thus curtail personal freedom of movement and restrict the choices that one has for work or leisure. Although these restrictions are often self-imposed, they are based on the very real possibility of discriminatory treatment and distressing experiences. It is easy to see that managing a spoiled identity has profound effects on the everyday interactions of Afghan men. These individuals exercise vigilance and are always cognizant of the potential consequences of their spoiled identity. The genesis of the structural and interpersonal stigma experienced by these men can be traced back to September 11 and the aforementioned encounters of defamatory comments and differential treatment must be understood within this context. In the immediate aftermath of this event, Afghan ethnicity came to be considered a negative attribute and the men found themselves the targets of surveillance and discriminatory practices. As such, Afghan ethnic identity in itself became a more salient factor in shaping participants' lived realities. The next section discusses participants' assertion of the importance of Afghan ethnic identity.

Collective Afghan Ethnic Identity

Despite diversity in experiences and perceptions, most participants expressed pride in their Afghan origins. Some had "passed" in the immediate aftermath of September 11 as a means of self-protection, yet all of the men proclaimed that they would no longer hesitate to announce their ethnic identity. Orbe and Harris (2001, 7) define ethnicity as "a cultural marker that indicates shared traditions, heritage, and ancestral origin" and Cornell (1988) adds the importance of an emotional bond or sentiment that originates in the past. Throughout the interviews, participants expressed such historical and emotional bonds to their Afghan identity.

Most participants noted that September 11 affected their personal identity by bringing their ethnicity to the forefront of their interactions. They continued this discussion by reiterating that prior to 9/11 they were members of just one of many different ethnic groups living in Canada. In the aftermath of this event, they were treated as a "risky" population, becoming targets of surveillance practices and differential treatment at the structural level, and defamatory comments at the interpersonal level. Despite all the negative experiences associated with their Afghan ethnic identity, they continue to assert that they are proud of their ethnicity. Even Najib, who claims that he has become pro-American, said:

I have always been a proud of being an Afghan, even if there are wars in Afghanistan... And I don't hide it...

Fong (2004) mentions that ethnic identity is an important part of personal identity, and argues that individuals try to communicate their ethnic affiliations, particularly if they believe that others hold an unfavourable view of their ethnic background that is unfair or untrue. All the interviewees expressed the view that being an "Afghan" constituted an integral part of their sense of self and that they have recognized the need to alter erroneous assumptions on the part of the public. A few of the men report deliberately introducing themselves as Afghan during social interactions with acquaintances or even with strangers. They contend that such interactions afforded them an opportunity to openly discuss Afghanistan and clarify any misconceptions about their homeland. Hamid, a young Political Science student said:

I want to say to people "I am from Afghanistan" because I actually want to change those people's mentality. Because generally when you ask about Afghanistan, all they think about is beating women, terrorism, and the Taliban regime. I really want people to

> *know how people react when you say you are from Afghanistan ... they have the sense of Afghanistan as the land of terrorism. And I want to be clear with them that it is not so.*

Yunis mentioned that he contacted some locally based radio talk shows when the topic of Afghanistan was raised in an attempt to inform and illuminate the audiences about Afghans and Afghanistan:

> *I listen to [a local talk-radio station] and when any subject comes about Afghanistan, I try to explain to make a little bit of clarification about Afghan's tradition. And I did a couple of times. And I was trying to explain to them who is this Taliban group and why they came to Afghanistan, who brought them in.*

He expressed the opinion that every Afghan living in Canada should take advantage of any opportunity to educate the public about misunderstandings regarding Afghanistan and Afghans:

> *This is the duty of each Afghani to complete [the Canadian public's] information because the media is always incomplete. And this is our duty to complete [information] for them.*

Indeed, Mullaly (2002) has argued that an ethnic identity is a political resource that can be used to further a group's interests, indeed ethnicity as identity could be understood as a new social movement. Clearly, some of the participants employ their Afghan ethnic identity as a political tool to at least challenge the erroneous beliefs held by the public.

Conclusion

It is important to remember that stereotypical depictions and prejudicial treatment of ethnic minorities are not new phenomena in the political and social discourses of North Americans (Mullaly 2002). For example, Aboriginal people and African-Americans have been systematically discriminated against in judicial, political, labour, and educational systems in Canada and in the United States (Mullaly 2002). However, the authoritarian and stigmatizing practices directed at Middle Eastern, Arabian, and Muslim people including Afghan-Canadians since the events of September 11, at both the structural and interpersonal levels are alarming. The participants' narratives highlight the speed with which the construction of a "risky" group can occur. It is clear that the stereotypes of Afghans, as supporting terrorism and as potential terrorists in large part shapes the treatment of these individuals, both in formal institutional settings and in informal everyday encounters.

It is our hope that this research will provide Afghan-Canadians with a framework for making sense of their experiences within the broader context of the systemic racial inequality that has dominated North American society. Perhaps an awareness of others' struggles with discrimination and prejudice can mobilize and motivate Afghan persons to become better organized in their efforts to fight against stigma, actively engaging in political and social discussion in order to challenge and eradicate prejudice. The events of 9/11 could be an impetus for this group to take part in educating the public about their culture, religion, and political history, as well as communicating their experiences of stigmatization and its effect on their lives. The principal author, as an Afghan-Canadian woman, took this initiative not only to provide a forum through which her fellow countrymen could speak to their experiences of stigma but also to begin her own personal fight against this social ill. What we need is not a "war on terrorism," as declared by George W. Bush, but a war against racism and prejudice that finds deep roots in North American political and social discourse.

Chapter Four

The Mark of "Disreputable" Labour

Workin' It: Sex Workers Negotiate Stigma

Chris Bruckert

Prologue

After abandoning high school and working at a number of minimum wage jobs, I eventually migrated into the sex industry. The job was a good, if not brilliant, fit. It provided me with adequate money, a pleasant work environment, great colleagues, and independence. Four years later, I drifted into other jobs and eventually into university. My time in the sex industry was not particularly significant—nor was it my identity any more than waitressing or sales clerking or telemarketing or cleaning hotel rooms or teaching university. That said, for many years I edited my biography to omit this specific part of my journey—at least until I was secure in my audience. For many years I lived not only the lie of omission but also a conceptual disconnect. After all, I did not "buy into" the discourse that I should be either traumatized by, or ashamed of, my work in the sex industry. More importantly, I had a nagging suspicion that by allowing myself to be invisible, I was implicitly supporting what I perceived to be the exploitative abolitionist rhetoric. I justified the decision to myself: What business is my past? What is the point? Did I really want to hurt my aging parents? These convenient truths masked a deeper reality—I was profoundly afraid of the consequences of "coming out." I was afraid of real material consequences—of being fired from my job, of not getting into graduate school, of being dismissed, of being appropriated by feminist scholars. Perhaps even more, I, a budding "serious" scholar, feared that on the basis of my past experiences I would become a token, a novelty, the embodiment of the liberal academy. Feeling dirty and dishonest, I was an *ambivalent* passer—and perhaps, for that reason I was not a particularly *good* one. Over and over again I let the mask slip—I spoke too passionately, or used too many insider examples, or employed the "wrong" pronoun. Far too often I heard the sharp intake of breath, the perplexed look and then observed the reflection in someone's eyes as they stripped away my veneer and reassessed me in light of this new (and apparently significant) identity. At the end of this private status degradation ceremony I found myself standing exposed as esteem was replaced by pity, contempt, dismissal, or titillation. Sometimes the experience was different. With those who either directly or indirectly shared my "spoiled identity," I saw suspicion replaced by connection. Such is the power of shared stigma that our differences slipped away (at least for the moment), our bodies relaxed, our vocabulary shifted, and our conversation deepened.

Ultimately, I knew I had to "come out." After all, how could I champion sex worker rights and continue to conceal my own experience? When the irony and duplicity became too troubling, however, I eased, rather than walked, out of the proverbial closet. More specifically I disclosed that I was a retired erotic dancer when I got my probationary (tenure stream) university position and only spoke publicly of my more "disreputable" past as a prostitute when I had the security of tenure. What about today? My whoring was a lifetime ago and in the meantime I have not only accumulated multiple markers of respectability—children, a doctorate, a professorship—but also constructed a public identity that integrates rather than denies my journey. What does this mean for me? Does it mean that I can be loud and proud with impunity? Not exactly. I still hear the sharp intake of breath. I still see the perplexed reassessment as my audience seeks to reconcile what they (wrongly) presume to be contradictory identities. I still sense confusion and the anticipation of a titillating story. But now I also see (or perhaps I only *think* I see) something else as well—something that speaks to master status. While I sometimes hear annoyingly patronizing congratulations—"Good girl!" "You've done really well for yourself!"—at other times I recognize the questioning of my accomplishments. Is she a *real* academic? Is she a rigorous researcher? How can she be objective? How did she get her job? Is she a token in the academy?

Does this matter to me? Like all stigmatized individuals, the answer is less than straightforward: sometimes it makes me angry, other times it undermines my confidence, often it spurs me on. But it always aggravates me!

> *I'm not friends with other dancers outside of work, other than Jackie. It's not because I don't like dancers, or don't want to be friends with them. It's just that I think most dancers need to realize we're in an industry that is not in the favour of women. We're being exploited… A club owner is not going to put you first. So we at least need to be there for each other and stuff. Instead of being another enemy to each other … I think a lot of dancers need to realize that as women we need each other. 'Cause I'm not there to be your enemy, I'm there to make money—just like you. I wish I could say that to them.* (Susan, erotic dancer)

Feminists have long drawn attention to the *whore stigma*'s implicit subtext of female unworthiness and dishonour, and demonstrated how the good girl/bad girl dichotomy splinters the female element and inhibits unified challenges to patriarchal power (Pheterson, 1996). Without questioning the validity (or indeed the significance) of this argument, my focus in this chapter is more specific, more immediate, and more concrete. I am drawing on the concept of stigmatized labour to explore how women working in the indoor sex industry (strip clubs, massage parlours, dungeons, brothels, and so on) experience, negotiate, and resist both interpersonal and structural stigma. Accordingly, this chapter is guided by a series of interrelated questions: What are the stereotypes that inform the stigma and how are stigmatic designations experienced? How are they implicated in the labour and the lives of these workers, and to what extent do they condition their personal and professional choices? How are stigmatic assumptions embedded in state policies and practice? What is their impact on workers' ability to realize their human, social, and labour rights? How do indoor sex workers negotiate their personal and social identities while managing and resisting the stigmatic assumptions of general and specific others? Finally, how does stigma "play out" for street-based sex workers whose ability to navigate and resist stigma is constrained by the public nature of their labour location, the cultural, economic and social capital at their disposal, and the layered discourses that denigrate, delegitimate, and silence.

Like many other chapters in this collection, I start with Goffman (1963a) and his definition of stigma as an attribute that reduces an individual "from a whole and usual person to a tainted, discounted one" (3). Interactively realized, it is "a special case in the typification of difference; one that is very much in the foreground of our attention and negatively evaluated" (1963a, 4). Since we are presumed to choose the *nature,* if not the *fact*, of our work, labour market location can be a discrediting attribute if the work is illegal, immoral, or improper.[1] That said, sex work differs from other "tainted" jobs such as morticians, custodians, and used car salesmen. Not only is sex work on the margins of legality, and subject to a specifically moral stigma, but the occupational stigma is constructed as a personal attribute so that the implications extend beyond the sphere of work and the label becomes a master status that has permanence across social *space*. It also adheres across *time*—even, as we have seen in the prologue, being an *ex*-sex worker is an identity marker that can be ascribed definitive value. It is also a *courtesy* stigma—contaminating associates, children, parents, and most especially, partners.

In this chapter I draw on the findings from a series of qualitative studies in which I was a researcher (Bruckert and Chabot 2010; Bruckert and Parent 2006, 2007; Bruckert, Parent, and Poliot 2006; Bruckert, Parent, and Robitaille 2003; Bruckert 2002). Specifically I am using forty-three interviews with erotic dancers and seventeen with women who work in the in-call sector.[2] I also draw on an additional twenty-seven interviews conducted with Ottawa-area street-based workers as part of a community-based research project. All the interviews were in-depth, semi-structured explorations lasting between one and three hours. This methodological approach reflects the researchers' profound commitment to starting from the perspective of participants, carefully attending to the voices of experience, and rigorously centring those voices in the analysis.

The Mark of the Whore and Beyond

> *[The public] have a very bad image of dancers. That it's like on Jerry Springer and like what they see on TV, you know? Of course they do. I did. I had a bad image of dancers until I became one. Like it's something you have to be involved in to actually understand.* (Kim, erotic dancer)

The sex workers who participated in the various researches were highly cognizant of the stigmatic assumptions of outsiders and appreciated that the nature of the stigma is neither straightforward nor self-evident. They recognized that the whore stigma that positions them as immoral and hypersexual persists: *"People do judge. You say you're a dancer and they'll pretend they don't judge but*

1 My point of departure is consistent with the subject position of workers and well supported in the literature that sex work is work (Benoit and Millar 2001; Jeffrey and MacDonald 2006; Lewis, Maticka-Tyndale, and Shaver 2005, 2006).

2 Within the sex industry the distinction between out-call workers who go to the homes or hotel rooms of clients, and in-call workers who provide services in their own homes or places of work, is significant.

they do. [They think] we will sleep with anybody... it's not true at all" (Kim, erotic dancer). At the same time, they were also aware that they are the subjects of a cluster of other stigmatic assumptions. These discourses form a constellation of "sticky" characteristics that "become attached, entangled like candy floss" (Goffman 1963a, 57) onto the public identity of the sex worker. One myth that persists is the notion that sex workers are vectors of disease; this prevails despite significant empirical evidence that sex workers are safe sex practitioners and that "HIV transmission is about unprotected sex, not prostitution, and prostitution does not inherently carry a risk of HIV infection" (Canadian HIV/AIDS Legal Network 2005, 26). Equally prevalent is the (mistaken) assumption that workers are substance (ab)users. Kate, a 19-year-old erotic dancer, explained what this meant for her:

> *People are very judgmental, and they're having negative opinions of dancers. They think that we're all drugged up... I'm not ashamed. But it's just not something... I mean I don't brag about [being an erotic dancer]. You know, so I just tell them, I saved up over summer to live on my own, or I have a job that pays this much. You never know what somebody's going to say.*

Sex workers must also contend with the paternalistic radical feminist discourse that positions them as victims without agency:

> *Every single day, every person you meet, you never know if you'll get judged. That is a tough thing to deal with. Especially if you are happy with what you are doing and you chose to do what it is that you do. It has been about a year a half that I do my own thing, I am independent, I make my own choices, I see who I want to see, I do what I want to do. Even that is not enough. I think about telling my mom and all I can hear is her saying "Oh my gosh! Who is making you do this?" Well, it's me; I choose to do this!* (Meredith, massage-parlour worker)

This is a particularly insidious stigma and one that workers take on with considerable finesse when they categorically reject such a construction yet acknowledge that, like other individuals who sell their labour power, they may be exploited *workers*. Ginette, a Haitian woman with ten years' experience in the erotic dance industry, spoke to this:

> *Certainly there are problems, but it is a choice. It is a choice like working at McDonalds where you go and earn minimum wage. Maybe that is not really a choice. But they do not see it like that; they do not pity you because you had no choice.* [translation mine]

In short, sex workers are presumed, in the first instance, to be immoral social agents. In addition, however, there is also a cluster of inferred characteristics: that they are diseased, abusers of illicit substances, and victims without agency.

As will become evident, stigma is experientially real for women in the indoor sex industry. In fact, for many sex workers, it is not the job itself—the sex, the intimacy, or the physical demands—but the stigmatized nature of the labour that is the most disagreeable element:

> *It's tough to always be judged and to never really know who is going to judge you... I have to say, it's probably the hardest thing, or maybe the only hard thing for me in this business.* (Tammy, massage parlour worker)

The next section turns to thinking about how this "stigma assemblage" plays out in the lives of women in the indoor sex industry before reflecting on structural stigma and the ways these same discourses and conversations inform state policy and practice. Appreciating that sex workers are social actors and agents, the discussion then turns to indoor sex workers' strategies for managing and resisting stigma. We end the chapter with some reflections on the implications of stigma for women labouring in the street-based sex industry.

Stigma Matters: Private Life

For sex workers, stigma is not an abstract sociological concept but a *lived* reality. Many of the women who participated in these researches had stories about being discriminated against based on their occupation and having to cope with people assuming their labour to be a definitive identity marker; the mistaken belief that sex work is who they *are* rather than one of the things that they *do*:

> *People who don't know me, they almost view me as not a real person when they get to know that I am a stripper... That I live very much outside of society. And I do live outside of society in that I engage in unconventional work, but I also very much live within society, I go to school, I have a job, I shop at the local grocery store.* (Sophie, erotic dancer)

The implications of this are real. Sex workers talked about being denied jobs when potential employers found out about their current or former labour in the sex industry, of being refused apartments, of having their bank loan applications declined. Others had faced negative judgments, or experienced a perceptual shift, when their neighbours, friends, or co-workers became aware of their occupation. Jan, an Ottawa-based erotic dancer noted:

> *The odd time when I have sort of let it come out, when people ask me, "What do you do?" [And then] especially with guys. As soon as I tell them what I do, it's like they start to look at you different. Like one minute, I'm sort of a friend or I'm like a person and then—I'm a dancer!*

In other cases, it is more than a perceptual shift. Karen, a 34-year-old single mother of two young girls, reflected on how an earlier attempt to exit the erotic dance industry by accessing social services was undermined when she was subjected to what could perhaps best be described as a "status degradation ceremony" (Garfinkle 1956, 402):

> *I walked in there, it was summer time, and my worker looked at me and said, "Are you stripping again?" This is in front of a whole group of people! A whole waiting room full of people! None of these people knew me from a hole in the ground, and she had the nerve to say that. Out Loud! Through her little cubicle because if she wasn't behind there she would have gotten it, you know what I mean? I couldn't believe it! I looked at her, I said, "I beg your pardon?" I got home and called her super, I mean nothing was done. I said, "No I'm not" [to her]. Because I looked nice. I was in a skirt in the summer time. She had the nerve to ask me that. It was just like unbelievable. They're the worst. They automatically assume because you can, you are. Or because you used to, you [still] do.*

At times the fear of being stigmatized, or stigma consciousness[3] (Pinel 2004) inhibits full participation in social life. Anne, another Ottawa dancer and single mother of two daughters, noted:

> *I've been too shy about signing my daughter up for play groups and stuff like that cause I'm afraid that they're going to find out about her mom being a stripper, and then they'll subject her to—to what not.*

A number of participants pointed out that even individuals who endeavour to be non-judgemental are nonetheless operating in terms of deeply embedded assumptions of difference. According to Jenny, a 31-year-old Aboriginal woman:

> *When you say 'I'm a stripper' people will automatically go, 'Ah, you know, it's a job like another'. Do they say that when you say 'I'm an accountant'— 'Oh, it's a job like another'?*

Angelica, a Montreal sex worker, drew attention to how the underlying assumptions sometimes play out subtly:

---

3 Stigma consciousness, defined by Pinel as "the extent to which targets believe that their stereotyped status pervades their interaction with members of the outgroup" (2004, 39).

It's hard to get a certain kind of support. Like, people that don't do it are always like "Well just stop doing it, then" you know, "Why are you doing it if it's hard?" [Laughs] It's like, well everything's hard! You know. Like if you're working, you're making six dollars an hour at a coffee shop you're gonna have to deal with people you hate. But that's part of your job. And it's the same thing... So it's hard to get that, like, full support.

Workers' engagement in a stigmatized occupation also has implications for their intimate lives. Some workers delay getting involved in a relationship until the end of their career, either because they do not want to deal with the complications or because they accept dominant discourses regarding "propriety:"[4]

I've dated a little bit but not really. I always said I'd never have a boyfriend while I'm dancing, you know, cause, to me, if a guy cared about you, why would he want you to show your body and be touched and stuff like that. (Judy, erotic dancer)

Some women spoke of their partners' unwillingness to offer support. As Karen, a Toronto area massage-parlour worker, explained: "*He definitely knows. But it's not like I'll come home and be like, 'This is what happened today,' it's not something that, you know, we discuss what goes on.*" Kim, an erotic dancer, explained how this lack of communication undermines intimacy: "*He didn't want to hear anything about my work. So obviously it was a go-nowhere relationship when you can't even vent to a person. You know 'cause we need to talk about our day.*" Even when partners were supportive, deeply embedded stigmatic assumptions emerge:

I'll never forget the one time... I made 400 dollars one night and I was just thrilled and he called me at work, and I was "Guess how much money I made!?" And he was like "How much?" "400 dollars!!" And he was like, "What did you do for that?" My heart just sunk. This was a person I was with for five years at the time! What was he thinking? If you don't know me! (Karen, erotic dancer)

In other cases, power/knowledge is enacted when a partner deliberately draws on the deeply rooted stigmatizing discourses to undermine the woman's sense of self. Doll, a dancer reflecting on a previous relationship, noted, "*He's like, you know, nobody will ever really love you while you're dancing. And I got that always stuck in my head, you know, like nobody's really going to care.*"

4 It is the stigma rather than the work that inhibits intimate relations. Many sex workers speak of their increased sexual confidence, improved self-image, and increased ability to identify their own sexual and personal needs—all of which can have positive implications vis-à-vis their intimate relations.

In short, working in a stigmatized occupation means workers must contend with a cluster of stigmatic assumptions that have a significant impact on their interactions and constrain their being-in-the-world.

Stigma Matters: Work Life

Not only do workers confront stigmatic assumptions in the social and intimate spheres, they also permeate the labour site. Angelica, a sex worker, complained, *"Clients assume that I'm really stupid."* Others spoke of clients' disregard for their personal boundaries as they wrongly assumed that any sexual or interpersonal service is available to be purchased.[5] Workers are also annoyed with the general failure to recognize the value of the services they offer:

> *My biggest challenge is the people that don't understand sensuality and who either do not respect or understand the concept of respecting providers ... What I mean by not respecting the services or the idea of the services that I offer. The whole "bang for the buck" attitude, like "what can I get."[...] I think women in the industries have incredible skills, how could you balance all that if you didn't have skills? But these skills don't relate to the mainstream.* (Tammy, massage parlour worker)

Erotic dancers are also frustrated with customers who believed them to be promiscuous. It should be noted, however, that rather than challenge the stigmatic assumptions regarding "availability," sometimes this script is subverted when it is used in their own interests. Rachel, an erotic dancer, reflected, "*I guess we all basically pretend we don't have boyfriends, or pretend we don't live with anybody—all those things like that you don't ever talk about.*"

The notion of stigmatized labour also alerts us to the assumptions embedded in managerial practices and policies. Sophie suggested that the (mistaken) assumption on the part of managers that dancers are providing sexual services undermines their ability to engage in open dialogue regarding regulations:

> *We do get some information [about laws] but it's said so casually and not officially, like "don't suck cock." There are also some posters in the dressing rooms... Once, I went to see a manager to have him clarify a rule that says that we are not allowed to straddle customers. Everybody does it though and I don't see a problem with that since my crotch is about a foot away from the customer's crotch and it's obvious that there is no genital contact.*

5 Individual sex workers have their own boundaries and are prepared to offer some services and not others. For example, some workers may offer oral or manual release only while others offer intercourse.

However, when I asked my question, the management assumed that I was doing something against the rules, which now makes it very difficult for me to go ask for clarifications.

In addition, within a strip club, a specifically paternalistic discourse that casts dancers as unreliable workers is evident. This stigmatic assumption revolves around the perceived lack of work ethic and the administrative problems engendered by the "*unreliability of girls.*" Not only are erotic dancers always referred to as *girls*—a rather obvious example of infantilization—but the discourse resounds with sexist, patronizing assumptions. In the rather revealing words of one manager I interviewed, "*No shit, managing a club is like having ten girlfriends on PMS*" (Craig).

Of course, stereotypes and the ensuing stigmas do not operate in isolation. Perhaps it is not surprising that in the non-institutional space of the indoor sex industry, an ambiguous regulatory location exists in which racism, sexism, and ageism are manifest.[6] The very existence of Asian massage parlours speaks not only to racial segregation but also to deeply entrenched stereotypes regarding women from Southeast Asia. In strip clubs it is not unusual to see the "other" marginalized[7] and excluded based on stereotypical and Eurocentric definitions of beauty (Bruckert and Parent 2006; Stella 2003). Sophie explained that:

Unless they have been working there for many years, many black dancers can only work the day shift, when for me, because I am white, I can work any shift I want. I just show up. The managers will often make racist comments to the girls. For example, once I was in the dressing room with a black dancer. She was busy brushing her weaves. The manager was urging her to go back to work and she told him she was busy brushing her hair. He responded "That's not your hair," a comment I interpreted as racist. They will also act in more subtle ways such as banning rap music, but not stuff like Marilyn Manson, which is not necessarily the kind of music a middle-aged white man would like either. In certain clubs, they will go as far as to ban artists like Rhianna. It's not rap, but she's black. Girls complain about it all the time, it bothers all of us. We all wish we could see it addressed.

6 Racism has long been characteristic of the sex industry. In their historical examination of Vancouver's erotic dance industry between 1945 and 1975, Ross and Greenwell (2005) demonstrate that racializing discourses and practices conditioned the industry and the experiences of the women workers, noting that "the gold" of the golden era was unevenly distributed among dancers. White striptease dancers dominated the "A-List" headliner category in ways that exposed the racial grammar of post-war "glamour" and "sexiness"—a grammar that simultaneously encoded dancers of colour as "novelties with limited marketability" (2005, 138). Their research uncovered a geographically and racially segregated industry—racialized women dominated in the working and under-class East End, rarely finding employment in the "upscale" West End clubs (Ross and Greenwell 2005, 141).

7 See Said's (1978) concept of orientalism and his argument that occidental culture has essentialized Asian peoples in ways that obscure diversity.

Many strip clubs appear to have "quotas" of racialized women. Joan is a 31-year-old black woman whose narrative is striking:

> *I'll give you an example. Just yesterday I was going to go and work at The Pussy Palace, and as soon as I went in there and said "hello" to a manager, he told me I could not work because there were already two dark girls working that day and that's their quota. He told me that's an everyday thing at all the bars; they all have their limits of how many are allowed to work. Well they always say that, but I've never heard the two—they'll usually allow three or four. I had to pay extra to get to the other bar where I could work.*

Moreover, racialized women must contend with negative responses and even rejection, not only from management, but also from clients:

> *I often face racism at work. Many people like me, but I have had others who say to me "Excuse me but I want nothing to do with blacks." This past Friday I had the same experience. I went very pleasantly to see a man who was seated and he looked at me in a way... and he said, "I would like you to leave my table." You see it was really my colour that he wanted nothing to do with.* (Dominique, translation mine)

In an effort to manage the consequences, some women attempt to exploit (and of course thereby legitimate) the discourse that would oppress them by carving a space for themselves as the exotic other. Joan, a 23-year veteran of the erotic dance industry, explains:

> *Actually, they sort of adore me. I think because I'm different. My features are different. I'm not black and I'm not white and I'm not mulatto. So I'm kind of Spanish/black/something and it's like a completely exotic look.*

The "quotas" and overt racism evident in strip clubs cannot be individualized to the sex industry but must be understood within the broader context of Canadian society. In their 2007 report, the National Anti-Racism Council of Canada stated,

> The lived experiences of racialized groups, are rooted in extreme and disparate poverty, inequality, racism, and general socio-economic insecurity and deprivation. [...] the poverty rate for racialized groups is three times the average of their white counterparts. Racialized groups within Canada are victims of structural and systemic racial inequality in a country that prides itself as a protector of human rights and promoter of equality. (NARCC 2007, 7)

In this context, racialized sex workers find themselves confronting layers of stratification and intersecting stigmas that merge and converge and profoundly affect their labour experience.[8]

Structural Stigma

Embedded in the conceptualization of sex work as stigmatized labour is the recognition of the historical process of moral regulation; when *disreputable* and stigmatized activities are enacted as work, the workers and their labour site are enmeshed in a regulatory web unknown to mainstream occupations. Workers are discursively constructed based on stereotypes, first as anomalous and then as at risk/risky in official policy and practice. These (dubious) "truths" take on an authenticity that then legitimates subsequent regulatory initiatives. In this section, we turn our attention to this structural stigma and reflect on some of the ways it conditions the work and private lives of indoor sex workers.

Sex workers inhabit an ambiguous legal location—while the exchange of sexual services for compensation is not, and never has been, illegal in Canada, there are a number of laws in the *Criminal Code*—most especially section 210, which prohibits being an owner or inmate of a common bawdy house[9]—to which women working in massage parlours or brothels and, to a lesser extent, erotic dancers, are vulnerable. Of course, this law has been the subject of a constitutional challenge by three current and former sex workers, Terri Bedford, Amy Lebovitch, and Valerie Scott. However, the March 28, 2012, ruling by the Ontario Court of Appeal in *Canada (Attorney General) v Bedford (2012 ONCA 186,* at 212) that "the impact of the bawdy-house prohibition on prostitutes, and particularly street prostitutes, is grossly disproportionate to its legislative objective" and is therefore unconstitutional has been stayed pending a ruling by the Supreme Court.

In practical terms, this means that in-call sex workers continue to organize their labour practices in an effort to minimize the likelihood of being charged (and engendering the additional and permanent mark of a criminal record) and, in the process, increase their vulnerability to violence. For example, they will not communicate openly on the phone. Simon, a masseuse, explains, "*Some people expect sexual services that I don't necessarily provide... I can't say, 'Yes, you are gonna have an orgasm at the end' or 'I am going to jerk you off' because of my fear of police entrapment.*" Moreover, cognizant of the potential for clients to lay a complaint

8 See Bruckert and Frigon (2004) for more on this issue.

9 In the Canadian *Criminal Code,* a bawdy house is defined as "a place that is kept or occupied, or resorted to by one or more persons, for the purpose of prostitution or the practice of acts of indecency." As such it can be a sex worker's home, hotel room, or even a parking lot.

with the police, sex workers endeavour to appease disgruntled clients. They are also hesitant to report violent clients or turn to the police when they are victimized. Sometimes this may be based on experience but it may also be based on stigma consciousness and the presumption that police will operate in relation to stigmatic assumptions. The following quote by Tammy, a massage parlour worker, exemplifies the latter:

> *What recourse do I have if I have a bad client? Can I really walk into a police station and say "I offer erotic massage services and this guy took it too far, raped me, and beat the shit out of me?" I would never do that; I would never walk into there and try to have them go after the people that know that we have no recourse. The laws are set up in a way to protect everybody but us.* (Tammy, massage-parlour worker)

In strip clubs where all erotic dancers, as well as managers and support staff, can be charged if one worker engages in sexual congress with a client, the women police each other. Diane was unequivocal:

> *I'm not doing time for nobody. Ah, if I see a girl lap dancing, if I catch a girl doing a twenty-dollar dance, I'll tell. I'll tell the management. Oh ya, I'll mark the girl. I don't care ... cause if we were to get raided, I'd be going to jail for her.*

Structural and interpersonal stigmas intersect when police officers, mandated to patrol the legal parameters, elect to reproduce the moral ones as well. This emerged most often with erotic dancers, whose labour is necessarily public. Karen, a 34-year-old Caucasian dancer, tells the following story:

> *I was coming out of the bar one night… I go and get in my car, cop car pulls up right behind me and blocks me in. [He] parks behind my car so I can't get out. This is in the winter time so I was sitting in my car waiting for it to warm up ... he's still parked behind me—[after] 4 minutes… He hasn't come over to my window. He hasn't done nothing. I can't back up 'cause he's right behind me… So I'm like what the heck? So I roll down my window and he finally comes over… and I'm like "Hi"? He was like "So, do you work here? What do you do here?" I said "Well, I'm a dancer." You know what I mean? He says, "Did you have a good night tonight?" I said, "Well it was pretty quiet you know"… I said "You guys have been out like crazy, putting blocks and this and that up and down the street, so it's been really dead." And he's asking me all these questions for like 10 minutes. Finally the guy got back in his car and says, "Alright then have a good night." Gets in his car sits there for two or three more minutes, then pulls away, and lets me leave.*

Doll, an Aboriginal woman and ten-year veteran of the erotic dance industry, recounted a similar incident that speaks not only of extra-legal interaction but also the existence of an electronic data double:[10]

> *One day I was driving my car and I got pulled over [and] they ran my license plate and my driver's license and it showed up that I worked at The Cobra … I find that really weird you know. 'Cause any time I get pulled over by a cop that's what's going to show up. It's not something that I'm happy about … And they told me that I hang around this pimp and I go, "Listen I don't hang around that guy" and they told me I was a liar.*

The implications of police, operating in relation to stigmatic assumptions are chilling as they effectively deny sex workers the protection and justice to which they, as citizens, are entitled:

> *So I got in a cab and called 911 on my cell phone 'cause I was so riled up and said, "I'm a dancer and I was just raped in the champagne room" and she said "Go to the police station on Main Street" … so the cab dropped me off there, I paid him and he left. And I gave them this case code that they told me to give them at the desk. And they looked at me and started laughing. They were like "Go home, you're wasting our time." That's what they said to me.*

Structural Stigma in Municipal Regulation

Structural stigma is not only apparent in criminal law and in the actions of state agents, but is evident in municipal regulation as well. Municipalities that have jurisdiction over health and space also draw on stereotypes and questionable "common knowledge" to legitimate the regulation of the indoor sex industry. In the next section we see how a specific cluster of stereotypes (disease, drugs, and contamination) justify regulation of the in-call sex industry. The discussion concludes by reflecting on the implications of the deeply embedded assumption that sex work is *not* work, the considerable evidence to the contrary notwithstanding.

While "bawdy-houses" are, at least for the time being, criminalized, many municipalities have laws governing body-rub parlours. In Toronto, a body-rub is defined as follows:

---

10 The data compiled on social actors and virtually stored becomes an electronic image of that person. Haggerty and Ericson writing on the surveillant assemblage explain that this data operates "by abstracting human bodies from their territorial settings, and separating them into a series of discrete flows. The flows are then reassembled in different locations as discrete and virtual 'data doubles'" (2000, 605).

> *kneading, manipulating, rubbing, massaging, touching, or stimulating by any means, of a person's body or part thereof*, but does not include medical or therapeutic treatment given by a person otherwise duly qualified, licensed or registered so to do under the laws of the Province of Ontario (Municipal code 545:1). [emphasis mine]

This licensing bylaw is discriminatory on a number of fronts. For example, it costs forty-five times as much for a body-rub parlour license as it does for a license for a holistic health centre.[11] The bylaw also severely restricts the number of body-rub parlour licences available and is rife with structural stigma. Here the assumption that sex workers are vectors of disease plays out in the requirement that applicants provide a health certificate stating that they are not carriers of infectious disease, and agree to a more comprehensive medical examination if the authorities have reason to believe that the applicant may suffer from an "illness, injury or any other physical or mental impairment" rendering them unfit to carry out the required duties (section 545.333). The inferred stereotype of criminality and substance use is evident in the "mandatory police record check" but also in the explicit prohibition against the possession of illegal drugs (section 545.356).[12] The latter is telling; of course the possession of illicit drugs is criminalized in the *Criminal Code*, but municipal officials appear to consider the "risk" warrants reiteration.

In the case of strip clubs or "adult entertainment parlours," structural stigma is also evident. Since the 1980s, municipalities across Canada have implemented bylaws premised on space management to regulate strip clubs. Framed in terms of city planning, this approach is based on assumptions of moral contamination. For example these bylaws include severe zoning restrictions and further specify that clubs must be located at least five hundred metres from schools, churches, and residential areas. Moreover, many municipalities demand that dancers, like workers in body-rub parlours, attain licences that are more expensive and restrictive than those required by other service workers.[13]

The issue of licensing is particularly ironic. In spite of the administrative recognition of their work and workplace that licensing suggests, workers in body-

---

11 For example, in Ottawa managers/owners of these parlours must initially pay the city $6,577.00 to obtain an operating permit and $6,381.00 for renewal. These fees are substantially higher than those required to operate, for example, a holistic health care centre ($143.00 to obtain a permit and $45.00 to renew).

12 For an excellent discussion on the implications of municipal regulation see van der Meulen and Durisin (2008).

13 For more on this see Bruckert and Dufresne 2002.

rub parlours and erotic dance clubs are consistently denied their rights as workers. Those in the indoor sex industry are not able to take advantage of the provisions of the *Employment Insurance Act* or the various *Human Right Codes* when their rights are infringed upon by, for example, racist policies or practices. Nor are they protected by legislation such as *The Occupational Health and Safety Act* in Ontario, *Loi sur la santé et la sécurité du travail* in Quebec, or the *Loi sur les accidents du travail et les maladies professionnelles* (*Industrial Accidents and Occupational Diseases Act*) in Quebec. Between 2000 and 2009, the Dancers Equal Rights Association (DERA),[14] an Ottawa-based organization, petitioned the Ontario Labour Board for recognition of dancers as workers and the enforcement of their statutory labour rights. The requests were ignored or categorically dismissed by bureaucrats, in spite of the evidence that dancers a) labour in legal municipally and provincially licensed establishments; b) meet the legal criteria of workers under the *Occupational Health and Safety Act*; and c) meet the *Employment Standards Act* four-fold test for employees (Smyth 2003).[15] In short, these workers are denied the income security, access to statutory protection, and legal recourse generally associated with employment. Sophie explained what this means to her:

> *I don't like that I have no recourse when I'm dissatisfied with my employment. I do have real world job experience and in those jobs if, for example, a co-worker treats you badly, you can go to your manager. If the manager doesn't listen, you go to human resources. If they don't listen, you go to the president and if they don't listen, you go to the labour board. At the club, I can't go anywhere. If I go to the manager and say "Hey, this is what happened," what does he care? There are no consequences for not listening. The only leverage I have is to leave and then I won't be able to make my house payments... So my options are to put up with it, stand up to them and be out of work or quit. If I do speak up, they will either not listen or I will get fired.*

The structural stigma that permeates municipal and provincial laws regulating (sectors of) the sex industry speaks to the importance of attending to more than criminal law, and pushes us to recognize the limitations of decriminalization in the absence of a broader challenge to stigmatic assumptions. As Stacey Hannem and I examine elsewhere (Bruckert and Hannem, forthcoming), legal-

---

14 In 2007, DERA amalgamated with the Exotic Dancers Association of Canada (EDAC) of Toronto and established the national Exotic Dancers Rights Association of Canada (EDRAC). In 2010 the organization ceased being active.

15 Reaffirmed in personal communication with Samantha Smyth, Acting Administrative Manager, EDRAC, September 9, 2008. While EDRAC fought on behalf of dancers, in-call sex workers are denied even the right to lobby for their inclusion under protectionist labour and human rights laws.

ized models in the Netherlands and United States (Nevada) continue to operate in relation to stigmatic assumptions of risk, disorder, disease, and immorality. As a result, sex workers in legalized regimes are subjected to mandatory health testing, licensing, restricted labour options, and geographic dislocation (see also Shaver 1985, 2012).

Personal Identity: Managing Sense of Self

Goffman's concepts of personal and social identity provide a conceptual point of entry to shed light on indoor sex workers' negotiations of stigma. In the case of the former, it is notable that sex workers are social actors invested in non-deviant identities but also cognizant of prevailing discourses; as such they must make sense of their participation in stigmatized labour in ways that do not undermine the self. Successful entry into the occupation requires workers, at the onset, to transcend stereotypical assumptions about the industry. That is to say, these individuals must first dispose of their own "stigma baggage":

> *I'd never been in a strip joint before—a female strip joint—in my life. I had no idea what went on until the day I went into one—to work. And, so I mean, I was raised with the persona that everyone is, ah, hos [whores]. So I went in there thinking "Oh my god, I'm going to have to be a cheap floozy" and then I danced, and then I danced for a customer and I thought, "Well is that all there is? This is easy."* (Debbie, erotic dancer)

Identifying different approaches to the management of personal identity highlights the importance of individual subjectivity and alerts us to the importance of attending to the intersection of identity, agency, and resistance (Bruckert 2002). When examining identity management, three distinct approaches emerge: normalization, relational identity, and constructing the self as exceptional. The first and most common approach was normalization of the industry *and* its workers. Many sex workers are extremely articulate in their deconstruction of the assumptions underlying the stigma. Most tended to normalize the industry as "just a job" and draw on the language of labour. At times they also integrate other discourses, particularly feminism (around gender roles and sexism) and sex radicalism, to undermine the prevailing stereotypical construction. The narrative of Angelica, a massage parlour worker who also offers domination services, illustrates this:

> *I just had an epiphany one day. I thought, I'm pretty, I'm young, I'm a woman, I've had to deal with harassment every day since I hit puberty... You know? I was like, I'm a sex*

> *object ... if I go to work at a restaurant and I get hired because I'm pretty, if I work in an office for ten dollars an hour and my boss is looking at my chest the whole time. You know? It's like sexism is a serious part of society that is just a given. People don't realize, and I was like, "it's time to start manipulating this for my own benefit. Because I'm going to be feeling it no matter what I do." It's there no matter what, so if I'm at the top of the ladder then I feel like I'm beating the man, you know. I literally get to beat the man!*

Other workers resolve issues around personal identity by assuming a relationally realized non-stigmatized personal identity. That is to say, they deconstruct the stigma in terms of particular sectors of the industry and draw attention to how they differ from "real" or "typical" sex workers. Here we see a moralizing discourse. Erotic dancers make careful reference to the all-important *line* that distinguishes them from prostitutes: "*We are not sex workers; we don't have sex!*" In-call workers suggest that there are substantive differences between themselves and street-based sex workers. This positioning reinforces the stereotypes of the "othered" sector, something that is evident in the narrative of Jacqueline, a Toronto area dominatrix:

> *I guess that the women who do this, we're not that image that they have of us, you know, that we're the girls who stand out on the street corner or whatever. It's not like that. We're all nice people, we're just trying to make a living. And, uh, I don't know that there's anything really wrong with what we're doing.*

While ideologically highly problematic, one can of course hardly fault sex workers like Jacqueline for reproducing the good girl/bad girl dichotomy and seeking to derive the benefits afforded to "good girls"—however marginal that "good" may be.

Finally, a small number of indoor sex workers reproduce very negative discourses about workers in general and position themselves (and perhaps a select few others) as different, as atypical. In the case of the dancers, some of them may reinforce the idea that many fellow dancers are prostitutes or they may talk about their colleagues as unreliable, volatile, dishonest, and drug consumers. According to Linda:

> *[Strippers are] intimidating. And they fight about everything. It's kind of inbred in you after a while and you can't really trust anyone there because if anyone ever asked you to borrow money it would never come back to me if I had lent it out ... You get to a point that if you let anyone know anything about you it always ends up spreading everywhere... I don't mean to generalize...*

By constructing a straw-stripper (or straw-whore) against which they position themselves as morally superior, these workers offer a powerful legitimation of the dominant discourse by "insiders." Debbie noted, "*I am not a typical dancer... I am a girl trying to make a living... it may be against some of my morals.*" Of course, by stigmatizing your own labour location, you risk self-alienation. Perhaps not surprisingly, Linda found that, "*I just don't feel like I fit in a lot.*"

Social Identity: Managing Stigma

Indoor sex workers are *discreditable* individuals, rather than individuals whose immediately apparent stigma renders them discredited. In fact, the decision to work in a particular sector of the industry is very often conditioned by concerns about stigma; for example, some in-call workers elect to not to work in the erotic dance industry and also to forgo the more lucrative escort trade specifically because of the risk of having their labour identity exposed. It may also condition labour practices—many dancers work far from home in an attempt to forestall inadvertently being "outed" as a sex worker.

Not infrequently, there is a tension between personal and social identity—individuals may have no shame (in fact, many are proud) and actively challenge the construction of sex workers as victims, as drug addicts, as immoral, and so on. However, while resistant, they are "stigma conscious" (Pinel 2004) and engage in information management to minimize the social costs of disclosure. Research reveals a range of approaches, from passing to full disclosure. There is no ideal strategy—having to negotiate stigma means that all tactics are fraught with the potential for negative repercussions.

At one end of the spectrum were women who essentially lead double-lives. For these workers, the use of a professional name operates as a stigma management tactic that aids the separation of their work and private spheres. Such workers disclose to very few individuals. For example Chrystal, a massage parlour worker from Montreal, had informed her mother with whom she resided, however, her partner of nine months was still under the impression that she worked in a convalescent home. Fiona, an Ottawa-area in-call worker explained:

> *I have a boyfriend and I would never tell him. I don't consider myself a cheater so it's a weird dynamic because I don't think at any point I'd want to tell him. But I also don't feel ready to quit. Do I think he would judge me if he knew? Absolutely!*

While isolating the worker from confronting stigmatic assumptions this is nonetheless a "loaded" approach. As research on the LGBTQ community has demonstrated (Kinsman and Gentile 2010), managing identity in this manner can be highly stressful. Certainly keeping an aspect of one's life, be it sexual orientation or occupational location, hidden from significant or more general others is not only personally disorienting, it demands continual vigilance because "*It's hard to always keep a part of you secret*" (Tammy, massage parlour worker). Individuals are forced to monitor talk and behaviour, create fictions, such as a job that does not exist, and avoid discussions about work in order to guard against disclosure and the loss of their non-deviant identity: "*I don't know if I can keep it a secret any longer—you know the lies are catching up*" (Debbie, erotic dancer). The existence of a discrediting, hidden identity may also render an individual vulnerable, as information can be employed as a strategy of control. The following story by Marie, an erotic dancer, speaks to this:

> *Well my parents were supportive. Not all the time. Not when they discovered it. They found out through one of my boyfriends—he was mad and he just opened my costume suitcase on the kitchen table, and my parents freaked out. And they didn't speak to me for two months.*

Workers who adopt this approach also tend to avoid any contact with other sex workers for fear of being inadvertently "outed": "*[I] won't take the friendship home, because then there's the explanation of how you met them or whatever*" (Gillian, erotic dancer). This denies workers the support of insiders, which can mediate the tension and stressors of labouring in a stigmatized occupation because "*you need support. It is hard for people who are not in it [the sex industry] to understand*" (June, erotic dancer).

Most workers, in an attempt to negotiate an ethically comfortable space that affords them access to support while minimizing the negative consequences of their occupational location, choose to disclose to some, but not all, people in their social circle. Some, such as Charlotte, a Toronto area dungeon worker, spoke of the need to be honest: "*They were old friends that I might have told because I didn't think it was fair to lie to them.*" Charlotte is necessarily aware that failure to disclose renders her vulnerable to being defined not only as a sex worker but also as deceitful. As these workers move towards greater and greater disclosure, they find themselves vacillating between managing stigmatic assumptions, hidden identities, and uneasy social situations.

Notably, even sex workers whose labour identity is largely public, were inclined to shield specific others (most especially mothers) from the information—not infrequently they are concerned about their loved ones having to engage in their own identity management. This tension is evident in the testimony of Rachel, an erotic dancer:

> *I think it's a great job. Anybody who thinks anything else just doesn't know. They still have this old mentality of it ... always drunk or stoned or you spend your money all the time. And they just think we're a bunch of low-lifes. And it's not like that at all. So right now, I don't mind telling anybody at all. Except my parents—cause they're kinda ... God-fearing people. So I'd rather not. My mother would probably commit suicide or probably think she'd failed or something or "Where did I go wrong?" So I'd rather not put them through that.*

Finally, some very politically active individuals flaunt their labour location and offer both private and public testimony. These workers are not only proud, they are defiant, and actively resist the dominant discourse that would have them feel shame. In the process, they also challenge others to confront their own stereotypes. Anais, a Toronto area dungeon worker, explained:

> *For me it's been an act of resistance. If you have control over what you do, and if your rights are not violated, and you're looked upon as a human being and as an actual worker, it is a legit job. Within society, it's a no-no to be a sex worker and advertize that you are a sex worker. As an activist and as a feminist, I find that it's a legit way of expressing an active resistance against a society.*

Such workers bravely confront stigma. Annabelle, an "out" brothel worker from Montreal, noted:

> *It's difficult to go against society; it's not easy, going against people's morality. We are a minority. It's not easy to fight against the whole population and against ideas that are so entrenched in people's heads...*

Conclusion

Stigma, both interpersonal and structural, is a *concept* for academics, an *impediment* for feminists, but for sex workers it is something that is *experientially real*—reverberating through their professional, social, and intimate lives. That said, how stigma is experienced, negotiated, resisted, and/or managed is highly variable, subjective, and conditioned by material, social, personal, and discursive resources. This latter point becomes even clearer when the experiences of street-based sex workers are considered. Indoor sex workers have access to resources that allow them to manage the stigmatizing information and even "closet" their labour identity. By contrast, not only do street-based sex workers regularly confront stigmatic designations by virtue of the visible nature of their labour, but their experience of stigma is layered and they have, for the most part, less cultural, social, and economic capital to draw on. Some street-based sex workers are so marginalized that the stigma of sex work intersects with other stigmatic designations to such an extent that it is difficult to extrapolate one from the other.

Their existence in the intersectional crevices helps us to appreciate how profoundly this population lives stigma. It is street-based sex workers who are the most readily available targets of the emotions engendered when an individual is reduced "from a whole and usual person to a tainted, discredited one" (Goffman 1963a, 4), marked as *other* and defined as someone who is not only *not like us* but is in some (often undefined) way risky or *threatening to us*. Sometimes this contempt/fear is verbally manifested by "*people driving by and calling me a bitch, not because they know me but because of what I do*" (Bianca, street-based worker); other times it is corporally enacted when "*people change sidewalks when I walk on one side of the street, they lock their doors, they roll up their windows*" (Marie-Claire, street-based worker). Sometimes it is violently enacted when community members "*throw rocks at me. This one man, he put mud in a bag, tied it with an elastic, and threw it at me*" (Janette, street-based worker); other times it plays out when the police who "*see me from a mile away and stop me, call me names... They can't tell if I am working or not. For them I am always just that junkie ho*" (Charlotte, street-based worker).[16]

It is also not surprising that street-based workers are particularly vulnerable to structural stigma. Stigmatic assumptions about sex workers permeate the paternalistic/punitive laws that seek to save at the same time as they punish. We see stigmatic assumptions of risk-contagion structurally embedded in police practices. When the Ottawa Police Service send "Community Safety Letters"[17] to individuals "found in the company of a sex trade worker" (Ottawa Police Service); not only is the worker presumed guilty, but those found in his or her company are immediately suspect by association.

Sadly, we need look no further then the tragic (mis)handling of Vancouver's infamous missing (murdered) women case for which Robert Pickton was ultimately charged and convicted.[18] Here we see how embedded stereotypes and

16 For more on the stigmatization of street-based sex work, see Bruckert and Chabot 2010.

17 These letters—sent to the owners of cars sighted in the company of sex workers—draw on stigmatizing discourses (and misinformation) when they advise the recipient of the "clear correlation" between substance use, HIV, and sex work (Ottawa Police Service).

18 Originally charged with twenty-six counts of first-degree murder, on December 9, 2007, Robert Pickton was found guilty of six counts of second-degree murder and sentenced to life imprisonment for a minimum of twenty-five years. On August 3, 2010, Robert Pickton exhausted his avenues of appeal and the remaining twenty charges were stayed.

structural stigma not only condition the lives of marginal individuals but can contribute to their deaths as well. This chapter ends with more questions: Why did the police refuse to investigate the disappearances of the women? Why did police insist that these women were simply transient despite considerable evidence to the contrary, including abandoned possessions and uncharacteristic lack of contact with their families? Why was Pickton not questioned when his propensity for violence against sex workers was known? Why were charges against Pickton stayed in a near-fatal 1997 attack on a sex worker, despite considerable physical evidence?[19] Why did the police not investigate the Pickton farm in 1998—before five of the six women Pickton was convicted of murdering were killed—when it was flagged by victims' families and by a former employee? Why, as the toll of "missing women" kept rising, did the police reduce the size of the investigating team? Why did the mayor of Vancouver—after announcing a $100,000 reward for information leading to the arrest of individuals responsible for a series of garage robberies perpetrated against middle-class citizens—flatly state that the city was not going to fund "a location service for hookers"? Why did we, the public, not have the sense of outrage we felt when we heard about Clifford Olson, Paul Bernardo and Karla Homolka, or Russell Williams? And why is there no commitment by our political leaders to address this injustice?

Many of these questions should be at the heart of the (euphemistically named) "Missing Women Commission of Inquiry." Any hope of naming, let alone addressing, injustice has been dashed by a process that gives rise to ever more questions: Why was a former Vancouver Police officer hired to write an "independent" report? Why were there twenty-five publically funded lawyers representing police and government interests while community and Aboriginal groups are denied funding for legal representation? Why were the Commission's narrow terms of reference established without consultation with the Aboriginal, sex worker, and community groups that called for the inquiry in the first place? And why was a constrictive timeline imposed and then used to justify refusing to hear from key witnesses? In short, *why* has the Commission "served to repeat the same discrimination and exclusion that we had hoped it would uncover"? (Coalition 2012).[20] Consistent with the findings of other authors in this collection (see for

19 On April 11, 2012, Crown Council Randi Conners testified at the Missing Women Commission of Inquiry that she stayed the proceedings on January 27, 1998, because of the victim's drug use which, in her assessment, made her an unreliable witness—physical evidence, including a key used to handcuff the victim found in Pickton's pocket, notwithstanding. Five years later when the clothes confiscated by the police that night were finally tested, DNA from three of the missing women was found (CBC 2012).

20 Taken from an open letter signed by a coalition of fifteen organizations many of whom have been active in seeking social justice for the women of the Downtown Eastside for years.

example Hannem, Chapter Six), I would argue that it is precisely the stigmatic assumptions that underlie what Lowman (2000) named the "discourse of disposal" that are enacted interpersonally, structurally embedded, and institutionally reproduced that facilitate social (in)action and perpetuate marginalization.

Chapter Five

The Mark of Sexual Deviance

What Keeps Men Who Have Sex with Men Up at Night?

Kevin Walby

Prologue

Men carry around numerous secrets
about the touching encounters they have with others.
We cannot share such stories
about touching other men. When the stories are leaked,
when the story gets out, it's over. Pigeonholed.
All of a sudden, the story is out of their hands.
I know many men keeping secrets.
They want to talk. They want to confess.
But they do not know anyone who would listen without injurious judgment.
Some have big secrets.
They are getting married, having kids. I receive wedding invitations—
them standing in a suit on some picturesque bluff
beside a picturesque bride in white.
They do not want the stories to be told.
They want the stories to be buried.
They would fight to the death
to keep those big secrets submerged.
They dare not speak about their noble affections.
This is what replaces affection: hush, fretfulness, unease. Only one thing is certain:

should the story get out, the life built up around their secrets would be levelled.
They want the stories to be buried.
Keeping secrets. Aching to confess.
All of a sudden... the story gets out.

Introduction

In February of 1975, John Damien was dismissed from his job as a horse racing judge by the Ontario Jockey Commission when his sexual orientation as a gay man became known. Concerned that same-sex orientation might make one susceptible to blackmail, the boss offered a cash bribe and told Damien to resign. Damien refused and was fired. Then his sexual orientation was made public through the media. Damien consulted the Ontario Human Rights Commission (OHRC) about his case, but the OHRC declined to help since, at the time, it did not prohibit discrimination on the grounds of sexual orientation. Damien and his supporters fought for many years for justice in the courts. It was only in 1986 that the OHRC included sexual orientation in its human rights code, twenty-two days after Damien died of cancer.

This chapter is about the regulation of men who have sex with men and their resultant experiences of stigma. Despite all kinds of legal change—including decriminalization of "homosexuality" in 1969 and legalization of same-sex marriage in 2005—discrimination against, and criminalization of, men who have sex with men still occurs in Canada and elsewhere. Many scholars have tried to conceptualize the discrimination and criminalization that men who have sex with men face. Some argue that we live in a culture of heteronormativity (Adam 1998; Butler 1990), which means that a segment of people are split off and constructed as "homosexual" as opposed to "normal." For Plummer (1975, 120), rendering men who have sex with men as "strange" is a first step towards regulating their bodies and conduct. Suicide, lower self-esteem, unemployment, and ostracism from family and community are possible outcomes of this regulation. Such outcomes are compounded when other factors such as ethnicity, class, disability, and health are accounted for.

Does the term "homophobia" best encapsulate the antagonism that men who have sex with men face? The term "homophobia," popularized in 1972 by psychologist George Weinberg, "crystallized the experiences of rejection, hostility, and invisibility that homosexual men and women in mid-20th century North

America had experienced throughout their lives" (Herek 2004, 8). But the term "homophobia" has been described as "overly narrow in its characterization of oppression as ultimately the product of individual fear" and at the same time "too diffuse in its application" (Herek 2004, 11). The stereotyping, persecution, and exclusion of those who engage in same-sex relations is based on more than an amorphous fear. How should we understand the exclusionary practices against men who have sex with men that continue to occur today?

"Stigma" is a concept that can be used with more precision to refer to processes of stereotyping and exclusion. Goffman (1963a) defined stigma as a social identity that spoils one's reputation. Existing conceptualizations of "stigma" are not without problems. Link and Phelan (2001) argue the idea of stigma focuses too much on individual perceptions and not enough on observable discrimination. In this chapter, I address the stigma associated with particular sexual practices, emphasizing that stigma is socially facilitated and not simply a private trouble.[1]

I begin by mapping how "homosexuality" was discovered as a deviant identity in the nineteenth century. I proceed to assess Link and Phelan's (2001) model of stigma, arguing that their conceptualization of stigma glosses over how identity management involves resistance of stigmatization in the making. Drawing from research I have conducted on the regulation of tearoom (or washroom) sex, male-with-male public park sex, and the male-for-male commercial sex trade, I discuss how an adjusted version of Link and Phelan's (2001) model of stigma can be put to use in the sociology of sexuality. I conclude by considering issues of identity regarding stigma negotiation by men who have sex with men.

The Construction of "Homosexuality" as a Mark of Sexual Deviance

The literature on stigma, mostly based in psychology, has by and large failed to conceptualize stigma as situated socially, culturally, and historically (Hallgrímsdóttir et al., 2008). Though taken for granted categorizations of sexual identity like "homosexual" and "heterosexual" assume fixity, it is important to reject transhistorical categorization and instead look at how sexual categories emerge and become socially organized. The way that male-with-male sexual activity is framed matters for the way the issue is regulated (Scott 2003; Kaye 2003).

1 The term "men who have sex with men" is useful since we are speaking of all men who have sex with men and not just those who identify as gay. Moreover, "queer" does not represent how all men who have sex with men think of themselves (Fox 2007). Neither does "gay." While broader issues important to the gay, lesbian, bisexual, and transgender community will be touched on, there is not the space to deal with all the specificities of these identities as it relates to stigma.

There have been periods when male-with-male sex was more-or-less accepted. For example, Rocke (1996) demonstrated that between the thirteenth and sixteenth centuries the Church in Florence (and in Italy more broadly) considered male-with-male sex a deadly sin, yet it was only during periods of mass loss of life from the plague that these acts became stringently policed, and only those Florentines who took the active role were criminalized as "sodomites." It was with the full-scale appearance of medical institutions in the nineteenth century that non-procreative sexual behaviour by men came to be viewed as an imprudent loss of semen. The emergence of Victorian morality introduced a public/private dichotomy upon which much sexual regulation would be based for the remainder of the nineteenth century. The attempt or actual commission of an act of "buggery" became offences in England under sections 61 and 62 of the *Offences against the Person Act* in 1861. It is in the work of early sexologists that "homosexuality" becomes associated with "inborn" characteristics. "Homosexuality" as a concept did not exist in the United Kingdom (UK) in police, medical, and legal circles in 1871 (Weeks 1981, 101). It was not until 1885 when England's sodomy laws were amended to apply specifically to "homosexuals" that the concept became embedded in law. In short, an act became an identity: "The sodomite had been a temporary aberration; the homosexual was now a species" (Foucault 1978, 43).

By the early twentieth century, many state officials as well as sexologists were eugenicists. The merger of eugenics, nuclear family values, and population statistics led to a hereditarian theory of population regulation that ultimately culminated with the Nazi use of the pink and black triangles to mark gays and lesbians. The downfall of the Third Reich did not result in the end of discrimination against gays and lesbians. The 1957 *Wolfenden Report* in the UK, for instance, called for broader policing of public sex acts and for the complete withdrawal from regulating sex in the private sphere. The *Wolfenden Report* became core policy, informing regulation projects in North America as well. All "homosexuals" had to be eliminated from the social body. For example, during the height of the Cold War, the Royal Canadian Mounted Police were involved in a "homosexual hunt," persecuting and jailing gays/lesbians, who were argued to be sick (Kinsman 2000). State officials and psychologists worked in tandem to develop a series of eye response tests they called "the fruit machine" to detect suspected "homosexuals" in the public service.

Male-with-male sexual relations have long been a target of social and moral regulation. These regulatory projects comprise the structural element of sexual stigma. We continue to see stigmatic assumptions embedded in criminal justice laws and practices—in, for example, the elevated age of consent (18) for anal intercourse between partners who are not husband and wife (CCC s 159) and the prohibition against anal sex involving more than two participants[2] (CCC s 159.3.a). These echoes notwithstanding, male-with-male sexuality is decriminalized in Canada, and since 2005 with the proclamation of the *Civil Marriage Act*, same-sex marriage has been legalized in Canada. Yet, as we will see below, stigma remains despite legal change.

Stigma Revisited

How do regulatory practices translate into an impact on the lives of men who have sex with men? The answer: stigma. Goffman's work has been crucial to the development of stigma studies. Key to the idea of stigma is conceiving of it as involving a "mark" and "stereotype." The mark is a presumed attribute of the individual. Goffman referred to these marks as stigma symbols: "signs which are especially effective in drawing attention to a debasing identity discrepancy … with a consequent reduction in our valuation of the individual" (1963a, 44).

There have been critiques of Goffman. For instance, Wacquant (2007) argues that Goffman did not address blemishes of place, or the territorial stigma that can limit mobility and comes from being associated with certain communities or parts of a city. Kusow (2004) suggests that Goffman-inspired analyses of stigma focus too much on the coherence of normative orders. To be fair, Goffman did argue that it is possible for stigma symbols to "mean one thing to one group [and] mean something else to another group, the same category being designated but differently characterized" (1963a, 46). Being attuned to how stigma differs in intensity from context to context is an important tenant of stigma studies (Campbell and Deacon, 2006).

Arguing that a clear definition of stigma has never been advanced, Link and Phelan (2001) maintain that stigma exists only when its component elements are present: labelling, stereotyping, separation, status loss, and discrimination. Link and Phelan's approach offers some conceptual clarity and a lucid understanding of how stigma affects the life chances of stigmatized persons.

According to the model proposed by Link and Phelan (2001), labelling is the first element of stigma. Labelling focuses on how some differences (or marks, or attributes) are selected out for scrutiny and become salient measures used for distinguishing or sorting "kinds of people" from one another. Being a member of a stigmatized group makes one a social deviant (Goffman 1963a, 143), while being a member of a group of "normals" but still considered "trouble" makes one

2 Note that the Quebec and Ontario courts of appeal ruled CCC s 159 to be unconstitutional in 1995 and 1998 respectively.

an in-group deviant. These differences are sometimes thought of as unchanging, but they are variable, depending on time and place.

The second component of stigma is the attachment of a stereotype to the label. Those bearing the mark are tagged as somehow lesser human beings. The fear that "homosexuals" insidiously seduce unsuspecting youths into a deviant subterranean world is the most common stereotype (Janoff 2005). Many people continue to think of men who have sex with men as perverted, mentally ill, maladjusted, effeminate, and sinful. What is called courtesy stigma can develop when "perceivers infer that the relatives or companions of a stigmatized person share some of that person's devalued attributes..." (Sigelman et al. 1991, 55). Third, stigma and its associated stereotypes are used to construct those who bear the mark as collectively different from so-called normals. Those who are stigmatized are imagined to be a homogeneous group, and a group that is somehow "dirty" or "dangerous." The stigmatized person must be imagined as part of a deviant community. A case in point: the rigid division between homosexuals and heterosexuals that still exists in many societies today.

Fourth, status loss can be a consequence of the stereotyping, labelling, and differentiation between "us" and "them." Status loss that moves a person downwards in hierarchies compounds other kinds of identity-based exclusionary practices (e.g., racism). Dodds (2006) showed how members of ethnic groups stigmatize HIV-positive men who have sex with men (of their group) and exclude them in ways that make it difficult to access social support and services. Status loss can be intensified when people do not conform to the status quo (Crawford 1994). Ostracism from familial or religious groups is common for men who have sex with men when they "come out" or are "outed."

The fifth component of stigma in Link and Phelan's (2001) model is discrimination, which may be individualized or structural. The status one had before the onset of discriminatory practices matters as pre-existing low status can intensify discrimination. Individual discrimination might take the form of an employer barring a man who likes sex with men from employment, while structural discrimination can be thought of as how an entire social group is excluded from full participation in an activity. As an example, the Canadian Blood Services policy of banning gay and bisexual men from blood donation has recently received criticism from gay rights organizations as a form of structural discrimination.[3] A "yes"

---

3 In the 1980s and1990s, the panic over HIV/AIDS (originally called gay-related immune deficiency) targeted men who have sex with men. Gay men were problematized as disease vectors to be contained, the gay community became the world of the monster, and the AIDS carrier became the monster itself (Redman 1997; Donovan 1995).

answer to the question "have you had sex with a man, even one time since 1977?" lands men on a donor blacklist, whereas answering "yes" to the question "In the past six months, have you had sex with someone whose sexual background you don't know?" results only in a six-month deferral.[4]

HIV and AIDS in North America have affected young men having sex with men more than other groups. That said, it is estimated that in Ontario only 17.2% of men who have sex with men are HIV positive (Remis 2008).[5] The point here is that the policy targets and bans all men who have sexually touched other men at any point in their lives when the majority of these men are not HIV positive and do not engage in sex without a condom.

Link and Phelan (2001) argue that the entire process—from labelling to stereotyping, separation, status loss, and discrimination—might take place over a few months or occur more rapidly. They argue that each element must be demonstrated for stigma to exist. According to Link and Phelan (2001), if there is labelling and stereotyping without separation, status loss, and discrimination, it is unfitting to call such an event "stigma."

Link and Phelan's model demands evidence of observable discrimination for "stigma" to be operating. The trouble is that these authors create a dichotomy between labelling/stereotyping (as individualistic and supposedly less integral components of stigmatization) and the structural aspects of separation, status loss, and discrimination. Link and Phelan fail to recognize how the structural aspects of separation, status loss, and discrimination are anticipated, felt, negotiated, and resisted by targeted individuals, often before the stigmatization process fully matures into observable discrimination. Link and Phelan thus ignore how identity management for the purpose of preventing discrimination entails an already existing process of stigmatization that the person is aware of and negotiates or resists through various strategies (passing, gradual disclosure, selective affiliation, discrediting of labels, and activism). In short, Link and Phelan focus too much on outcome instead of process in establishing what is, and what is not, stigma.

Male-with-male Sex and Stigma: Some Examples

Notwithstanding its limitations, Link and Phelan's model is valuable insofar as it synthesizes past contributions to stigma studies into a coherent theoretical

4 This indefinite deferral also applies to people who have taken money for sex since 1977, which presumes that people selling sexual services practice unsafe sex when in fact sex workers are often safe sex experts committed to protecting themselves and their clients from infections and disease (Bruckert and Chabot 2010).

5 The statistics are inconsistent, but see AVERT 2010 for an example.

package. In this section, drawing from my research on the regulation of tea-room sex (Walby 2009a), male-with-male public park sex (Walby 2009b), as well as the male-for-male commercial sex trade (Walby 2010), I briefly show how Link and Phelan's (2001) model of stigma might be drawn upon to inform an analysis of empirical material.

What tearoom sex, male-with-male public park sex, and the male-for-male commercial sex trade have in common is that openly gay men and closeted men who like sex with men are engaged sexually and then become problematized by policing or medical agencies. The concept of stigma is useful for conceptualizing antagonism against these men, but the experience of labelling, stereotyping, separation, status loss and discrimination is not experienced equally by all. The experience of stigma depends on what kind of work these men do, what kind of sexual activity the label invokes, and other issues related to life course and status.

The first case study is about the regulation of tearoom sex. Between 1983 and 1994, the Ontario Police Commission condoned the use of video surveillance equipment in public washrooms in order to apprehend what they called "sexual offenders" (gay men cruising in tearooms). Cameras were placed above urinals or in the ceiling of public washrooms. Ultimately more than 500 men from southern Ontario were charged with gross indecency. The process started when, based on a complaint about juvenile involvement, the Orillia Opera House was raided by city police. The story hit the papers, and was followed the next day by reports of police dragging accused men out of schools while they were teaching. Suspects were subsequently followed and harassed by the media and endured taunts of "fag," "homo," and "son-of-a-bitch" from onlookers at the courthouse. Several men required psychiatric care as a result and the Simcoe County Board of Education fired three teachers who were charged. Notably although anxieties concerning juvenile involvement in male-with-male sex were mobilized to justify the regulation, the charges laid did not include sexual interference with minors.

The Orillia case provides an example of how men having sex with men become stigmatized, subjected not only to labelling and stereotyping but also, especially for those who lost their jobs, separation, status loss, and discrimination. The stereotype of "homosexuals" corrupting the minds and bodies of unsuspecting youths was fundamental in motivating Orillia's stigmatizing response. Results were similar in other Ontario cities where police conducted such surveillance projects and raids. Stigma as a concept, in the meaning that Link and Phelan (2001) provide, is a solid fit for this case, because all elements of stigma were operating upon these men.

An examination of how tearoom sex has become problematized demonstrates the way stereotypes regarding men who have sex with men can be part of a process that leads to status loss and discrimination. As was the case in Orillia, the regulation of male-with-male public park sex in Ottawa (Walby 2009b) involved a process of stigmatization through outing. This case study of National Capital Commission (NCC) conservation officer work demonstrates one example of how notions concerning "appropriate" sexuality are shaped and reinforced through policing and surveillance. The NCC is a public organization responsible for so-called "beautification" projects around the Ottawa region. NCC conservation officers are peace officers who monitor the parks under their jurisdiction, write up occurrence reports, and coordinate what they call "blitzes" with the Ottawa Police as well as the Royal Canadian Mounted Police.

Public park sex between men is regulated by the NCC because of, firstly, complaints regarding discarded condoms and the imagined potential for spread of disease to children, and, secondly, the fear that "gay" men lure children into the bushes to abuse them. Stereotypes concerning the corruption of youth became embedded in regulatory practices. Through their surveillance and occurrence reporting, which attempt to ban queer sex from public, NCC conservation officers are involved in the (hetero)normalization of sexuality. Men found to be having sex in parks are usually "outed" to family and/or co-workers. Consider the following excerpt from a conservation officer occurrence report:

> While patrolling the Ottawa River near Bates Island I observed three males performing oral sex. The minute they saw me they all ran away. Intercepted two individuals 10 minutes later. One left in his vehicle. I got the plate. It almost caused an accident. Called the RCMP for assistance and they arrived … one male gave a fake ID … I issued tickets on site … Constable St-Amour from the RCMP and myself went to the address to serve the client. Arrived there and spoke with the wife and explained the situation. Gave the ticket to the wife and she saw a picture to confirm ID.

The process has real implications in the lives of those targeted. In this example, the NCC officer identified the man's sexual behaviour to his family. Men who have sex with men in public parks are less worried about HIV/AIDS and sexually transmitted infections than they are about gay bashing, police, and community harassment (Flowers et al. 1999). Though the NCC conservation officer's work might be based on stereotypes, there is no labelling and there is not necessarily any separation or status loss *per se* in all cases. Certainly if the man who fled from the NCC officer lost his family or job as a result, it would have meant stigmatization as per Link and Phelan's (2001) model.

Tearoom trade and park sex are highly visible forms of male-with-male sex, which makes them more easily subject to stigmatization (Plummer 1975). I have also conducted interviews with male-for-male Internet escorts who sell sexual services to men in Ottawa, Toronto, New York, Montreal, and London (UK). Compared to the cases of tearoom regulation and park sex surveillance, the example of male-for-male Internet escorts demonstrates how the issue of stigma, as it pertains to men who have sex with men, has multiple layers. Many sex workers experience stigmatization, especially on-street and transgendered workers. As Leon (bar hustler, escort) puts it:

> *The judgments come, people talking about you selling yourself and turning tricks and doing drugs. We do not want him in our establishment anymore. In Toronto, it came to a point where I was down and out. There was stigma depending on the environment. There are so many kinds of bars. You go in and you know this is not happening. Other bars are more upscale, and you feel the judgment.*

Supporting Wacquant's (2007) claim about stigma and location, place matters when it comes to stigma, since for Leon:

> *the smaller the city, doing that work, word gets around quick, and it will limit you from getting hospitality work, telemarketing work, any kind of work. It is hard to combine sex work with a real life job unless you have your own business and clientele.*

The intensity of discrimination also depends on where else one works when publically identified as selling sex to men. In 1995, Gerald was released from Ryerson University and his job as a contract journalism instructor when it became known he sold sex to men. Gerald said there "*was sensation in the papers with much mockery and nasty calls … people yelled at me in the street, it was bad for a while.*" The union eventually won a settlement for Gerald, meaning that there was some recognition of discrimination. But the event has now led Gerald to manage his relations strategically: "*Mostly I do not feel stigmatized, but I only hang around with people who knew me before or got to know me because of this… [the Ryerson incident] is not something I would want to go through again.*"

Internet escorts experience stigma, but because Internet escorting is less visible due to an individualized labour process (anonymity being the name of the game) they talk less about discrimination and more about managing labels and stereotypes. For instance, Byron (escort, agency owner) describes how he negotiates stigma but points out that discrimination against male escorts is not nearly as intense as for other sex workers: "*There is stigma. I close myself off more from those who are not in the business. I do not feel it as much, and I do not see it as much, but I know it is there. I know prostitutes and call girls experience worse.*" While Byron says he can sense stigma almost as if it is stuck to him, he does not mention any separation, status loss, or discrimination accompanying the unease. His management of stigma, his closing off from those not involved in escorting, is an attempt to manage the blemishes of character that could accompany being outed as selling sex to other men.

Often stigma is experienced in relation to health care agencies (van Brakel, 2006) including labelling and stereotyping from doctors. One escort describes a conversation he had with a doctor:

> *He asks, "Oh, how many?" and I'm like "I don't know... a hundred just this year"... but at the same time when you have someone like my father who will sleep with two or three women in a year but won't wear any condoms, will go see a prostitute ... Who is more dangerous? I want the public system to exist for everyone and to have any sex worker doing thousands of clients a year to still have a doctor who won't get out the red marker and say, "Oh, shit. Maybe you should stop." And thinking that you're just a disease.* (Jacques, escort)

Not all experiences of labelling and stereotyping are overt. If the individual is engaging in some form of identity management but has not experienced status loss and discrimination, it does not mean, as Link and Phelan (2001) propose, that stigma is absent. Instead, identity management strategies, such as selective disclosure or contestation of labelling, suggests they are experiencing stigma in the making, and are taking steps to avoid the advancement of this process into status loss and discrimination (Plummer 1975). For instance, one escort (Tyler) mentioned, "*I would feel terrible if my mother or father or immediate family found out what I do, they would be very quick to judge, I know they would judge me.*" The model proposed by Link and Phelan must be adjusted to account for stigma negotiation or "sensed" stigma and the tacit manner in which processes of stigmatization emerge in the lives of targeted individuals.

The world of male-with-male Internet escorting is clandestine, so stigma might be less immediately salient because stigma assumes some public disgrace. This work is "*under the radar because most [of us] don't want people to know what we do*" (Steve, escort). Keeping secrets implies management of stigmatization in the making:

> *I don't put out the neon lights to everybody ... you don't know how people are going to react. I have never gotten a real negative reaction but I think it's also because I've been careful about who I told.* (Donald, escort)

This sort of partial closeting is a form of managing the elementary forms of stigmatization. Interestingly, self-identified gay escorts experience labelling and stereotyping from other men who have sex with men. Tyler said:

> *I have been very good at keeping that part of life a secret to most of the people in the [gay] community ... I outed myself as a sex worker to a few friends of mine and these are people that I trust ... I think if you are too open about what you dò as a sex worker you get labelled as a hustler and you are put in the category, you are pegged as this and whatever prejudices come with that. Gays can be just as discriminatory as other people, if not worse sometimes.*

Similarly, Sam (escort) feels that when other men in gay chat rooms find out he sells sex they sometimes make derogatory comments: "*He read [my ad] and then he called me a 'prostitute,' it was not a compliment, it was an insult.*" The interesting point here is that labelling and stereotyping occurs within the gay community itself. As Mark (escort) from London (England) put it, "*Sometimes you hear or read snide comments, like he is 'commercial.' So there is some stigma. There is no pressure from the outside; it is all from the gay community.*" Other escorts described being rejected by men in dating scenarios because of their work. These examples hint at how gay men also engage in the labelling and stereotyping characteristic of stigmatization, even against men who have similar ideas regarding pleasure and sexuality.

Despite legal changes, male-with-male sexual relations occurring in settings such as tearooms, parks, and commercial sex trade encounters are still targeted by regulatory agencies and continue to face the labelling and stereotyping intrinsic to stigma. Even when their relations with other men are more clandestine, identity management implies a process of stigmatization in the making that must be handled strategically. The question then is, how do men having sex with men negotiate stigma along with identity?

Identity and the Negotiation of Stigma

Earlier I focused on the structural elements of sexual stigma germane to regulation, policing, and surveillance. Even though many overt forms of discrimination have disappeared, stigma remains. Legal change does not translate automatically into equality, insofar as stereotypes concerning gays and lesbians are firmly entrenched in the way we think about sexuality (Ward 2008). Link and Phelan's (2001) conceptualization of stigma pins the designation on a negative economic or social outcome. This ignores how identity management to prevent status loss and discrimination is a marker of labelling, stereotyping, and stigma in the making that is felt, negotiated, and resisted by targeted individuals. In this final section, I discuss stigma and identity negotiation.

Gay and lesbian identities are not fixed (Kaufman and Johnson 2004).[6] That said, it has been argued that "the most momentous act in the life of any lesbian and/or gay person is when they proclaim their gayness—to self, to other, to community" (Plummer 1995, 82). For lots of men, the process is quick. For others, coming-out takes time. The more an individual publically identifies as homosexual, the more he might have to live with stigma, because more people might be labelling him as "one of those kinds of people." Yet the more an individual comes out, the more likely he will find networks of support and others dealing with similar experiences. Disclosure of sexual orientation can be daunting, but is mediated by self-acceptance and community integration that can make coming-out a less dangerous, even positive experience.

"Gay" as an identity category intersects with other aspects of men's identities. For instance, African-Canadian men who have sex with men must tread warily in communities of Caribbean diaspora because of a certain type of heterosexist thinking based on traditional gender expectations (Crichlow 2004). "Buller man" is a slang term used to refer to men who have sex with men who are forced to develop strategies for participating in the communal (heterosexist) structure of these communities so as not to "out" their interest in same-sex pleasure. Many of the men Crichlow interviewed managed intersecting identities to avoid stigma. Crichlow's book is autobiographical as well; he discusses some of his encounters with racism in Toronto's gay communities. Similarly, gay Asian men in Toronto negotiate stereotypes regarding what it means to be gay and what it means to be Asian (Poon and Ho 2008). Thus, analysis of stigma regarding gay identity must consider intersecting identities as well.[7]

---

6 Throughout the chapter, I have been speaking of an activity (men having sex with men) and not an identity. Here the discussion shifts toward the latter.

7 Gay transmen may experience stigma to a greater degree. Transmen are individuals who were assigned female identity at birth and born with female sexual and reproductive organs but identify as men, or have had sex reassignment surgery. Penis and chest reconstruction can be important procedures for female-to-male transsexuals who seek bodily changes of their sex organs. Transmen have typically been presented as pathological by a medico-psychiatric discourse (Cromwell 1999). They are accused of having Gender Identity Disorder (GID), said to be a persistent sense of acute discomfort with one's assigned physical gender. GID is a psychiatric classification currently listed in the Diagnostic and Statistical Manual of Mental Disorders. Transmen do not follow traditional pathways to masculinity, but they undeniably practice masculinity (Green 2005). The experience of transition varies depending on whether they openly transition and remain in the same set of relations (e.g., a workplace) or if they find new relations or a new job as part of transitioning. If a transman does not successfully "pass" in masculine environments, he can face antagonism. If a transman prefers other men as sexual partners, he can be doubly stigmatized. Schilt's (2006) research suggests that transmen come to reap the benefits of "becoming man," receiving more authority and more respect in their workplaces. But Schilt did not examine how experiences differ depending on sexual orientation. Noble (2006) provides more of an analysis of transmen, racism, and heterosexism. There has been little research into the issue of gay transmen and stigma.

Intersections are not limited to issues of ethnicity. It is important to reflect upon the strong correlation between homophobia and HIV/AIDS stigma. This can be a major problem, because men who have sex with men may be less likely to get tested for HIV/AIDS or access care and treatment services for fear of stigmatization, especially if no queer-friendly health services are available. Fear of one's HIV status being known is related to fear of being ostracized from family or community. There can be increased anger and decreased sympathy for men who acquire HIV from other men (Herek and Capitanio 1999; Herek 1999). As White and Carr (2005) show in their study of HIV/AIDS stigma in Jamaica, the co-construction of HIV/AIDS and "homosexuality" intersects with class, because of the increased visibility of poorer people. HIV/AIDS stigma not only works to divide the gay community from the rest of the public, but also can lead to factions within the gay community (Courtenay-Quirk et al. 2006).

Official anti-stigma and sensitivity training by public health agencies has been recommended for communities that continue to stigmatize men who have sex with men and/or men with HIV/AIDS. Another option for confronting stigma is community involvement by gay and HIV-positive men themselves—anti-stigma activism from the bottom up. Community involvement may buffer and/or compensate for the adverse effects of stigma at the same time as creating integration amongst participants and educating the public about gay/lesbians issues and HIV/AIDS (Ramirez-Valles et al. 2005). Participation in the gay rights movement or mobilization around AIDS can give men who have sex with men a sense of community. At the same time stigma can be ruinous, leaving people ostracized and feeling worthless (Meyer 1995), without work or access to health care. For others stigmatization can be a process of authentication, of self-formation and coming to be fully accepted in a supportive group of peers. These bonds form what Nardi (1999) has called "invincible communities," alliances of solidarity that provide people with networks for dealing with stigma.

Not all attempts at negotiating stigma are collective. Some people do not have the resources or connections and might not be able to engage in stigma reversal, or discredit the labels of the "normals." Using the terms reactive, intermediate, and proactive strategies, Siegel and colleagues (1998) have developed a comprehensive analysis of how HIV/AIDS-related stigma is negotiated. The first strategies are reactive, seeking to hide HIV status, sexual orientation, or both. Concealment strategies aim to hide discreditable attributes. "Passing" can take the form of dissociation (behaving as if one is not part of the group one is associated with), omission (excluding details about one's life to manage personal information), or using accomplices as association ploys (Kanuha 1999). For instance, Connell (1992) has discussed the "very straight gay" sort of masculinity some men who have sex with men adopt in order to pass or to be accepted in heteronormative contexts. Selective disclosure means talking about HIV only with one's most trusted allies.

Siegel and colleagues (1998) also discuss intermediate strategies, such as gradual disclosure, selective affiliation, and discrediting the labels of moral entrepreneurial groups. Gradual disclosure is coming-out but being careful and strategic about timing and context. Selective affiliation is aligning with those who have encouraging attitudes towards men who have sex with men. When challenging the idea that same-sex orientation was a "sickness" in the 1960s, men who have sex with men became empowered against psychiatry and its attendant regulatory agencies. Some men who have sex with men can engage in pre-emptive disclosure, community education, and collective activism around HIV/AIDS politics. In these forms of collective action, what "gay" means is important. The notion of a "gay" and "lesbian" identity or a totalizing queer community is tricky because of how arbitrary the boundaries of community can be (Valverde 1989). Adopting the notion of a distinctively gay culture might be one way to increase militancy around organizing a radical gay politics against stigmatization. But it might also lead to a separatist orientation (Schur 1980).

The potential for violence, confrontation, and harassment that men who have sex with men face should not be discounted. Many situations men who have sex with men might consider risky are confrontations where they must challenge heterosexist language that they encounter in the course of their everyday lives. Some of these men's most political moments are mundane occurrences. For example going to the gym or meeting potential business clientele can necessitate identity management (Linneman 2000). Whatever strategies are pursued, negotiation of stigma implies negotiation of sexual identity and intersecting identities. Even in a workplace that has passed employment equality regulations, for example, one may not have the support or resources necessary to come "out" (Ward 2008; Leinen 1993). Being "in the closet" is stigmatization in the making, which necessitates identity management.

Conclusion

The contemporary situation looks brighter for men with diverse sexualities. In 1973, the American Psychiatric Association removed "homosexuality" from the *Diagnostic and Statistical Manual of Mental Disorders*. In the early 1970s, most states in the USA had anti-sodomy laws while only a few do today. The *Criminal Code of Canada* was amended to decriminalize private "homosexuality" in 1969. Gay and lesbian political organizing and alternative media have had a major impact in changing public perception. Connell (2005) argues gay men have "pioneered in areas such as care for the sick, community education for responsible sexual practices, [and] representation in the public sector" (19). Canada became the fourth country in the world to legalize same-sex marriage in July of 2005. Increasingly, it appears okay to be gay, especially in Canada's cities where support networks are developed. Despite optimistic change, stigma continues to affect the lives of men who have sex with men, especially when gay identity intersects with other identity categories. Stigmas are elastic—they are able to persist and accommodate countless concerns regarding urban disarray, moral order, sexuality, and normative gender behaviour (Hallgrímsdóttir et al. 2008). There are serious limits to legal reform as a method for diminishing stigma for men who have sex with men. The legalization of same-sex marriage has galvanized a new generation of socially conservative politicians and anti-gay rhetoric. Straight men do not want to associate with men who have sex with men for fear of being labelled gay (Kimmel 1997). Moreover, straight men deride one another through use of labels like "queer," "gay," and "fag" in ways that can contribute to stigma against men who have sex with men (Burn 2000). Men who have sex with men and those with HIV/AIDS are still at risk of being ostracized. Men who have sex with men in some ethnic communities risk similar ostracism from familial and religious circles. Transmen are still labelled and managed by psychiatric institutions. And stigma can make men who have sex with men feel guilty, inhibiting stable relationships.

All this suggests that there is more anti-stigma activism to be done. Focus on landmark events, such as the 1969 Stonewall riot, should not eschew small moments of resistance, the kind of bottom-up anti-stigma activism that helps ensure that men who like sex with men can spend their nights not worrying about stigmatization in the making.

Chapter Six

The Mark of Association

Transferred Stigma and the Families of Male Prisoners

Stacey Hannem

In August of 2006, shortly after beginning my PhD research, I was invited by the women who attended a family support program to accompany them at a candlelight memorial vigil on "Prisoners' Justice Day." This day of remembrance was established by incarcerated prisoners to honour the memory of those who have died in prison, whether due to violence, neglect, or natural causes. The women—wives and mothers of prisoners—and a few children, spent the late afternoon constructing placards and posters describing the cause and listing the names of prisoners who had died inside the walls of the penitentiary. The vigil was to take place later in the evening on the downtown steps of City Hall. A summer festival drew large crowds to the downtown and the women and children with their candles and posters received considerable attention from passers-by, some curious, some disdainful. A few stopped to read the lengthy list of names; many drew near only to turn quickly away.

About an hour into the vigil, one of the children complained that she needed to use a bathroom and her mother got up to take her to a nearby coffee shop. As they turned to leave, the little girl, who was about seven years old, held out her sign, a sheet of Bristol board, to me. She asked, "Can you hold this for me?" The sign read in brightly coloured marker and glitter, "We support our loved ones in prison. I love you, Daddy." I smiled at her, "Sure," took her sign, and propped it up in front of my knees where I sat on the concrete steps. Several minutes after they left, a well-dressed woman in her late forties approached the building. She appeared pleasant and she made eye contact with me as she neared to read the signs. She took in the sign at my knees and her demeanour immediately changed. The smile left her face, her eyebrows arched, and her lips pursed. My heart dropped into my stomach. "Hmph. Prisoners' families," she said to a female companion who had approached behind her. She gave me a look that could only be described as one of contempt, turned on her heel and walked away. I was incredulous. I felt as though I had been slapped. I felt at once embarrassed and angry. Perhaps more telling was my internal dialogue: "How dare she judge me! I don't even have a father in prison! I'm a researcher! I'm a PhD candidate!" In disbelief, I turned to Laura, the executive director of the agency and leader of the support group, "Did you see that?" She smiled sadly at me. "Now you see how it is. This is what these ladies deal with all the time."

> *I think it all comes down to one issue. It's that families are being considered as criminals—where we're not. So we're being treated negatively to start with. We're being looked at in a negative light to start with. I think if they saw that most families are just like them. Like normal citizens. It would change their entire outlook and they would treat us completely differently than they do now.* (Anne, a prisoner's wife)

As the authors throughout this volume demonstrate, symbolic and structural stigmas are attached to those characteristics that are best described as "undesirable" or risk-laden within a particular social and political milieu. Certainly criminality, sexual deviance, ethnic minority status, and mental illness are some of the most salient markers of risk and dangerousness in Western culture and have been stigmatized and subject to programmes of intervention. Occasionally, however, circumstances arise in which an individual who carries no identifiable stigmata is labelled and marked by his or her association with another (stigmatized) person. In his work, Goffman identified that stigma can be transferrable, attaching itself to those who are related to, or associated with, discredited persons and even (less acutely) to those who are "twice-removed" from the stigmatized individual (1963a, 30). Goffman also observed that the contagion of stigma can serve to exacerbate the effect of the original stigma as relatives, friends, and acquaintances may choose to remove themselves from relationships that are viewed as potentially socially damaging and others, upon learning of the discrediting characteristic, will avoid involvement with stigmatized persons (1963a, 30). Most recently, Gwenola Ricordeau's (2008) study of the family of prisoners in France has confirmed this phenomenon. Friends' and family members' fears of being labelled can then contribute to the social isolation and outcast status of the (ex)prisoner and have a detrimental effect on family relationships.

Transferred stigma or "courtesy stigma" as Goffman called it, bears further exploration through a thorough theoretical discussion of the existence and implications of this particular societal idiosyncrasy. In fact, with the notable exception of a few essays that detail the prejudice and isolation experienced by the families of prisoners, the mentally ill and delinquents (see, for example, Barton 1988; Fishman 1990; May 2000; Sharp 2005; Condry 2007), the notion of stigma by association, has rarely been addressed in the sociological literature. This chapter will discuss the phenomenon and effects of transferred stigma and the myriad of ways in which stigma affects the families of criminalized persons,[1] both at the individual, symbolic level and at the collective, structural level.[2] We will also engage with substantive examples of how these two levels of stigma reinforce one another and perpetuate negative stereotypes of prisoners' families. First, however, I will briefly discuss the methodology of this study. I will also explore the often-overlooked role of gender in the transference of stigma and its significance to this research.

The information presented in this chapter is based on conversations with twenty-eight individuals who had experienced the incarceration of a male family member (Hannem 2008). They were recruited primarily from agencies who offered support services to the families of incarcerated men. These "conversations" took the form of seventeen in-depth, semi-structured interviews and three small focus groups comprised of thirteen individuals.[3] Most of these individuals were women. Though a concerted effort was made to contact male family members of prisoners, they were difficult to locate owing not only to their smaller numbers but also because they tend not to use available family support services.

---

1 While I utilize the family members of prisoners as a particular example of the transmission of stigma, note that many of the concepts presented here may also be applied to the close associates of other groups of labelled and stigmatized individuals, such as the family members of mentally ill persons, homosexual persons, those who work in the sex trade, and others.

2 See chapter 1, this volume, for a thorough discussion of symbolic and structural stigmas.

3 The observant reader will notice that this, in fact, totals thirty "conversations"; two individuals participated in both a focus group and an interview, bring the total number of persons to twenty-eight.

Gender and Transferred Stigma

While the vast majority of incarcerated persons throughout the world are male, many of these men are engaged in relationships with women[4] who are greatly affected by the collateral punishment of incarceration. The difficulties confronted by these women are forgotten or ignored by correctional administrators, legislators, and the public, and their circumstances are rarely discussed when creating social and criminal justice policy. Traditional patriarchal norms make women more vulnerable to the effects of transferred stigma by constructing their identities in relation to that of their male partner. In the case of prisoners' wives, this occurs in two intersecting ways: first, through the woman's own ethic of care and her identity as a supportive "wife," which increases the likelihood that she will continue the relationship with her incarcerated spouse/partner; and second, through the patriarchal economic system that often places her in a precarious situation of financial dependence or marginal economic status, relative to men.

When a man is sent to prison, the female partner who is left behind may become a *de facto* single mother, but will often make a concerted effort to keep the family unit intact, despite involuntary separation from her partner. Girshick (1996) attributes this tendency to the woman's own ethic of care and personal identification with the "wifely" role that she plays in caring for her family, but also to more general societal expectations that a woman will be invested in her relationship and family.[5] In a patriarchal society, a woman's social identity is closely linked to that of her male partner and his social status, particularly if she does not have a career or other significant public identity separate from her partner/husband and family. This phenomenon allows for the stigma of a man's identity as "criminal" or "deviant" to be more easily passed to his wife or female partner. Conversely, men are more likely to be insulated from transferred stigma by an independent social status (including professional/work identities) that does not rely on marital or kinship ties. This autonomous identity appears to reduce the likelihood of transferred stigma significantly, as others relate to the non-deviant

---

4 Admittedly, research around prisoners in same-sex relationships is lacking and certainly warrants further exploration.

5 When a woman is imprisoned, it is relatively rare that her male partner would endeavour to sustain the relationship throughout the period of incarceration or assume the care of minor children (Casey-Acevedo and Bakken 2002; Maidment 2006b). More commonly, the relationship will dissolve, or the woman may have been a single mother at the outset of her sentence. In these cases, again other women bear the collateral cost of incarceration as children are sent to live with and be raised by maternal grandmothers or aunts. In the absence of these supportive kin relationships, children are placed in the foster care system.

established master status. In short, we find that transferred stigma can be a gendered phenomenon, disproportionately affecting the wives, female partners, and mothers of incarcerated men.

The case of prisoners' families is not the only situation in which we find that women are more greatly affected by the transference of stigma from a family member or associate. Although the potentially gendered nature of stigma has not been the focus of much empirical study, several examinations of courtesy stigma have found that women may be more prone than men to the effects of associating with discredited or stigmatized persons (see also Kampf 2008; Smith, Mysak, and Michael 2008; Grey 2002). For example, in Gray's (2002) study of the experiences of parents whose children had high-functioning autism, he found that mothers were more likely to describe incidents of discrimination, avoidance, and hostility than were fathers. Clearly there is space for further examination of the role of gender in the transference of stigma, and/or "courtesy stigma." However, an understanding of the gendered nature of transferred stigma and the mitigations of social roles is integral to comprehending the experiences of the family members of incarcerated men, to which I now turn.

Living with Transferred Stigma

All of the family members that I spoke with had stories of negative social experiences, rejection, condemnation, and avoidance behaviours. They reported the loss of employment, difficulty in finding work, isolation, and lack of support. Even friends and extended family often pull away, leaving the individuals to deal with the incarceration alone. Brenda, the partner of a prisoner, described her experience:

> *I lost many friends after I made the decision to stay with Tom. I lost many friends the day it happened and people never bothered to phone. You know, for some, it may have been because they didn't know what to say. I have no idea because I never heard from them. And I struggled with that an awful lot.*

While it is difficult to ascertain exactly what forces are at play when an individual applies for employment, four of the wives/partners that I spoke to felt very strongly that their status as the family member of a "criminal" had a negative impact on their occupational opportunities, either preventing them from obtaining employment or causing them to lose a job. In one case, the cause/effect relationship was made very clear when a woman from a small community was told that she could not return to her place of employment because the family member of one of her husband's victims also worked at that location. In another case, Catharine, the wife of a prisoner, strongly suspected that her inability to find work in her chosen field was the result of her relationship with her husband:

I went back to school, took a business course, and had opportunities to apply to law offices and things like that. And my own family members were calling and saying "Oh, you know, she's married to a prisoner." And you just don't get the opportunity in law offices to work when you're considered to be on the other side of the fence.

Other family members reported a strong sense that if their employers or potential employers knew of their situation, they would be discriminated against. It is unclear if this feeling was always founded in real possibility; however, it is interesting to note that the mere *anticipation* of negative reactions from others is enough to alter an individual's behaviour and lead them to engage in proactive stigma management. In this sense, one can certainly argue that stigma exists as a relationship between the (potential) stigmatizer and the (potentially) stigmatized, and is not merely imposed from the outside and restricted to observable evidence of discrimination.

A common reaction to the anticipation of stigmatic attitudes or behaviour is to manage one's identity through selective disclosure or "passing," keeping the discreditable characteristic a secret whenever possible (Goffman 1963a). All the family members in the sample reported at least sometimes choosing to keep their situation a secret from others, or feeling that it was not relevant information that needed to be disclosed in many situations:

In the community where I live in now, no one knows. So I haven't had any repercussions that way, and I haven't felt anything socially. (Brenda, a prisoner's wife)

(Do you tell people?)
No. No, oh gosh! Especially studying at [the university], straight A student... I guess, for me it's nothing that I ever want to talk about. Nobody knows here. I don't have a lot of close friends [at university] either, so I don't, feel the need to tell them. But, uh, no. I'm not comfortable. Here no. It's a different environment... I'm here for school and that's pretty much it. But when I'm [at home] I go out, I see people that know my brother or know my family, that's a little different. I have to deal with them. But here I don't even have to worry about it or think about it. So nobody knows about it here. (Kim, a prisoner's sister)

[I tell] some people, you know, but most of the time we sort of just say he's out of town or whatever, because it's easier. (Francine, a prisoner's mother)

> *I told myself, as long as my parents are alive, I'm not going to say anything, and then I had the children and so, I have now two conditions. I'm not going to say anything while my parents are alive and until my children tell me that they're willing to have everybody know. If it was just me, I wouldn't care so much, but because there are other people around, I decided to keep it quiet. (What do you tell people?) That he's not around. Like, we're just not together. Which is hard 'cause it makes him seem like a total bad person, 'cause he gave up his children.* (Anne, a prisoner's wife)

However, "passing" can be a double-edged sword. While it can make daily life easier, choosing to keep one's situation a secret means that one is unable to share day-to-day experiences and to interact freely with co-workers, friends, and other acquaintances. While passing may be a very functional choice for dealing with the immediate potential of stigma in occasional impersonal interactions, it may in fact be counter-productive in the long term for continuing relationships. Family members who choose not to disclose their situation to those with whom they interact on a daily basis find that the very act of passing perpetuates their own isolation and avoidance behaviours. These individuals are not willing to risk the potential of negative reactions and so relinquish the possibility that some people will react in a supportive and compassionate manner:

> *It's a very isolating thing, I think, unless you talk to other people who are in the same situation. And not everybody wants to talk about it. I mean, it's not something you go around saying, "Oh, you know, my son's gone to jail," whereas if somebody has a serious illness or something like that there's not the same stigma, I suppose you would say. Yeah. So, yeah, it's isolating.* (Francine, a prisoner's mother)

Wives, in particular, report a tendency to self-isolate and to withdraw from social situations in which their undisclosed status as the spouse of an incarcerated man may become problematic. Concealing the fact of an incarcerated son or brother may be easier since parents and siblings usually live relatively autonomous lives and casual acquaintances would not expect them to be present. However, a woman who has to make up excuses for the absence of a partner is placed in a much more difficult position. For example, if acquaintances or co-workers are unaware of the woman's marital status, or believe perhaps that the individual is separated or estranged from her spouse, they may offer to introduce her to "eligible" individuals. This can be a potentially embarrassing and troubling problem for a woman who has chosen to remain faithful to her incarcerated spouse. Two women spoke of the impact of their hidden marital status on their social lives:

I think the only negative repercussions I put on myself, where I consider myself as being in a couple, although I'm by myself all the time. ... I don't go out with whatever single friends I still have left, because I'm not trying to meet anybody. And those that are in a couple relationship, if they invite me it's usually to try and fix me up with somebody, so I've kind of pulled away from a lot of, um, I don't pull away from the relationship, but from social occasions. I've become more of a recluse because of it. (Anne, a prisoner's wife)

I've had co-workers who said, "I know this guy and he'd be just great for you!" And they don't know about Paul, so that's awkward, you know? And so, I guess I just prefer to, well not avoid, but I usually don't go out if they invite me or whatever. It's just easier not to get into a situation that might be embarrassing. (Daphne, a prisoner's wife)

Consequently, many prisoners' wives find themselves in self-imposed exile, isolated from social interaction not by others' avoidance, but by their own anticipation of negative reactions.

Occasionally, situations do arise in which passing becomes difficult, or even impossible. One of the most salient examples of this is the experience of entering the penitentiary as a visitor. Nearly all the family members in the sample had visited the prison where their loved one was incarcerated ($n = 27$), and all but one reported that their interactions with penitentiary personnel were negative at least some of the time. Only one wife felt that she was consistently treated well by the correctional officers. Another wife and one parent reported that their treatment was predominately positive, with the exception of a few negative moments. However, the vast majority of the family members reported multiple incidents of rude or demeaning treatment perpetrated by correctional officers in the visitor centre and many reported a general feeling that prisoners' family members were not respected by the corrections staff or treated courteously.

[I've visited in] maximum, medium, and minimum [security], and halfway house, community. It's intrusive because most of the staff see you through the same glasses as they see the offenders. They see you as the offender as well. There's very little respect given to families. And interestingly enough, the higher the security level the worse it gets. I remember one time, there had been an incident in the maximum and I was waiting to go into a PFV [private family visit], and I was signed in. And you know, most of the staff know who you are and you have no idea who they are, there's just too many of them. And one staff member was talking about watching videos that night and another staff member asked him, "What are you gonna watch for videos tonight?" and he said, "Oh, I think I'll get Catherine's Cock-up, *which is a common porn video. And because of my name it was directed to me. Families just don't deserve, nor do they expect that kind of disrespect.* (Catharine, a prisoner's wife)

Um, sometimes you get guards who are just polite and do their job and then other times you get people in that box, the glassed in box who can be really abrasive. I have seen people be really badly treated. One time I saw a lady go there and I mean she wasn't a girl, she was probably a mom. And when she asked to see her son and went to put her things away and then came back and said, "Oh, um, I meant to leave some money," and the guy behind the glass said, "Look, there's the notice. You're supposed to do that before you do anything else!" Well, okay, yes, the notice is there, but maybe she'd never been there before, and that's stressful going to a place like that. I mean I think he could have just said, "Oh, well, next time, could you do that before you do anything else?" And that kind of rude response to people I think is unnecessary. And it creates bad feelings with families. So, I think that some people should not be selected for the front line, shall we say. (Francine, a prisoner's mother)

They're crappy at [the prison]. Really crappy. I can't tell you exactly how because it's more a feeling, a condescending, patronizing type of thing than anything. It's not like you can give a story and say, "Well, they did this, or they did that." It depends on the guard. Some of them are miserable as hell. They'll wait 'til everybody's checked in before they'll let one of us through [to the visiting room]. You know, some of them will let four at a time go. Others don't care. And that takes a good twenty minutes off your visit. (Isobel, a prisoner's wife)

The negative treatment that family members often experience when entering the prison to visit can be very demoralizing and in some cases results in them choosing to visit less often or not at all. Even the prisoners will sometimes elect to forego visits in order to spare their loved ones the embarrassment and stress of prison visiting.

I went to visit him when he was at [the first prison], I think about five times. And I probably visited him maybe three or, I don't know how many months he was in [the second prison], maybe it was only two. But I went up about three times, I think, or maybe more. I don't know. It's very different at [the second prison], the visiting. The guards are really, really asinine. And he told me, "Don't keep comin' up here." He said, "Don't worry about it." He said, "I just stick to myself." He said, "You don't have to put up with their shit. Much as I like seein' you, I know you're just down the road." So anyways, I didn't go to see him in [the second prison] as much as I thought I would. (Isobel, a prisoner's wife)

Well, this is the thing: when he has been in prison he doesn't want me to visit. He has always said it's not a place I want my mom to come to, which makes it difficult because you're relying on letters and the telephone, and it's a respect thing. He said, I don't really want my mom, you know, and that's okay. (Francine, a prisoner's mother)

Family members do acknowledge that the treatment that they receive varies, depending on the individual staff members with whom they interact. Some correctional officers who work at Visits and Correspondence (V&C) are viewed as being more respectful and better to deal with than others, and the family members seem genuinely to appreciate these individuals for treating them with respect and courtesy. As Munn (this volume) suggests, this may stem from the tendency of marginalized persons to interpret everyday acts of civility as expressions of exceptional kindness.

There are some very, very nice people. And there are some very, very, very bad people. Yeah. Well, it's like in the world. But some people are there for the pay, and possible success and advancement and the potential of power that's there. Others are there to make a difference. Usually they don't last a long time, unfortunately. But when they do, either they change, or they burn out. (Anne, a prisoner's wife)

[At the prison], we had this one chaplain who just saw me as a pathetic woman who comes to visit her husband in prison, like "how pathetic." There was this other chaplain who was, and remains, even though William has moved from that prison, just truly compassionate and beautiful and helpful to us through the death of William's mother—that's where we got to know this person. I never felt judged, I felt really supported. I felt valued as an intelligent and strong woman. So the range of experience was extremely broad and still is. Because he now has this case officer who is so compassionate, but his parole officer who I talked to for the first time the other day, I can tell, she just really thinks that I must be crazy and it's a horrible feeling to feel pitied. It's truly awful. So it's very, very wide-ranging. (Danielle, a prisoner's wife)

The Intersection of Social and Structural Stigmas

Clearly, the disrespectful treatment of visitors is not the official policy of the Correctional Service of Canada (CSC), which is purportedly based on a core value of "respecting the dignity of all persons." However, the seeming prevalence of antagonistic encounters between correctional staff and visitors at penitentiaries across Canada, and at various levels of security, suggests that the phenomenon may be more institutionally pervasive than merely the result of certain individuals' prejudices. It is likely that the attitudes of the correctional officers are reflective of a larger institutionalized stereotype of prisoners and their families as risky individuals who pose a danger to institutional security and possibly to the public as potential perpetrators of crime. This assumption is enacted in prison security policies, which direct disproportionate scrutiny at visitors and family members while neglecting to inspect the behaviours of staff, volunteers, suppliers, and professionals to the same degree. Family members are keenly aware of this discrepancy and describe a feeling of being targeted and treated "like criminals." The discretion[6] given to Institutional Heads of federal prisons to determine the type and scope of searches to be used is exercised in a way that is consistent with the belief that prisoners' family members pose a threat to the "good order of the institution." They are subjected to greater scrutiny than either staff or those designated as "professional visitors" or volunteers because it is believed that they may bring illicit substances into the prison.

Professional visitors or volunteers are screened for a general visiting list and enter the prison as representatives of a religious or charitable organization who will interact with the prisoners for therapeutic purposes. They may, for example, address such issues (deemed "criminogenic needs" in correctional-speak) as alcohol and drug addiction, as is the case with AA or NA volunteers, or promote the social integration of prisoners, as with various visiting programs such as *The Infinity Lifers' Liaison Group*. Professional visitors or volunteers cannot be on the visiting list of a specific prisoner and cannot have family visiting privileges. If a volunteer develops a personal relationship with a particular prisoner and is placed on his or her personal visiting list, volunteer visiting privileges will be lost. The individual will only be able to enter the prison for the express purpose of visiting the inmate who has requested the visits. Two of the women in the sample who met their men during his period of incarceration had previously been volunteer visitors; each was obliged to stop her volunteer involvement when she wished to pursue a relationship with an incarcerated man:

> *When I decided I wanted to see more of Jim, I had to give up [my volunteer work]. They don't allow people to visit one person and volunteer at the prison. Not even at another prison, which I don't really understand. I'm not sure what they think I would do! It's pretty stupid really, 'cause I enjoyed the volunteering work.* (Megan, a prisoner's wife)

---

6 The commissioner's directive on the searching of visitors to federal penitentiaries states, "In all facilities except minimum security and Community Correctional Centres, there will be a routine non-intrusive search of all visitors upon entering the institution" (Correctional Service of Canada 2004a, 3). The precise nature and procedures for these searches are determined by the Institutional Heads of each prison who are required by the directive to establish an Institutional Search Plan unique to the security needs of the institution under their care (Correctional Service of Canada 2004a). Although the directive states that there is also to be a protocol for searching staff upon entry to the prison, policy allows the Institutional Head a substantial amount of discretion in dictating the scope and types of searches employed.

Although I could not find evidence of this policy in any written CSC documentation, it is uniformly observed. According to informal conversations with CSC executives, the purpose of not allowing family or personal visitors to volunteer at the institutions is to decrease the possibility of these individuals being used to assist prisoners in exchanging contraband or trafficking drugs into the prison. The rationale for denying them the opportunity to volunteer at another institution is to prevent the possibility of cross-contamination, or drugs being moved from one prison to another via the volunteer/visitor. The two women who had previously been volunteers noted that their treatment at the institution changed with their newly acquired status as the personal visitor of a prisoner. They found that they were more frequently subjected to electronic screening for drugs and they perceived that the correctional officers' respect for them had decreased.

The Correctional Service of Canada maintains that family members and friends of inmates are sometimes placed under a great deal of pressure by their incarcerated loved one to bring illegal drugs and other contraband, such as prescription medications and cash, into the prison. In many cases, the family member has not previously been involved in this type of illicit behaviour but believes that her loved one will be in physical danger if the contraband is not obtained, and so is compelled to act out of care and fear. This places the family member in a precarious situation; discovery of the trafficking can result in the permanent loss of visiting privileges at best, or criminal charges and jail time at the worst.

The Correctional Service of Canada discourse is not completely without foundation. Jane, the wife of an ex-prisoner, started a support group for the families of prisoners and spoke to the reality that family members sometimes bring drugs into the prison. She made the point that some prisoners are willing to use and manipulate their family members for their own gain, without regard for the safety or well-being of their loved ones. Jane also described her own experience:

> *When I was involved with John and people found out that I worked in a pharmacy, I was approached about bringing things in. And they said that they were going to mess with him. So, John called me that night and I said, "I just want you to be prepared," and he says "Why?" I said, "Because someone found out I work in a pharmacy. They want me to supply them with drugs. I'm not doing that, so you'd better be watching your back because they said you're going to end up hurt." He said, "Don't worry, I'll take care of it." I said, "That's good 'cause I can't." So I was lucky, 'cause whatever he did on the inside was not my issue, that was his issue. Right? That's the way I looked at it. That's a prison issue. That has nothing to do with me as a person. But I mean, it was scary being approached by people you don't even know, who come up to you because they figure you can do something for them, right? But I would have lost my job, I would have lost my*

> *children. I would have lost everything, just to do that sort of thing. So I understand the pressure that some of these families are under. But I also believe that they need to have a way out and sometimes they don't have that way. Because if they tell, even if they went to CSC and told them "I'm being pressured to bring drugs in," the first thing CSC's going to do is stop their visits. So they lose, right? But they'll bring them in, and then they have to do it the next time, the next time. So, you have to do it in a way that these women are not going to lose, or be under suspicion if they do, or report the ones that they know are bringing them in.* (Jane, the wife of an ex-prisoner)

As Jane's narrative highlights, the correctional response to families who encounter pressure to bring in contraband is highly problematic as it prioritizes the preservation of institutional security over the well-being of families. This policy affords a family member faced with this kind of scenario little recourse given that reporting the situation to CSC will likely result in the loss of visiting privileges, at least temporarily if not permanently. If a family member reports that she is under pressure from her partner/son or another inmate to traffic drugs, CSC rationalizes the removal of visiting privileges as the easiest and most expedient means of ensuring that the family member will not succumb to the pressure to introduce contraband and of protecting the family member from any recourse that may result from refusal to comply. They reason that if the family is not able to enter the prison then they are relieved of the burden of dealing with the requests for drugs. The structural stigma that marks prisoners' family members as risky to the security of the institution means that any attempt to report perceived threats or pressure to traffic in contraband is perceived by prison staff as confirmation of elevated risk. In practice, this policy is perceived by family members as punitive and it reduces the likelihood that they will report such a situation to CSC. This places family members who are approached or threatened in a difficult position of weighing the legitimacy of the danger to their loved one with the possibility of criminal sanctions if they are detected attempting to bring drugs into the institution. Ironically, the policies intended to stymie the flow of drugs into the prison may place family members—particularly wives of prisoners—in a position where they feel that they have no palatable recourse but to bring drugs into the institution.

In 2004, CSC introduced mechanical screening devices to detect trace amounts of chemical and drug residue at visitor security. The Ion Mobility Spectrometry Device, or "ion scanner" as it is commonly referred to, is a constant source of frustration for family members who visit the prison on a regular basis. Two of the wives who participated in this study specifically identified the introduction of the ion scanner as having profoundly negatively changed their experience of visiting at the prison. They characterized the use of the ion scanner as assuming criminal involvement where often none is present and reported feeling that they are treated as potential, or actual, criminals when the scanner detects traces of drugs and the alarm goes off (rings):

> *They put in that ion scanner and for the first little while they were gauging it because it wasn't picking up the small quantities of whatever they pick up. I wasn't ringing, and in my head I thought, "Well I don't do drugs, I'm not in contact with drugs, I'll never ring." And then all of a sudden, I started to ring. But it wasn't regular. Some women rang almost every week when they went. It never got like that with me. But, I started to really resent the fact that I was treated like I had done something wrong when I hadn't. And I'm so straight it's crazy! I'm probably straighter than three quarters of the employees in there! I do nothing! Nothing! I sit home and take care of my kids. I have no time to do anything else! And to be looked at that way...* (Anne, a prisoner's wife)

> *Certainly at the start I felt like everyone was looking at me. I was very leery of the ion scanners and I got frustrated. Yeah, I got frustrated I guess, because for the first few months I tested positive, for [drugs] all the time. And I've never used drugs. And because I just moved here, I didn't know anyone so I never went to anyone's house and no one came over to mine. I always showered right before I got in my car to go see him, so I couldn't understand it. And once it was very high and it was high three times... So they got someone out to speak with me. And my visits were never cancelled. Now it hasn't happened for a year, I guess. But there's a lot of nervousness going into it.* (Brenda, a prisoner's partner)

Family members taking prescription medications often find that they will set off the ion scanner. Three of the interviewees recounted instances where their use of legally prescribed medications caused them difficulties and anxiety at institutional security. These types of stories were also a common topic of discussion during the focus groups:

> *I was taking an anti-fungal for my athlete's foot that was recurring, both the cream and the capsules. One nice person at the ion-scanning machine was nice enough to explain to me that, yes, that can make it ring for heroin. 'Cause apparently they're both made with opiates. So, I rang positive. But he looked at it and he said that the ratio of some kind of chemical versus the other kind of chemical showed him that it was probably not [illegal] drugs. And my son said, "Oh it must be the pills you're taking." And I said, "David, I'm taking an anti-fungal, it can't be that!" And the guy said, "Yeah it is"... And he gave me the name of the product that I was using, without me naming it.* (Anne, a prisoner's wife)

> *You know, the first time I was introduced to the ion scanner was a social at a medium security institution. I had an intolerance to dairy products and I had taken a lactate pill, which is, you know, to help process lactose, before I went in, because I knew they were serving pizza—that was on the menu—and there was cheese. And they scanned my hands. Well that was before they knew not to scan hands, okay? And it came up a barbiturate. And then I realized that if you have anything on your hands, the ion scanner is going to identify the closest possible chemical. So that was my first experience. One time, a lady went before me and tested positive for cocaine and then I went behind her and tested positive for cocaine. Well, you know, they're supposed to change their gloves and the insert that goes into the scanner and use a new swab every time, but you know what? These people are human and they don't know enough about this machine anyway. So, when they tested me the second time, they did all that and tested again and I came up clean. The ion scanner ... I don't think that they know enough about it. I know they need something to try to prevent the transfer of drugs into the institution because of security and many other factors, but I'm not sure that the ion scanner is the way to go. It's not accurate enough. It's just not. So, it's intrusive when you test positive and you know full well that you're not a drug user and never have been.* (Catharine, a prisoner's wife)

While correctional staff can use the ion scanner readings to distinguish between the higher levels of drug content consistent with illicit drugs and those lower readings indicative of a legal medication, individuals often find that the reaction of the staff is not understanding or sympathetic in these instances of "false positives." In fact, correctional service personnel will not use the term "false positive" to describe these instances where a visitor registers a positive reading on the ion scanner even though they are not carrying drugs. CSC maintains that the ion scanner is a machine that merely scans for the presence of chemical particles and therefore is not capable of error, as suggested by the term "false positive." Even when legitimate prescription medications cause a positive reading on the ion scanner, family members are treated as suspect and often detained for lengthy periods, taking away from valuable visiting time. Family members who are not involved with drugs, but who scan positive often feel that they are treated in an arbitrarily harsh manner rather than being processed in a professional and efficient way:

> *I was positive for some drug thing. They have an ion scanner. I take prescription drugs; that's the only drugs I take. And one time they said I was takin' cocaine and another time it was marijuana, another time I forgot what it was, heroin or something. And of course I never touched anything like that. And I was scared stiff. And I had to sit there and wait until they got somebody to come and say it was okay for me to come in there, or do a strip search, or whatever the hell they were going to do. And so I sat there for*

> *an hour and a half. Finally, they got the guy on the phone and he just said, "Oh, just let her in. That's fine." So I had half an hour [left to visit].* (Isobel, a prisoner's wife)

Anne interpreted the rude treatment by correctional staff in the aftermath of a positive drug scan as a form of humiliation, meant to shame her for her relationship with an incarcerated man. The lack of explanation and information increases the anxiety and fear experienced by family members and results in frustration with the correctional staff:

> *It's very frustrating [when you test positive on the ion scanner]. And then, if you get somebody that doesn't explain anything to you, you go sit down and think, "I don't understand." And then the guard will say to you, "Oh, you rang!" [Sarcastic tone] "I mean, nobody else did." Like ahhh! Hey listen, I know I don't do anything! And if I can ring that means if you were tested, you would probably ring! You know, like, give me some credit. But you don't get it, because you're involved with somebody who, in their eyes, doesn't deserve it. And that gets to be frustrating.* (Anne, a prisoner's wife)

In focus groups, women described feeling targeted and under suspicion as the primary focus of Correctional Service Canada's drug prevention policy. In fact, the guidelines for the Ion Mobility Spectrometry Device prescribe its use for scanning visitors to the institution only. Visitors are defined as "immediate member[s] of the family (mother, father, sister, brother, spouse or common law spouse); anyone who has been approved to visit the inmate; or any other member of the public entering the institution that is *not a CSC employee*" (Correctional Service Canada 2004b, 2, emphasis added). There is no reference to scanning employees and contract staff on a regular basis. The institutional emphasis on visitors as a potential source of drugs creates a divisive, in-group/out-group mindset between the correctional staff and the visitors, which serves to exacerbate the stigmatic attitudes that individual staff members often present to prisoners' family members. Most of the family members emphasized that the problem is not the routine drug screening, as they understand and are willing to comply with the requirements of institutional security, but the suspicion and disdainful treatment that they received as a result. Family members, overall, do not believe that the correctional staff members are adequately screened for drugs and that undue blame is placed on visitors for the quantity of drugs available in prisons:

> *Well, let's put it this way. A person coming in can't bring a heck of a lot in, for the amount of drugs that are in prisons. So think about it. The suppliers, the people bringing in the meats, that sort of thing. Um, the guards. I mean in KP [Kingston Peniten-*

tiary] ... ten, fifteen years ago they had massive scandal—I think it was ten guards that were named. Two committed suicide, whether they actually committed suicide or not... That whole thing was drug related. I mean, John [her husband] said himself that when his father died when he was in prison, one of the guards came up and gave him a drink. Actual liquor. Said, "You probably need this." It should not have been in the prison, right? [...] So I mean the only way that you could have zero tolerance in a prison is that you test everybody. (Jane, the wife of an ex-prisoner)

To me, the only difference between some of the guys in there and the guys guarding them is a uniform. Which is pretty sad. And when Karl was being released this time, he went before the parole board. And they said to him, "So where do you think the drugs come from in prison?" And Karl looked at them and said, "Your own people." And they said, "Well how can you say that? How do you know that?" And he said, "Well, because just this week one of your guards was let go because he was one of the main carriers. He came in with a lunch pail and they, for some reason, checked his lunch pail, and there he had this big parcel." And Karl said they didn't say anything. That was the end of that discussion. And his parole officer sat there and said, "I can't understand why anybody would do drugs in jail. Why would you want to do drugs while you're in prison...?" (Laughs) They just don't get it! ... But the other thing is that it's also the monetary system in the jail. The guards bring it in, the guards make a lot of money. On a lesser level, a carton of cigarettes is way over the top, like a hundred bucks or something like that. (Francine, a prisoner's mother)

The 2007, the Correctional Service Review Panel[7] reported that they were informed by "staff and unions that visitors are considered one of the major sources of drugs coming into the penitentiaries" (Correctional Service of Canada Review Panel 2007, 31). Notably the role and interest that union and staff members may have in protecting the reputation of the Correctional Service of Canada and its employees was not questioned nor remarked on, and the panel did not recommend any changes to institutional policy regarding the screening of correctional staff. However, they did recommend the enhancement of visitor screening and included the advice of the Canadian Centre for Abuse Awareness that "any visitor convicted of attempting to transport illicit drugs or narcotics into institutions be banned for life from entry upon CSC premises..." (Canadian Centre for Abuse Awareness, as cited in Correctional Service of Canada Review Panel 2007, 31). They recommended the increased use of drug dogs, ion scanners, and searches

7 The Correctional Service Review Panel was an independent panel appointed by the Conservative government under Prime Minister Stephen Harper to review the operations of the Correctional Service of Canada and to formulate recommendations for improving the correctional system.

of visitors to the institutions. This narrow focus on visitors as the primary source of drugs trafficked into the prisons—which seemingly excludes CSC staff and contractors from suspicion—reflects a stigmatic view of prisoners' family members and associates as a risk to institutional security and, by extension, to public safety. Conversely, the correctional staff are perceived to be protecting the public from the dangers associated with criminality and drugs and are therefore themselves not risky, nor subject to suspicion. Power, then, shapes official knowledge about the sources of drugs in prison, and affects institutional policy in a way that overtly blames prisoners' family members for introducing drugs into prisons and ignores the possibility of staff involvement in the institutional drug trade.

Given the strict screening policies for visiting federal correctional institutions, and the sheer quantity of drugs that passes through the prison system, it is highly unlikely that the bulk of drugs available in prisons are trafficked by families. Prisoners and ex-prisoners also report that correctional officials are often involved in the drug trade (see Marquart and Roebuck 1985, for example) and the lack of screening for staff entering the prison certainly supports this as a possibility. There have been high-profile cases of correctional staff caught trafficking drugs into prisons, and even prison officials have been known to voice their concerns. Lord Ramsbotham, the former Chief Inspector of Prisons in the United Kingdom, commented on prison staff involvement with drug trafficking to the British media: "Without the staff, these things couldn't get in" (Cox 2008). The notion, then, that family members and visitors are primarily responsible for introducing contraband into the prison is a discourse that serves to mask the reality of a flawed system that relies on maintaining the illusion of strict divisions between the keepers and the kept.

While some family members may attempt (and sometimes succeed) to carry illicit substances into the prison on their persons, the unfortunate reality is that the actions of a few affect the treatment of prisoners' families as a whole. The rude and disrespectful treatment that family members often experience does not directly contribute to institutional security, but it does serve to reinforce the hierarchy of the institution, which places staff above visitors and inmates. The institutional policies that focus risk management disproportionately on visitors allow individual staff members to justify the stigma that they place on family members and perpetuate negative interactions between family members and staff on an individual level. This intersection of institutional security policies and the treatment of visitors exemplifies the complex, dyadic relationship that exists between structural and symbolic forms of stigma in which one reinforces the other in a continuous circle. This symbolic stigma of association with criminality initially prompts the definition of prisoners' families as risky individuals, justifying increased surveillance and risk-management responses. The risky identity and associated danger to institutional integrity that is assigned to family members, then prompts the maintenance of an in-group/out-group division that justifies the denial of basic respect and courtesy to prisoners' family members and manifests in increased symbolic forms of stigma at an interpersonal level. Family members argue that were staff subject to the same levels of scrutiny and suspicion upon entrance to the institution, they might come to appreciate that the individuals entering the prison are not uniformly "risky" and rather than prejudging families on the grounds of their association with a prisoner would treat visitors as individuals. This leads us to the question of why the individual identities of prisoners' family members are so effectively obscured by the stigma of association with criminality. In the final section of this chapter, we engage with the social psychology of stigma transference and the polluting qualities of deviance.

The Process of Transferred Stigma

The notion of deviance as contaminating has a long history. Mary Douglas' (1966) work on "pollution and taboo" illustrated the fact that many popular fears and perceptions of risk or danger are based on culturally specific, symbolic understandings of purity and defilement. Association or proximity to these "polluting" characteristics is seen as leading to contamination and susceptibility to negative outcomes. This fear of pollution or symbolic contamination can be understood as a motivating force behind others' rejections and avoidance of families affected by incarceration. One wife, Danielle, attributed others' reactions to their fear and to a sense of disbelief and uncertainty that accompanies the discovery that you have spent time with someone who was capable of committing a terrible crime. There is a sense that one's safety has been violated through proximity to a potential victimizer. The knowledge that one could have become a victim of someone whom they knew and trusted is a difficult truth to assimilate:

> *I think that this is a case where it's just unimaginable that a person who everybody knew and loved could be capable of these terrible crimes. So in some ways it increases the stigma because it really shakes people's understanding of safety and feeling of safety .... the crimes happened at a store in the middle of the afternoon, not in a dark alley or late at night. So I really understand people's fear.* (Danielle, a prisoner's wife)

However, even in circumstances where the actions of the offender did not pose a threat to others' perceptions of their physical safety, the family members of many prisoners may also, inadvertently, pose a dilemma for others and challenge their understanding of the social order.

In a "just world" (Lerner 1965, 1970, 1980), the tragic events that lead to the criminal conviction and incarceration of a family member would only befall "deserving" families—those who are morally corrupt, involved in marginal and questionable activities and lacking in character. The fact that many families affected by the incarceration of a loved one are, for all intents and purposes, "normal," hard-working people calls into question the belief in a just world and fundamentally challenges the stereotypes and expectations that have been constructed around those associated with "criminals." Rather than grapple with the idea that the tragedy of a violent or criminal offence could just as easily happen to them or involve one of their kin, individuals attempt to explain away the anomaly by casting the innocent family member as equally culpable for the crime, or by searching for character flaws that would provide a justifiable explanation for the situation:

> *I found that my husband's crime was my crime. And that's how the greater community sees it. I mean there were people in my own faith community who said, "I just don't understand why somebody would do that." I mean, people stopped talking to me in my own church. And they're right; they didn't understand it. They did not understand it, and didn't want to. And because people don't understand it, they think that there's something wrong with you. They think that you're not intelligent. They think that you're a mess. They think that your life is out of control. There are all kinds of things that people think when they don't understand something. And most of it comes from their own fear; but instead of dealing with their own fear and identifying that, it's easier to place [blame] elsewhere.* (Catharine, a prisoner's wife)

> *There are people who are kind and love you and there are people who don't want us anywhere close and would prefer to pity me or think that I'm crazy, or delusional, or co-dependent, or whatever other things they'd like to call me to make sure that I'm different from them; because [they think] it could never happen to them.* (Danielle, a prisoner's wife)

The threat that these families pose to others' feelings of safety and insulation from the world of criminality has the effect of inciting reactions of avoidance, discredit, and blame. The fear elicited by the actions of the offender is deflected to their family by virtue of their relative exposure. Danielle emphasized that the fear and anger displayed by her friends and acquaintances had a much larger impact on her than it did on her incarcerated husband who was isolated from the unkind words and judgements of others:

> *It was all directed toward me. No one ever wrote a letter to my husband saying, "I hate you, how could you do this?" But people, even friends wrote letters or emails saying,*

> *"How could you ever go and see him?" or "I don't ever want to hear his name." I was really the person who paid a huge price for his actions. And there were really times when I wished that someone would come and take me and put me in solitary confinement and let me have the time to think and the safety from the outside world and make him come and deal with the fallout from his actions. Not that I wish that on him, and not that I wanted to go to prison, but ... [I was] totally and completely vulnerable to the judgement of all of society.* (Danielle, a prisoner's wife)

In this light, we can think of transferred stigma as both a function of social stereotypes and judgement of the moral characteristics of those who associate with criminals. More than a mere "courtesy stigma,"—as Goffman (1963a) imagined it (a replicated and diminished version of the original stigma that tainted the convicted family member), transferred stigma takes on a life of its own and is transformed in its particular constellation to reflect moral judgement of the actions and character of the family member. The individual is viewed as not merely "the wife of a convicted criminal," but as the *kind of woman* who would choose to maintain a relationship with a convicted criminal, with all of the associated negative stereotypes and characteristics that the status entails.

It is important to note that not all individuals react negatively toward the family members of incarcerated men. In the minority of instances ($n = 3$), family members reported receiving support throughout their ordeal from community members and extended family and not feeling stigmatized. George, one of the two men I interviewed and the father of an incarcerated man, shared that he and his wife were initially reticent to disclose their situation to others, but as they became more open about their son's incarceration they were met with understanding and compassion, rather than the stigma and rejection they had anticipated. The majority pointed out that reactions to their situation tended to be mixed and while some of their friends, family, and acquaintances were supportive, many were not:

> *Some people I found just really rose to the occasion and the challenge of being fully compassionate. And other people just were so fearful and angry that it was all taken out on me.* (Danielle, the wife of a prisoner)

Since family members reported that not all individuals reacted toward them in an overtly negative manner, it is possible that the community members who are most understanding and most likely to be accepting are those who have themselves experienced an undeserved tragedy and borne witness first hand to the fallacy of a just world.[8] For example, the family members of other prisoners are particularly likely to be understanding and to recognize that the offence does not necessarily reflect on the offender's family:

> *Because of the neighbourhood I grew up in, I knew a lot of people [who had family members in prison]. Most of my girlfriends' brothers [have been in trouble with the law]. I have another girlfriend, my best friend, whose brother is in jail for murder and he's going to be in there for a long time. Yeah, so my best friend she understood. She wouldn't say anything. She understood and didn't criticize me or look at me any different.* (Kim, the sister of a prisoner)

This phenomenon is reflective of other studies of prisoners' families in marginalized communities in which the commonality of imprisonment mitigates the experience of stigmatization. For instance, Schneller's (1975, 1976) study of "the social and psychological effects of incarceration on the families of Negroes [*sic*]" found that social stigma was not a significant problem for these families due to the prevalence and normalization of criminality and incarceration in the ghettoized black community. Although the sample in the present research was not large enough to reflect this, one could assume that a similar trend of normalization might be found amongst families on Aboriginal reserves and in urban, ghettoized communities with high rates of criminal conviction and incarceration.

Acknowledging the origins of transferred stigma in the stigmatizers' worldview and fears allows space to consider the families of prisoners as individuals and to compare their personal characteristics to established stereotypes. The participants in this research were eager to emphasize that they felt unfairly stigmatized and wanted others to see them as "normal" people who happen to be dealing with the serious, personal tragedy of a loved one's crime and imprisonment. Unfortunately, our sense of social responsibility has not yet evolved to the point where the devastating effects of incarceration on families are addressed in a meaningful and positive way.

Transferred Stigma and Collateral Damage

As we have discussed, much collateral damage accompanies the imprisonment of a loved one, including social isolation, financial hardship, emotional trauma, and family breakdown (see Hannem 2008; Hannem 2011; Fishman 1990). Some of this damage may be viewed as the direct result of stigma, such as when loss of

8 The scope of this chapter does not allow further exploration or comment on this phenomenon, but further study of public views toward stigmatized individuals could provide insight into the role of personal experience in the assignment of stigmatizing values.

employment or inability to find work due to one's status as the family member of a prisoner causes financial difficulty, or the rejection and avoidance of former friends and family lead to depression and isolation. However, many collateral effects, while not *caused* by stigma, may be exacerbated when stereotypes and symbolic stigma are used to excuse inaction.

The marginal status that association with criminality bestows allows the public the luxury of indifference to the plight of these families. In this case, marginality is inextricably tied to blameworthiness and to the stigma that accompanies moral deficiency. The neo-classical belief that criminal behaviour is the result of rational choice is a popular conception that justifies blaming the prisoner for his own criminality and for the resultant impact on his family. The male prisoner, as "head" of the household, having made the choice to commit the crime is then deemed responsible for the family's ensuing difficulties. Since the family's hardships can be tied directly to the immoral actions of the prisoner in breaking the law, there is a sense that society is divested of responsibility for the effect on the family, and is under no obligation to mitigate the impact of the criminal justice system on the lives of the family members of prisoners. Members of the public will suggest that "he should have thought about his family before he committed the crime!"

Similarly, the family member's choice to maintain a relationship with an incarcerated loved one is interpreted as evidence of moral culpability and the ensuing hardships are viewed as "just deserts" for whatever moral or personal failing has led the individual to be in a relationship with an incarcerated man. As a result, symbolic and structural stigmas are left unaddressed and the collateral damages of incarceration are at best ignored, and at worst condoned, by the public and by government agencies.

The individuals who came forward to participate in this study did so because they wanted to make a difference: to make others aware of their experiences and to open a dialogue about the injustice of punishing families who are legally innocent for their loved ones' crimes. It is time that we begin to question the unintended effects of our criminal justice policies and to seek more effective means of dealing with crime and those who are most affected by it: offenders, victims, families.

Chapter Seven

The Stigma of Mental Illness

"Slashing" and Managing the Stigma of a Scarred Body

Jennifer M. Kilty

Prologue

It was night—snowy, dark, and cold—a typical Canadian winter evening. I was twenty years old and living with four other young women while attending university and working towards my undergraduate degree. We had been drinking prior to going to the local neighbourhood pub, and we continued to drink throughout the evening while at the bar. Maloney and I shared a bathroom in the downstairs part of our large two-floor apartment. I was tired when we returned home from the bar, and I remember desperately wanting to get into the bathroom to brush my teeth so that I could retire to my bedroom to sleep. I banged on the bathroom door to get Maloney to hurry up. I was impatient. Another roommate, Sarah, came downstairs and upon seeing me waiting to get into the bathroom, opened the bathroom door. Our initial thought that Maloney was playing an innocent prank was quickly wiped from our minds as we took in the reality—our friend sitting on the edge of the tub with a steak knife in her hand and blood dripping down the side of her arm from a wound she had just self-inflicted. I remember standing in the doorway just staring at the blood. Sarah took the knife from Maloney's hand and held a towel to her arm. I just continued staring at the blood. That evening and in the years that followed, Maloney did not want to talk about it, and so we didn't. However, Sarah and I watched Maloney closely and I found myself periodically counting the knives in the kitchen drawer.

It was after the fateful night in January that I described in my prologue that I began to read all I could find about self-injurious behaviour. I wanted to learn what this behaviour was, what it meant, and most importantly, why my friend would do this to herself. I discovered the book *Rock-a-bye Baby* by Anne Kershaw and Mary Lasovich (1991), which told the tragic life story of Marlene Moore. Moore served time in both provincial and federal prisons in Canada and was described as a chronic self-injurer. Moore's story is one among many about self-injurious behaviour in prisons for women in Canada and around the world. Mirroring how self-injury is addressed in wider society, the carceral context also largely ignores this behaviour in terms of research and documentation. Self-injury is, however, constructed as risky behaviour, not because of the potential for infection, disease transmission, or an unintended more serious laceration, but because these women's actions testify to the fact that they remain ungovernable in the carceral context. In this chapter, I respectfully attend to the experiences and understandings of these "ungovernable women" and, drawing on Goffman and other theorists, think through the implications of embodied and lived stigma.[1]

Self-Injury and Criminalized Women in Context

The act of purposefully committing some form of injury[2] to one's own body evokes an image of an individual in crisis, an individual who is distraught, an individual who is out of control, or an individual who is mad. Much of the earlier research on self-injury, primarily rooted in the psy-[3] traditions, focuses on whether or not individuals who self-injure are actually attempting to complete suicide (Ross and McKay 1979; Heney 1990; Favazza 1996). This question not only detracts from understanding self-injury as a strategic method of coping, but it simultaneously reconstructs the behaviour as irrational and as more dangerous than it is. Moreover, all of these images elicit some form of stigma whereby the individual engaging in self-injurious behaviour is marked—at both the symbolic and structural levels. In this chapter I examine how stigma operates on these symbolic (micro) and structural (macro) levels but also how in the carceral context

1 Given that women commit a disproportionate amount of self-injury in comparison to men, this chapter examines self-injury by women. Future research should include a fully gendered examination of self-injury.

2 The term self-harm encompasses a broad range of actions that include but are not limited to self-cutting, head banging, swallowing foreign objects, burning or branding the skin, and deliberate scratching or picking at the skin or an already existing wound. This chapter will focus more specifically on the act of self-cutting—which I call self-injury.

3 I use the phrase "psy-" as an umbrella term to describe the psychological and psychiatric sciences that locate differences in behaviour in a biologically and/or psychologically problematic individual.

it generates the notion of self-injury as a contagion; self-injury is viewed as liable to spread to other incarcerated women because of the stereotype of criminalized women as mentally unstable, weak, and susceptible to adopting self-injurious behaviour as a negative coping strategy. Focusing on how criminalized women construct and explain their own self-injurious behaviour, this research aims to centre their voices and narratives in order to shed light on the experiential realities of an extremely marginalized population.

Self-injury, like female criminality more broadly, is often explained through the medical model as a psychiatric problem surfacing because of the woman's inability to adequately deal with the changes that occur during adolescence, pregnancy, and menopause. For example, Favazza (1996) locates some of the causation of self-injury in faulty female biology:

> The female genitalia, for example, are partially internal; menstruation cannot be controlled; changes in body contours at puberty may be dramatic; during pregnancy the foetus is experienced as the "other within"; the lactating breast belongs both to the child and to the mother. Thus, there are elements of ambiguity, paradox, and discontinuity in females' experiences of their bodies. (293)

Favazza's explanation suggests that self-injury is a "woman's problem" that occurs when women perceive their bodies as unknown, unknowable, and as not their own. In this light, self-injury is presented as a pathological, and thus irrational, attack on an alienated body. In a similar vein, the *Diagnostic and Statistical Manual of Mental Disorders, 4th Edition* lists self-injury as a symptom of other illnesses, such as borderline personality disorder (APA 2000). Similar to the commonly identified roots of personality disorders in women, psy- literature often presents correlative evidence between self-injury and physical and sexual trauma (Jones 1986; Heney 1990; Miller 1994; Connors 1996; Peters and Range 1996; Heney and Kristiansen 1997; Fillmore and Dell 2000; Turell and Armsworth 2003). Some authors have even claimed that self-injury is a form of trauma re-enactment (Miller 1994). Consequently, psy- discourses fail to acknowledge the social and environmental impact of, for example, imprisonment on a woman's self-injurious behaviour (Ussher 1991; Pollack and Kendall 2005; Maidment 2006a, 2006b).

Much feminist literature constructs self-injury as a coping strategy, often but not necessarily rooted in past trauma, and/or as a potential resistant practice (Heney 1990; TTFSW 1990; Faith 1993; Miller 1994; Hyman 1999; Fillmore and Dell 2000; Kilty 2006, 2008). Feminist therapist Jane Hyman (1999) claims that self-injury is a way of expressing emotion without using words. This is important for women in prison, who are frequently discouraged from, and even punished for, expressing their anger or frustration (Ross and McKay 1979; Heney 1990; Faith 1993; Fillmore and Dell 2000; Kilty 2008). Rather than relying on a psy-medical model, this research adopts the view that "contemporary self-injurers [are] not merely pathologically impulse driven; [they] carefully think about, consider, defer, and plan their behaviour" (Adler and Adler 2007, 559). However, the use of self-injury as a way to cope does not lessen its potential harm or the stigma it generates. This chapter offers insight into the experiential realities of women in prison who self-injure, the ways they negotiate their identities as criminalized women and as slashers,[4] and how they manage the stigma associated with this self-harming method of coping. Next, I root the paper's theoretical framework in identity-work discourse as it relates to the construct of stigma and the experiences of criminalized women who self-injure.

Theoretical Framework: Identity and Stigma

Too often, stigma is presented as the unfortunate result of everyday stereotyping. By contrast, this book illustrates that stigma is actually an inherently active process that affects the material and lived realities of many marginalized groups. Given the fact that stigma is generated based on beliefs about an individual's identity or due to more specific identity markers (Goffman 1963a), it is useful to begin the current analysis by examining the impact of said stigmas on the women's senses of self. There are two main streams of thought regarding identity, which are often problematically presented as a dichotomy. First, identity has been described as static, as innate, or as biologically and/or psychologically hardwired into each of us, making it an essence that is simply maintained (Gergen 1991). This view suggests identity is a fixed construct that allows individuals to preserve their perception of self over time, giving them a sense of control over who they are and how others will perceive them. The second stream of thought constructs identity as a dynamic process; as something we negotiate and something that continues to evolve and develop in conjunction with the experiences we have throughout our lives (Gergen 1991; Giddens 1991).

Stuart Hall's work offers us a useful bridge between the micro-level identity projects inspired by Gergen and Goffman's work and the analyses of governance offered by much of the governmentality literature. Hall uses the concept of identity to refer to:

4 Many women self-identify as "slashers"—a term used specifically to describe the practice of self-cutting.

> a meeting point, the point of suture, between on the one hand the discourses and practices which attempt to "interpellate," speak to us or hail us into place as the social subjects of particular discourses, and on the other hand, the processes which produce subjectivities, which construct us as subjects which can be "spoken." Identities are thus points of temporary attachment to the subject positions which discursive practices construct for us. (1996, 6)

Hall's conceptualization of identity as a kind of suture is both intriguing and useful. It provides the space required to begin examining the link between identity as a construction, and the sociohistorically located institutional discourses that constrain or "hail us into place."

In prison, technologies-of-the-self focus on "hailing into place" and/or correcting what correctional experts view as personal weaknesses or flaws in identity. Cruikshank's (1996) work on self-esteem and Hannah-Moffat's (2000, 2001) extensive work on the notion of empowerment provide a useful theoretical point of entry. Both strategies promise to deliver a technology of subjectivity that will help eradicate criminality in women by waging a revolution-on-the-self and the way the individual woman self-governs (Cruikshank 1996). In the correctional context, some of these practices include confession (to psy-experts, correctional officers, and social workers), journaling (which is a kind of self-confession), as well as engagement in correctional programming (for substance use, the development of healthy relationships, parenting skills, job skills, and even cultural awareness). Correctional officials operate within a conceptual framework built upon the concept of self-care, which in turn reflects the stigma associated with certain kinds of behaviour (i.e., substance use, "bad" or uncaring mothering, and most pertinent to the current discussion, self-injury). Correctional discourses that construct criminalized women as inherently dangerous and irrational (which suggest they have a fixed or static identity) and correctional emphases on self-care (which suggest women can change) exist in tension.

Discourses of self-care are embedded in correctional approaches to psy-care, correctional programming, and correctional policy (Kilty 2006); more specifically, they require that women prisoners be substance-free, financially secure, and "good" mothers. Self-care reflects neo-liberal doctrine rooted in a discourse of choice and built on the premise that you are "in it alone." Subsequently, prisoners must remodel their identities by psychologizing their own narratives, thoughts, actions, and behaviours in accordance with correctional demands. In order to self-care, criminalized women must create substance-free, acceptable work(er), and mother(hood) identities (Boyd 1999, 2004). Ultimately, self-care is entrenched in psy-language and is enacted through identity maintenance, construction, and negotiation.

Given that self-care operates via identity and thus stigma management, it is important to understand how women prisoners both resist and engage with identity transformation. The concept of "folding" (Hall 1996) allows us to do this as it holds a view of identity (stigmatized or other) as something that is adaptive (fluid), yet also as something that can maintain constitutive aspects over time (fixed). Conceptualizing identity as a series of cleavages or folds—that are malleable and conditioned by time, space, sociocultural context, and historical experiences, as well as who we are with—incorporates both discursive approaches to understanding identity (fluid and fixed) and thus allows for discussions of individual agency and identity as resistance. More specifically, criminalized women often "fold" inward aspects of their identities that are perceived as displeasing or threatening to their ability to self-care—(i.e., identity as a self-injurer/slasher). In the carceral context, it is only through self-care that psy- and correctional experts view women as able to generate a post-criminalized identity. However, a criminalized and/or slasher identity does not evaporate. This chapter focuses on how women are able to negotiate their identities as criminals and as slashers by folding this aspect inward in order to allow the negotiated self (or the managed, mastered, and responsibilized identity) to be on display to others.

Methodology

This research emerges from twenty-six in-depth and semi-structured interviews completed between May and September of 2006 (Kilty 2008). Of this total, twenty-two interviews were with former women prisoners and four were with social workers who work with "at risk" and criminalized women and girls living in the community. Of the twenty-two former prisoners, eight (36 percent) had served federal as well as provincial prison time, and fourteen (64 percent) served only provincial prison time. Exactly half (eleven) of the women had engaged in self-injury. Participants were located following initial contact with social workers at two local chapters of a woman's organization that provides housing, services, and programming to "at risk" and criminalized women. Staff members assisted by distributing an information sheet to women who used their services, and the women were able to contact me directly to arrange a meeting. Snowball sampling subsequently occurred as women who did not use the organization's services contacted me wishing to participate; this is a positive sign of how initial participants viewed the interview experience. I offered each participant a twenty-dollar honorarium and offered either a ride home or bus tickets to help compensate for travel costs.

This chapter offers a Foucauldian discourse analysis[5] of the narrative portrayals of different kinds of stigma (symbolic and structural) as they relate to self-injurious behaviour, which is constructed as engendering a kind of contagion effect amongst women in prison. This approach to discourse analysis draws on Foucauldian constructions of power/knowledge and requires that we account for inequality in our analyses because it perpetuates the marginalization of certain groups (Van Dijk 1993). Discourses are therefore active. Active scripts have the power to "constitute a discrete order of social relations characterized by the detachment of discourse from the locally situated speaker and her particular biography" (Smith 1990b, 123). In the prison context, these scripts constitute "institutions within the prison," by which I mean the multiple sites of discourse,[6] for example, psy- and treatment discourse, medical discourse, correctional and rehabilitative discourse, and correctional historiography (the correctional biography of the prisoner). Each one of these sites has the ability not only to create its own discourses but also to delegitimize those of the women.

Studying self-injury requires an understanding of participant's experiences as embodied subjects and as sites for research. Coffey (1999) suggests that:

> the body is negotiated in everyday life, serving as an agent of cultural reproduction and as a site of cultural representation… The body has been recast as a site of discourse and action; as a form of representation; as intimately linked to biography and the crafting of the self (59).

Body-work is symbolic, physical, observational, organized, managed, and governed, both by the self and through discourses. A key part of this research is the need to engage in a theoretical analysis of prison discourse as a site that attempts to manage, control, govern, "empower," rehabilitate, treat, cure, and watch the bodies of its prisoners.

The process of identifying inequality means that we must render visible the discursive strategies that legitimate control and naturalize (maintain) the social order (van Dijk 1993, 254). Stigma, more broadly, is in itself a discursive strategy and

5 Discourse analysis emerged from linguistics as a method to analyze the production and meanings of written and spoken language and texts. Different disciplines have since generated their own approaches for conducting discourse analysis. Most prominent among those from the social sciences and humanities is Foucauldian discourse analysis, which rather than examining the component parts of speech, examines the social and institutional contexts that give rise to the meanings that underlay statements and texts.

6 For the purposes of this chapter, discourse, reflecting Foucault's (1977) construction of power as relational and thus always already present, produces and constrains the production of truths. Discourses can effectively foster inclusion and exclusion, as well as institutionalized inequalities.

practice that legitimates control and naturalizes the social order. In this chapter, I illustrate how symbolic stigma reflects a kind of moral judgement regarding body mortification and corporeal markings, where psy-experts view self-inflicted wounds as indicative of psychological maladjustment. Similarly, self-injurious behaviour elicits forms of structural stigma (Hannem, Chapter Two) that increase social and political marginalization of those bearing self-inflicted scars. Moreover, I examine how the carceral context exacerbates stigma as psy-experts and correctional officials require prisoners to engage in self-care, and view self-injury as indicative of madness, manipulation, and even a contagious dangerousness. Foucauldian discourse analysis is a useful methodological tool in deconstructing the role that the different forms of stigma play in the lives of women who self-injure in prison. I begin by examining the women's experience of symbolic stigma.

Symbolic Stigma: On Slashed Skin and Corporeal Markings

Reflecting Goffman's (1963a) micro-level analysis of interpretive interaction with respect to discrediting behaviours and identity markers, discussions of self-injurious behaviour as it is experienced in the carceral context provides fertile ground on which to examine the impact of stigma on this group of marginalized women. To begin, self-injurious behaviour elicits a kind of symbolic stigma (and stigma consciousness) (Pinel 2004) where many criminalized women feel psychologically and socially marked because of how they perceive others' reactions to their scars, wounds, and continued self-injurious behaviours.

Goffman (1963a) discusses in detail the social and psychological impact of visible stigmata, but he focuses more explicitly on those forms of stigmata over which the individual has little or no control such as, for example, a physical disability. Self-injurious behaviour, strictly speaking, generates a form of visible stigmata—most commonly in the forms of burn marks, scars, open wounds, scabbing, and stitches. However, because these marks are self-inflicted, they do not generate the same kind of sympathy or empathy that would otherwise be the case. Bolstering the impact of the current neo-liberal political climate, this assertion also exemplifies the undercurrent of responsibility and blame that contribute to the foundation of stigma for self-injurious behaviour. More to the point, the women interviewed for this study reported that their self-inflicted scars elicited fear, shock, incomprehension, and apprehensiveness rather than sympathy. For example, several women noted that both in prison and while living in the community, they received poor care in hospital emergency rooms when they went for stitches following more serious self-injurious incidents (Aylesworth and MacPherson 2008; Hadfield et al. 2009). According to Julie, "*the nurses and doc-*

tors treat you last because you cut yourself. They act like you deserve to wait longer than other people."

Furthermore, the symbolic stigma associated with self-injurious behaviour is based on an attribute (corporeal scarification) that can be either discredited or discreditable, based on the locations of the scarring. Only some scars may be easily hidden and thus allow the individual to reveal the discrediting information when they feel more comfortable doing so. However, control over disclosure is not guaranteed. For example, several women with whom I spoke discussed the stress and fear of being "found out" because they were unable to ensure complete concealment of the scars on their limbs:

> *I always try to wear long sleeved shirts to keep them [scars] covered up. Because I see the way people looked at me, the way they stared at my arms if they were out in the open. Summer time is harder because sometimes it's just too hot to wear a long-sleeved shirt. I was at work and my boss noticed the scars because I had taken off my cardigan to cool down. He always treated me differently after he found out that I cut, like I couldn't handle anything stressful, like I was delicate.* (Jane)

The symbolic stigma of being a "slasher" was something the women were worried about both inside[7] and outside of prison. While inside, the women feared prison authorities would interpret their self-injurious behaviour as a failure to internalize psy-expertise and thus as a failure to self-care, which could limit their opportunities for release. Outside of prison, the women were primarily concerned with how others in positions of authority, for example their employers, co-workers, nurses, doctors, or therapists, would view them if they were to find out about their self-injurious behaviour. The women feared people would view them as potentially dangerous or as a liability, and that this stigma would make it difficult for them to maintain social and intimate relationships, or to secure work. Similar to earlier literature on the symbolic meaning of tattooing in prison (McDonough 2001), the women were fearful of not being able to gain employment due to the symbolic stigma associated with self-injury, often noting that scarification "*shows you've been in prison.*"

Due to the stigma women experienced during interactions with individuals who do not self-injure (Goffman's "normals") it is not surprising that they sought

7 While inside prison, the women were concerned about correctional staff finding out that they had engaged in self-injurious behaviour, as this invoked the self-injury policy that would result in their removal from the general population and placement in administrative segregation. This policy is itself a reflection of the symbolic stigma of self-injury but its response is structural in nature. I will discuss the concept of structural stigma in detail later in this chapter.

to manage symbolic stigma, and thus to try to "pass" as a "normal," predominantly through the practice of concealment. The women demonstrated their creativity when implementing different kinds of concealment practices. The most common technique was covering up their scars, wounds, and stitches with long-sleeved clothing; this practice often included a refusal to wear shorts, bathing suits, skirts, and low-cut or midriff-baring shirts. Similar to injection drug users (Boyd 1999, 2004), the women identified that it was common for them to have a certain place on their bodies that they preferred to cut. For example, Brooke stated, "*see I always cut here on my arm or on my stomach. I mean, how often do you walk around showing your stomach? This way no one will see my scars.*" Having such a preference usually made it easier for the women to hide their scars, as they were not required to cover their entire bodies, having only to actively conceal one area.

The women also discussed using make-up to cover their scars. This was a riskier and thus more challenging strategy as it was not foolproof and did not provide the same level of comfort that their scars would go unnoticed by others. For example, Sheryl stated:

> *For the marks on my lower arms here [she indicates the area on her arms that is heavily scarred], my wrists, and my neck—I try to put some concealer on. You know, to make them less noticeable. But I have to be careful not to let it rub off, or to get it on my clothes. I mean, why would someone have cover up all over their pants or shirt? But you can still see the scars through it—but I suppose only if you actually sit and look at them.*

It was clear that the women actively attempt to minimize the symbolic stigma they could potentially experience if others noticed that they engage in cutting. At the same time, and echoing earlier findings (Heney 1990; Fillmore and Dell 2000), it should be noted that all of the women described self-injurious behaviour as serving an explicit coping function for them (as a form of emotional release, self-punishment, and as a way to exhibit control of the self and over the body). For example, Joan stated:

> *It's easier to focus on the cut on my arm than it is to focus on my fucking life is shit, I'm in jail again, I've lost everything; I have nothing. It's just how mine comes out, because I'm not dealing with things that bother me, I'm not talking about them. So cutting kind of releases the pressure. Makes me focus on that.*

The fact that women cut themselves in order to cope with life stressors, including but not limited to their imprisonment, suggests how few avenues for self-expression exist within the carceral context. This finding also points to how women prisoners simultaneously recognized and felt the stigma of being a slasher and as a result were embarrassed that they cut to cope (Strong 1998; Jeffreys 2000):

> *I just don't want people to judge me because of my scratching. It's not who I am; it is just something I do. It helps calm me down. But I know what it looks like—people think you're loony. So I don't really talk about it to anyone. It doesn't impact how I am as a person, or as a friend.* (Joan)

When faced with interpersonal interactions, it is this fear of judgement that causes criminalized women to fold that aspect of their identities inward, expressing a side of their selves that is stigma-free and disassociated from their carceral life and history. Concealment practices are the key component to the women's ability to engage in the process of folding within their attempts to manage stigma and negotiate their identities as self-caring and thus responsible women.

While the women found ways to conceal their scars, correctional authorities actively reconstructed concealment as a risk factor to the women's individual and collective security. Given the prison's assemblage of psy-medical and punitive correctional discourses, the adoption of self-care as a technology of surveillance and governance (upon which one's security classification and even release can be partially based) is not surprising. The concept of self-care reinforces the neo-liberal belief that all behaviour is the result of individual choice. Interestingly, Mary, a lifer, distanced her own self-injurious behaviour from that of other women as a way to reclaim her identity as (now) a prudent, self-caring, and sane prisoner who has learned to be in control of her self-injury:

> *When I worked in the laundry, I had to go and take the stuff down to segregation for the girls, and that wasn't a pretty sight. So, some of them just sat there and rocked back and forth staring at the wall in their baby-doll dresses. I mean, some of these girls just never came back to reality when they cut. Some of them couldn't get a hold on it. I stopped when I realized that it just wasn't the right way to cope with things.* (Mary)

Some women, like Mary, created a new discourse against which they judged themselves as different, distinct, and separate from other women who also practiced self-injurious behaviour. For some criminalized women their identities as a prisoner and as a self-injurer/slasher are intertwined—further entrenching their experiences of stigma in their material realities. Mary's strategy of resisting the stigma associated with being a slasher exemplifies the individualism espoused in self-care talk, which consequently makes it more difficult to collectivize and resist this form of stigmatization, or to effect change with respect to how others understand self-injury. Next, I examine how correctional officials apply the symbolic stigma of self-injurious behaviour to other criminalized women who do not practice self-injury.

Self-Injury as Contagion

Stigmatization is a process that enables and contributes to informal social control, the outcome being the increased fracturing of social and political interaction (Anderson and Ripullo 1996, 26). Goffman (1963a) describes courtesy stigma—where one applies stigma born from certain attributes or statuses to others who are in some way associated with or who resemble the in-group member from whom the stigma originated—as a secondary step in the process of stigmatization. However, Goffman's description of courtesy stigma does not encapsulate individuals, such as women in prison, who are already stigmatized. Given the correctional emphasis on actuarial models of risk management that use aggregate data to predict risky behaviour, it is not surprising that those in positions of administrative power generate heightened or intensified social discrimination of the larger population—that being all incarcerated women. Therefore, at least for the present discussion, the discrediting attribute (self-injurious behaviour) essentially operates as the bond that links symbolic and structural forms of stigma.

While Goffman (1963a, 47) suggests that courtesy stigma emerges from our social interpretation of the "with" relationship, for women in prison the "with" relationship is actually based on the aggregate data used to predict risk and govern the prisoners and the institution. For criminalized women who self-injure, the "with" relationship exists only in the sense that both are imprisoned women. There is no requisite sense of companionship, nor is there necessarily a built or building relationship between the two parties. Therefore, I speak of self-injury as contagion and not as courtesy stigma because it is not the act of self-injury or the status of one woman being a "slasher" that taints our understanding of other women in prison. Rather, they are discredited and stigmatized by virtue of their criminalization, which carries the implicit assumption of mental ill-health. Therefore, the women's base or master status as criminalized causes them to be marked as *potential* slashers. In this light, we are able to see more clearly how the stigma associated with criminalization[8] opens the door for the application of other related forms of stigmatization.

8 For a more detailed examination of the role and impact of the stigma of criminalization, see both Munn and Hannem, this volume.

Given the correctional homogenization of women prisoners' identities, Goffman's (1963a) assertion regarding the sticky quality of personal identity and stigmatic attributes is essential to our current discussion:

> Personal identity, then, has to do with the assumption that the individual can be differentiated from all others and that around this means of differentiation a single continuous record of social facts can be attached, entangled, like candy floss, becoming then the sticky substance to which still other biographical facts can be attached. (57)

The correctional reliance on psy- constructions of criminalized women as inherently maladjusted engenders a unique form of stigma; by virtue of their identities as criminalized women, the stigma of being pathological is thoroughly entangled with the correctional biography of each woman. The seeming prevalence of self-injury amongst woman prisoners has led psy- and correctional administrators to attach that social-biographical fact/possibility onto all women in prison, whose weak mental well-being is considered typical and thus normative in that environment.

The correctional zeal to stigmatize and treat imprisoned women as *potential* slashers emerges from early and ongoing findings in psy-literature that describe self-injurious behaviour as prompting a kind of contagion effect, particularly when it occurs inside a total institution such as the prison (Cookson 1977; Ross and McKay 1979; Heney 1990; Favazza 1996; Carlen 1998). This finding illustrates both the correctional obsession with risk prediction and management and their construction of women as weak-willed or mentally vulnerable (Castel 1991; Hannah-Moffat 2000, 2001). The social workers I interviewed identified the Correctional Service of Canada's overemphasis on risk and security, to the detriment of any consideration of women's needs, as the foundation for constructing self-injury as a behaviour that is potentially threatening to the security of the institution:

> *But I guess from a prison perspective, from their perspective, well because their only concern is safety right? In prison, it's always about safety, safety, safety. Anything that can be threatening has to be stopped. So they try to stop self-injury by putting the women in segregation, which doesn't really work.* (Steph)

To suggest that the self-injurious behaviour on the part of one woman will incite others to engage in the same behaviour ignores the significance and role of women's individual identities—both in terms of agency and decision-making and in terms of resistance. Moreover, this framework ignores the empirical evidence that illustrates how self-injury serves a strategic coping function for many criminalized women (Heney 1990; Liebling 1994; Fillmore and Dell 2000). This framework illustrates how psy- and correctional experts stigmatize self-injury by suggesting that there will be some kind of transference of the behaviour from one incarcerated woman to another, as though women can "catch" self-injury. This evidently illogical assertion exemplifies how the penal apparatus has absorbed psy-interpretations of self-injury[9] into existing correctional discourse regarding the management of this "risky" population (Mathiesen 2000).

On the most basic level, incarcerated women are commonly subject to derogatory comments made by correctional staff members, which demonstrate the assumption that to be a criminalized woman is to be mentally unwell. Not only is there a lack of resources for women who wish to seek psy-care, but there is an increased stigma for those trying to access the services that do exist. Some women are actually taunted and mocked by correctional staff regarding their mental health status:

> *I had a male guard come in and say, "Okay, time to go for your mental walk" when he was bringing me to see the psychiatrist. Yeah, then he'd call ahead to the front desk to let us go through the doors, saying, "Psycho lady on the loose, psycho lady on the loose" so they'd open the doors quicker.* (Emma)

The comments made by the correctional staff toward Emma demonstrate how a woman seeking psychiatric care to deal with her self-injurious behaviour has the dubious distinction of carrying the dual stigma of having been both psychiatrized and criminalized (Lloyd 1995), as well as how correctional workers construct self-injury as an indicator of madness.

We now reach the juncture at which the symbolic stigma associated with self-injurious behaviour meets the structural stigma cultivated by correctional bureaucrats and management staff. It is the simultaneous adoption of the psy-construction of self-injury as a mental health need/risk that inherently generates an institutional security risk and the application of stigma to criminalized women more broadly (as if the women are all potentially mentally weak willed, unstable, or ill), that allows for the generation of structural stigma. It is important to reiterate that the correctional reliance on psy-explanations of self-injury is problematic because they rest on traditional positivist assumptions about women. As such,

9 It should be noted that I am highlighting the correctional reliance on the psy- assertion that self-injury is indicative of mental illness. I question the validity of such a claim; particularly given that self-injury is associated with a diagnosis (borderline personality disorder) that is highly contested by critical and feminist researchers (Clare 1976; Busfield 1986; Healey 2003).

psy-perspectives inaccurately present self-injury as indicative of some form of madness[10] and thus as an irrational behaviour, thereby rejecting the empirical findings of feminist research on self-injury, which argue that this behaviour can be a way to cope with life stressors (Heney 1990; Liebling 1994; Fillmore and Dell 2000; Kilty 2006, 2008). This is not to suggest that self-injury is a "good" or positive coping mechanism. Rather, it is important to acknowledge that the strict nature and governance of the prison environment inhibits other less harmful strategies of coping, making unavailable these other potentially more positive alternatives. In this light, self-injury is not inherently pathological or irrational but is rather practically useful to the women. In the next section, I examine how correctional policy and discourse, while relying on psy-understandings of self-injury, actually co-opt psy-discourse to ensure that it corresponds to punitive correctional ideology, policies, and practices.

Structural Stigma: On Quarantining and Reconstructing "Mad" Women as Manipulative Bad Women

There is a looming and unaddressed paradox between how psy- and correctional discourses explain self-injury and what prison policy deems an appropriate response to the behaviour. On one hand, correctional discourse reflects psy-explanations of self-injury as a mental health concern and indicator of mental pathology (see Wichmann et al. 2002). Despite psy-'s entrenchment in positivism, correctional discourses also rely on the Enlightenment concept of choice, where prisoners are penalized for making the "wrong" choices (Hannah-Moffat 2000, 2001). In the carceral context, the tension between these two approaches results in the reconstruction of self-injury as a bad and even manipulative choice that threatens the security of the institution. It is on the grounds of institutional security that both federal and provincial prisons for women in Canada justify the use of physical restraints (in either a restraint chair or a restraint jacket) and/or the practice of administrative segregation for women who cut themselves (CSC 2002a, 2002b). Reflecting Foucault's (1991) assertion that disciplinary and governmental modes of regulation co-exist, segregation operates on two levels, a disciplinary response is invoked when criminalized women fail to self-care in a manner that aligns with the interests of the institution, which also serves to quarantine those deemed at risk of inciting similar maladaptive behaviour in other women.

10 Self-injury is not a clinical psychiatric diagnosis in and of itself—it is, however, listed in the *Diagnostic and Statistical Manual of Mental Disorders* as a symptom of other diagnoses, namely Borderline Personality Disorder.

The use of segregation/quarantine as a response to self-injury reflects the correctional view that self-injury is a manipulative and dangerous behaviour (Heney 1990; Kilty 2006, 2008). For example, one study found that the staff they interviewed minimized the women's "genuine need for caring attention and nurturing" because they saw self-injury as "acting out" behaviour (Fillmore and Dell 2000, 53). The reconstruction of self-injury as manipulation demonstrates the correctional fixation on security and risk factors, and its failure to address women's needs (Hannah-Moffat 2000, 2001). Moreover, the disjuncture between positivist (determinism) and classical (free will) conceptualizations of self-injury facilitates structural stigma regarding this behaviour. We are able to disentangle how this structural stigma is produced by using a Foucauldian inspired "top-down" analytic approach (Hacking 2004). As aforementioned, and in relation to their criminalized statuses, women in prison are unilaterally stigmatized as being, or as potentially being, mentally ill. For example, all of the twenty-two former prisoners I interviewed took prescribed psychiatric medications while incarcerated. Given our fear and stigmatization of mental illness (Goffman 1961; Corrigan and Londin 2001; Kirby 2005) it is not surprising to see the extent to which criminalized women are psychiatrized (Kendall 2000; Sim 2005; Pollack 2006), nor how the combination of their psychiatrization and criminalization engenders their construction as risky and dangerous.

Indicative of my earlier claim that women in prison do not make up a homogeneous, uniform, or even unified population, there is a division in how women prisoners understand, explain, and label self-injurious behaviour. Participants who did not engage in self-injurious behaviour more readily adopted the explanations proffered to them by correctional and/or psy-officials. For example, when I asked Nellie if she saw women cutting and what she thought about that behaviour, she stated:

> *Yes I did. They're suicidal, they're sick in the head. They got a serious problem. I saw that a lot, yes, and those women are fucked in the head. You'd have to be to cut your own skin open. They need to be locked up. (Do you mean restrained, physically?) Yes. So they can't kill themselves.*

Nellie's script illustrates the interconnected application of stigma—based on a woman's status as criminalized, psychiatrized, and her identity as a "slasher." In this light, the "slasher" is "othered," reconstituted as a specific kind of woman who is distinctly different from the rest of the population of incarcerated women. She is "sick," and has something wrong with her. Nellie suggests that she is in need of both psychiatric help and correctional restraint. However, can we effectively "manage" mental illness in prison? Is the prison ever an appropriate environment for holding, let alone treating, individuals with mental illness?[11] Arguments for and against mental health treatment in the carceral context abound (Kendall 2000; Pollack 2006; Pollack and Kendall 2005); what is most pertinent to this discussion is how correctional officials respond to women when they self-injure.

Understanding the common assumption that many criminalized women are mentally disturbed in conjunction with their status as a "slasher" and the stickiness of this label (psy-construction of a contagion effect), we can see how structural stigma is fostered. Structural stigma comes in the form of the policy of isolating women who self-injure by putting them in segregation (CSC 2002a). For example, a social worker with whom I spoke stated:

> *When I spoke to the guards, they said that they put women in seg[regation] so they can watch them and prevent them from harming themselves further, but also to prevent other women from doing the same thing. You saw that even in the old P4W [Prison for Women] where they put all those women in seg, yet so many of them committed suicide while they were in there.* (Tammy)

Following a self-injurious incident, the woman is strip-searched to try to ensure that she does not have anything on her body with which to harm herself further, despite the fact that strip-searching has been linked to increases in both the frequency and severity of self-injury (Ross and McKay 1979; Heney 1990; Liebling 1994; Heney and Kristiansen 1997; Carlen 1998). The woman is then placed in administrative segregation to prevent repeated incidences of self-injury as well as the occurrence of a contagion effect where other women follow suit and begin cutting (CSC 2002a). Many women describe the detrimental impact of being left alone in segregation, under the guise of preventative security measures, in what is known as a "baby doll gown" (a simple paper covering, similar to those given in hospitals or doctor's offices):

> *I got nothing but time to focus on the negative and the fact that I'm being punished for hurting myself. I mean, what's it to the prison that I slashed you know? How is it an offence against them? So, yeah, it is self-destructive. To me, unless somebody is a threat to others I can't see it being a healthy place for anybody. When you slash you do it alone. And to be alone in seg, doing that to yourself, you could die. At least if you're in a group, somebody will see it and say something. I don't ask for help, it's private and embarrassing, you know?* (Joan)

---

11 For a more critical evaluation of the existence of mental illness and psychiatric diagnoses, please see Szasz 1961, 1971; Ussher 1991; Healey 2003).

I argue that the continued practice of segregating women who self-injure is not simply a preventative security measure, nor is it just a way to monitor the individual woman. Segregating women who self-injure is a form of punishment; it is the same response utilized when a prisoner is charged with an institutional misconduct. In this light, women's needs are not only reconstructed as risks (Hannah-Moffat 2000, 2001), but self-injurious behaviour itself is reconstructed as bad behaviour by prisoners who fail to self-govern responsibly—or who fail to self-care.

All of the participants who were segregated following a self-injurious incident were adamant that their placement in segregation was not going to stop their behaviour. For example, Marsha stated:

> *Why would being in seg stop me from cutting? It's so stupid! It only gets worse. I felt like shit in my cell, and I felt worse in seg. At least in the house I had some of the women to talk to, a bathtub to go relax in, you know? In seg, I'm just sittin' there, doin' nothin' but thinking about how I'm in jail again, and how I keep fucking up.*

Heney (1990) found that women in prison wanted to talk with a counsellor or a friend following a self-injurious incident, and that being isolated in segregation only made matters worse. More to the point, using segregation as a response to self-injury speaks to structural stigma, for as Hannem (Chapter Two) states, "This stigma is *structural* because the difficulties that arise from it are not so much a product of the stigma itself, or any inherent problems that arise from the condition, but of the institutional and conceptual structures that surround it." Given the empirical evidence, using segregation as a response to self-injury actually increases the behaviour it is intended to curb. Ultimately, structural stigma exemplifies how corrections co-opts psy-interpretations of self-injurious behaviour, absorbs these interpretations into existing punitive correctional policy, and finally uses these explanations to justify stigmatizing and discriminating against women who self-injure.

Similar to their negotiations of the symbolic stigma experienced because of their corporeal scarification, women prisoners attempt to resist and/or manage this form of structural stigma primarily through concealment. For example, the women identified self-injury as an extremely private and personal act; all the women described cutting while they were alone in their rooms or cells, and that they usually cut at night. In addition, the women also practiced storytelling about how they received their injuries, as well as cutting themselves on parts of the body that are easily hidden. Concealment is therefore a personal management strategy used to mitigate both the symbolic and structural stigmas associated with self-injury. However, incarcerated women also engage in stigma management practices that reflect the neo-liberal discourses that serve to foster the structural stigma to which they are subject. For example, some of the federally sentenced women discussed engaging in harm reduction strategies, such as tool sterilization and self-stitching with in-house first aid kits, in order to practice "self-care" and to demonstrate how they are "responsible cutters." Ultimately, in the current neo-liberal carceral context, a woman's ability to resist the institutional discourses that constrain and confine her, as well as her ability to negotiate her identity as a slasher, is bound by her skill of embracing the discourse, and contingent behaviour of, self-care.

Conclusion

Self-injury remains a behaviour that we know little about, despite the spotlight that periodically shines on it (Adler and Adler 2007). By virtue of its very nature, self-injury is a behaviour that shocks; the images of the act itself—a young woman, alone, upset, crying, knife wielding, cut flesh, the bleeding—combine to elicit incomprehension, morbid intrigue, and symbolic stigma. Incarcerated women are able to negotiate their identities as "slashers" through specific management techniques, such as concealment. What is more, in drawing on the work of Stuart Hall (1996) we are able to see how women in prison engage in a process of identity "folding" in order to facilitate the concealment of their corporeal self-scarification.

Correctional responses to self-injurious behaviour have historically been punitive, exemplified by the policy-driven response to continue the use of administrative segregation for women who self-injure (Ross and McKay 1979; Heney 1990; CSC 2002a; Wichmann et al. 2002). Within the carceral context, incomprehension about the genesis and nature of self-injury is transformed into fear and into a new form of structural stigma. The generation of structural stigma is due to the correctional reliance on psy-literature that suggests self-injury can cause a ripple or copycat effect amongst other women (Cookson 1977; Ross and McKay 1979; Heney 1990; Kilty 2006, 2008; Adler and Adler 2007). In this chapter, I have shown how, in practice, correctional policy actually redefines self-injury as a threat to institutional security (CSC 2002a, 2002b; Kilty 2006). While the redefinition of women's needs as risk factors is not a new phenomenon (Hannah-Moffat 2000, 2001), the connections between this redefinition and the forms of stigma outlined in this chapter offers a new avenue for theorizing both self-injurious behaviour and the experiences of incarcerated women.

The work outlined throughout this volume, employing a theoretical framework inspired by both Goffman and Foucault, has allowed me to link micro and macro forms of stigma as applied to women who self-injure in prison. Hannem (Chapter Two) defines structural stigma as "the result of a carefully calculated intent to manage individuals within a particular population, based on the risk that they are perceived to present, either to themselves or to society." This definition provides a point of entry to appreciate how using segregation as a response to self-injury is not simply a way to monitor women in distress—it is a way to manage a population deemed to be simultaneously at risk and risky. Because segregation is inherently a form of punishment, while there may be no intent to *harm* the women, this political response *creates* harm including increasing both the severity and frequency of self-injurious behaviour. Given this knowledge of how stigma is generated and applied symbolically and structurally to women prisoners who self-injure, in conjunction with our recognition of the unintended consequences of said stigmas, federal and provincial correctional services should revisit their policies regarding how to address self-injury when it does occur. Most importantly, we must advocate for the abolition of segregation as a response to women in distress, as it reflects a strict form of punishment rather than an intervention conducive to their ability to cope.

Chapter Eight

Speaking Out

On Being a Nigger[1]

Charles Huckelbury, Jr.

> In the folds of this European civilization I was born and shall die, imprisoned, conditioned, depressed, exalted, and inspired. Integrally a part of it and yet, much more significant, one of its rejected parts.
>
> —W. E. B. DuBois in *Dusk of Dawn*

Notwithstanding recent attempts to depict race as an artificial construct of governing bodies, I consider myself white. Sixty-four years ago, I was born into an upper-middle class family that traces its roots to northern European immigrants who entered this country not long after the Mayflower landed at Plymouth. I did not question in my formative years, and do not question now, the gifts endowed by nature and the abilities honed by nurture that have enabled those of European decent to, in effect, decide for better or worse, the fate of the planet on which we live. I came of age in the sixties and enjoyed the privileges and perks (usually assumed as my right), which included an education at excellent universities and exposure to art and culture that extolled European civilization above all others. Before the ravages of six decades took their toll, my hair was light brown leaning to red. My eyes are blue, and my skin freckles in the sun, indicating that my particular phenotype is far more comfortable in colder climates where melanin is not required to shield the body from intense ultraviolet radiation. And yet, in society's eyes, I am a nigger.

---

1 This article originally appeared in the *Journal of Prisoners on Prisons*, volume 8, 1/2 (1997). Revised by the author in 2010 and reprinted with permission of the University of Ottawa Press.

Imagine if you will, the shock of this discovery, flying in the face of everything I had come to believe and defying the logical extension of what I saw as a European progression that had lasted relatively uninterrupted for over two millennia. During the turbulent sixties, I had managed to remain aloof, refusing to acknowledge the claims of racial and ethnic minorities of being victimized by society in general. I believed that any man or woman could do whatever his or her talents dictated. Meritocracy and the Jeffersonian ideal of an intellectual aristocracy appealed to me; ability and opportunity were the twin pillars on which my philosophy rested. If life was a metaphorical foot race, then everyone certainly deserved an equal place on the starting line, but never did I presume that everyone would, or should, finish in the same position.

Of course, my peers were all white, and although I recognized certain disparities in abilities, I never questioned the freedom for all of us to expand to our personal limits. I projected this same assumption onto people of colour, refusing to listen to their cries against a racist society that denied them even the most fundamental opportunities for self-improvement. I believed that they simply lacked substance or else preferred subsistence, living as social parasites. I pointed to obvious success stories like Thurgood Marshall[2]—it would be Barak Obama today—to demonstrate the rewards discipline, intellect, and motivation brought, never believing that a man or woman would permit anyone to dictate what happened to him or her and their children.

I do not remember the first time I either heard or used the word "nigger," and obviously do not recall the context of either incident. Both doubtless referred to blacks in general, since during the fifties, the more reactionary elements of society used the term inclusively instead of preferentially, some even going so far as to use the n-word as an ethnic umbrella, under which *every* person of colour was gathered. I had heard African-Americans refer to each other as niggers, and in my naiveté, I could not understand the hostility when a white person dared to use the same epithet. Never could I grasp the magnitude of the insult. Indifferent to historical precedent and the stigma slavery had stamped on the soul of every African descendant brought forcibly to this country, I blithely passed on the periphery of the black population, content with my own existence and wholly unconcerned about the ten percent of the nation that remained disenfranchised.

In 1974, all that changed when I was sentenced to life in prison. I quickly discovered that skin colour does not confer nigger status; one's position in

2 Thurgood Marshall was the first African-American Supreme Court justice and the attorney who successfully brought *Brown v Board of Education* (1954) which desegregated American schools.

society does and is imposed by the prevailing power structure, that is, society itself.[3] As a student of history, albeit one with an incomplete education, I soon discovered the parallels between slavery and incarceration, and the environment in which I found myself clearly demonstrated that I had been relegated to the status of nigger. White, black, red, yellow, or brown, *every* convict was a nigger, with our rights circumscribed by both our confinement and the law of the land. Like Dred Scott,[4] I was property, not of any individual but of the state and its monolithic prison system, and were I to escape and make my way north via some latter-day underground railroad,[5] I could be returned at the discretion of the owners, that is, the State of Florida. Whereas the United States Constitution counted male slaves as three-fifths of a person for demographic purposes, convicts did not rate that high; we were, and are non-persons, niggers in the most authentic sense of the word and consigned to the social oblivion historically enforced by every court in the country.

In 1896, for example, the United States Supreme Court ruled in *Plessy* v *Ferguson* that separate facilities for races were legal and just. I discovered the same attitudes and applications in prison, at least with respect to separation. We were segregated not by race, but by our refusal to obey the law. Yet unlike the aftermath of the *Plessy* decision, no effort was exerted to make our position ostensibly equal to those outside. No one cared much about such rudimentary things as food, clothing, or education, and society assumed that we could survive on less than they. Indeed, many expressed outrage that we had what few comforts we did and publicly stated that we should be flogged and fed fish heads and rice twice a day. More moderate suggestions, including ones concerning education, were met with pre-*Brown* v *Board of Education* rhetoric, the polemics usually taking the form: "Why educate the bastards? They're no good anyway and too stupid to learn." I began to hear Old Massa's voice loud and clear.

Our loved ones suffered along with us, required to commute to and from the prison on the weekends in a generally futile effort to keep the family together. Given the long sentences most of us had, no tactic could have preserved such a union, where the husband or father would be absent for twenty to thirty years—and often permanently. As it was in the days when the men, women, and even children were sold separately, convicts watched as their wives, sons, and daughters left them forever. After all, niggers did not need families; we were not "normal"

3 For an excellent discussion of this phenomenon, I recommend Paulo Freire's (1989) *Pedagogy of the Oppressed*, New York: The Continuum Publishing Company.

4 Supreme Court case of 1857 holding that runaway slaves were property and could therefore be recovered by their owners anywhere.

5 Surreptitious means of transporting escaped slaves into "free" states.

and therefore could claim no societal obligation to maintain our nuclear families. We had no civil rights, and our human rights were constantly in question. Like the Spaniards in the New World, society needed a reminder that their niggers also possessed souls, but we had no Las Casas[6] to plead our case.

Whatever label one puts on it, incarceration *is* a form of slavery, or at the very least, indentured servitude, and manifests a blatant teleological philosophy. No concern is ever given to the propriety of the act itself; only the end result is important. And for convicts, that end result is the total, coercive humiliation of a human being, breaking him psychologically and constantly reminding him that he is less than his fellows, that he is in fact a nigger.

We are thus transformed into second-class citizens, if in fact citizens we still are. Guards are the functional equivalent of overseers, the crackers of the plantation, and have "carte blanche" to treat us in whatever manner they choose. They beat us and kill us with impunity. We are required to shine their shoes or boots, serve their food, or fetch and carry. We must defer to their every whim and often pay for rebellion with our lives. Lord Acton's[7] observation on the corruptive ability of absolute power found its proof in the antebellum South, and its modern affirmation stalks the corridors of today's prisons. Niggers we are and niggers we will remain in society's eyes and in the eyes of those it appoints to keep us in our places.

And yet, and yet… the pendulum does swing. Slaves were freed by the Thirteenth Amendment, protected by the Fourteenth, and enfranchised by the Fifteenth. Society at that time, at least part of it, recognized that even its niggers had never abrogated their rights, even when they were held in physical and psychological chains, deprived of their families, kept illiterate, and reduced to the status of chattel; they had those rights, basic human rights that Jefferson recognized, ripped from them as soon as they were placed in chains. Efforts to redress those wrongs led eventually to the giant strides made by the Civil Rights Movement of the sixties, although resistance was concerted and often brutal. Blacks ceased being niggers, at least in more enlightened discussions, not because society's opinion had changed—it had not—but largely because they were now seen as political fodder whose bloc votes could be courted and won by the most patronizing office seekers. But at least publically they were recognized as human beings worthy of consideration.

6 Bartolomé de las Casas (c.1484–1566) was a Spanish missionary and historian, known as the Apostle of the Indians, who was the first to criticize the oppression of Native Americans by their European conquerors.

7 John Emerich Edward Dalberg-Acton (1834–1902). British historian and liberal philosopher, noted for the statement, "power tends to corrupt, and absolute power corrupts absolutely."

Compare these advances with those articulated by the United States Supreme Court under Chief Justice Earl Warren. Beginning in 1961, prisoners' rights became a *cause célèbre*, attracting activists of every stripe and resulting in several landmark opinions (*Miranda*[8] and its progeny) that police and prosecutors continue to criticize. No longer could we be beaten until we confessed to whatever crime the police were having difficulty solving, and we could request and receive legal counsel as soon as custodial restraint was instituted. Moreover, conditions in many prisons were so deplorable and the lack of due process so egregious that the federal courts had no choice but to intervene to eliminate gross Eighth Amendment violations. Like the African-American community before it, the convict community began to achieve titular recognition as a group of human beings worthy of fundamental rights. Indeed, the court eventually decreed in *Furman v Georgia* (1972) that the State could no longer kill us arbitrarily and capriciously. We had come a long way, baby.

Now, however, we are suffering the effects of a uniform retrenchment at all levels. Gone is the acceptance that we are also human beings, unquestionably flawed but humans nonetheless. And like African-Americans before us, we have become a political football, only this time the politicians make no effort to hide the animosity in their public faces; without the franchise,[9] we do not count except as beasts of burden to bear the victors' spoils.

In every election, one issue leaps to the forefront and becomes the linchpin of the campaign. In the late sixties and early seventies, it was the war in Vietnam and civil unrest at home. In the mid-seventies, Nixon gave the Democrats all the ammunition they needed to regain the White House, but Jimmy Carter fell victim to an orchestrated economic attack by OPEC that raised gasoline prices and produced the infamous—and erroneous—malaise he is accused of describing in those affected chats.[10] In the eighties, along came Ronald Reagan and his confrontational tactics with the "evil empire."[11] But accompanying these obvious issues was a more subtle effort to shift public opinion regarding crime and punishment. In the last two decades of the twentieth century, when the country was at peace (except for intermittent excursions to validate the Monroe Doctrine,

8 *Miranda v Arizona* (1966). On the basis of this decision, U.S. police officers are required to advise detainees of their rights when they are taken into custody.

9 In the United States, prisoners are not entitled to vote. Indeed, for those with felony convictions this right is not reinstated upon their release from prison. As of 2002, the Supreme Court of Canada in *Sauvé v Canada* [2002] 3 SCR 519 held that prisoners have a right to vote under section 3 of the *Canadian Charter of Rights and Freedoms*.

10 This speech took place during the 1979 oil crisis.

11 Speaking during the cold war, Reagan was referring to the Soviet Union and Communism.

kidnap heads of state, or protect oil-rich proxies), when a strong economy and low unemployment guaranteed prosperity for most, and when no other external or internal threat loomed, crime and criminals became the hot button in successive campaigns for local, regional, and national races.

This trend continued following the events of September 11, 2001, which ushered in an era of profound American insecurity and increased efforts to isolate and marginalize social pariahs. Citizens no longer felt safe in either their homes or their jobs, and the resulting suspicion produced a mindset that effectively eliminated any ideal of equality. The proclaimed "War on Terror" held many Americans hostage to their fears and generated policies that permitted the government to detain indefinitely anyone declared dangerous (including American citizens). These draconian measures are periodically validated by individuals like the Time Square bomber and Umar Abdulmutallab, the Nigerian citizen who attempted to detonate an explosive device aboard an inbound jet over Detroit on December 25, 2009. Moreover, the virulent suspicion of anyone who does not conform to the preconceived paradigm of how a citizen should appear and act has produced the immigration wars that continue to divide the country. It also generated the abuses at the infamous Abu Ghraib prison in Iraq, committed primarily by National Guard troops who were employed as prison guards in the United States.

Yes, we are it; society's niggers are always good for a vote on one end of the political spectrum or the other. No one wants to be perceived as soft on crime, and with monsters like Ted Bundy, Jeffrey Dahmer, John Wayne Gacy, and others[12] constantly making headlines, support for more repressive laws and confinement is easy to find, especially when public servants convince the body politic that niggers neither deserve nor require a millisecond's consideration. If, as Emerson[13] observed, "a foolish consistency is the hobgoblin of little minds," then the attitude cultivated and maintained by society toward its prisoners clearly demonstrates the limited imaginations of a people responsible for increasing the prison population to over one million men and women, executing mental defectives and minors, and raising paramilitary police tactics to an art form.

This is not to say that, like the African-American community and their enslaved forebears, we are blameless. Most assuredly we are not, and I make no attempt either to argue with detainment for criminal behaviour for society's protection or to claim kinship with a people whose only offense was to be chained and transported by force to this country. Unlike expatriate Africans, we are active

12 In Canada, Russell Williams, Robert Pickton, Paul Bernardo, Karla Homolka, and Clifford Olson.

13 Ralph Waldo Emerson. "Essay on Self Reliance" (1841).

participants in our own confinement. But culpability is not the issue; society's insistence on creating a permanent underclass and the philosophical posture that denies our fundamental humanity are, and the members of that underclass—niggers—have no chance to rise above the station society has selected for us. Indeed, it is society's intent to keep us there, just as slaves were kept in their place by brute force and repressive legislation. Like the plantation owners in the antebellum South, the majority of Americans today do not discriminate, if you will pardon the irony. Slaves were seen as all of a piece; unworthy of inclusion on equal terms into the family of man. Today's convicts are likewise deprived of any preferential assessment: all of us are scum, all are irremediable, all are equally despicable.

One factor, however, escapes most analyses when treatment of, or attitudes toward convicts is discussed. Whereas for 350 years, slaves had no logical reason to expect manumission, our eventual freedom is guaranteed in over 90 percent of cases. Treating humans like niggers is always morally reprehensible, but from a utilitarian position, it hardly matters as long as that status remains invariant. If a society never intends to free those it holds in captivity, then treatment is irrelevant, and one's keepers can exercise their will without restraint.

The obvious concomitant to perpetual captivity is the ability of the captors to break their prisoners' spirit and convince them that they are in fact niggers deserving of their fate. This has historically proven difficult. Southern chain gangs and the new supermax prisons to the contrary, it is futile to attempt to break the human spirit by force alone. We are simply too resilient and in some cases, far too stubborn. Surprises, of course, do occur, as in Nat Turner's[14] short-lived rebellion, John Brown's[15] futile raid on the federal arsenal at Harper's Ferry, and the insurrection at Attica,[16] to cite but a few of the more notorious examples.

But—and the but is monumentally significant—if one's keepers have no choice but to release their charges after a specified time, then it does not take a giant leap of logic to understand that their attitudes should reflect that awareness. Perhaps society can impose nigger status on those it loathes, and in some instances, make

14 On August 22, 1831, Turner and seven other slaves killed their master and his family and, with about sixty slaves from neighbouring plantations, launched a two-day revolt. More than fifty whites were killed during the uprising, and an unknown number of blacks were lynched in reprisal by white mobs. Tried and convicted, Turner and fifteen companions were hanged.

15 On October 16, 1859, Brown seized the US arsenal and armory hoping to incite a slave insurrection. Captured and convicted, he was hanged two months later.

16 On September 9, 1971, prisoners at the Attica State Correctional facility in New York seized more than thirty guards as hostages. Four days later, more than one thousand heavily armed state troopers and corrections officers stormed the prison. Forty-three persons, including thirty-two prisoners and ten hostages, were killed in the action. Although first official reports stated that the dead hostages had had their throats slashed by the prisoners, autopsies subsequently revealed that they had died of bullet wounds from the intense rifle and shotgun fire by police and prison guards.

that label stick. What happens, however, when that nigger gains his freedom and during the course of internalizing his status, comes to understand that a perpetual state of war exists between him and the society that sees him as a nigger? What happens when he begins to act like the nigger society tells him he is?

A prisoner observed some years ago that ex-convicts have only three options upon release: we can reintegrate into society and become productive, contributing members; we can become public wards and strain a struggling system already on the brink of collapse; or we can resume the role of predators. The first option represents the most beneficial, both from society's and the ex-convicts' perspectives, and it makes the most sense. The second evolves from hopelessness and an anomic loss of self, derived from the indoctrination that convinces the susceptible mind that he is unworthy and therefore need not try to change his status. But the third is the creation of anger and a gut-wrenching, mind-bending need to pay somebody—anybody—back for the years of being treated like a, yes, like a nigger.

A journalist once examined the maximum-security unit at Pelican Bay (California) and interviewed some of the men inside, one of whom was frighteningly candid. He said that things had been done to him inside that no slave, no animal should have to endure, and that someone was going to pay for it. This individual was ending his sentence; no parole, no supervision of any kind, and he made the point that he could go wherever he wanted, do whatever he decided, and he was mad enough (and bad enough) to get the job done. This is the unavoidable result when society creates niggers by permanently subjugating a race or class of people, keeping its collective foot on the necks of those it tries to hold down and never letting them up either to breathe freely or even to catch a glimpse of blue sky instead of the dirt in front of their faces.

Niggers of any colour eventually get angry, and in my thirty-seven consecutive years in prison, I have seen scores of them. Most are long-term prisoners who will have two or sometimes three decades of prison behind them when they are released, and they are mad. They are mad like you would not believe. Their families are gone, they are largely unemployable, and the vast majority are psychologically unstable. I stress here that these people are going to be released because they have done their time—you cannot stop them. They will be living in your neighbourhoods and shopping in the stores where you, your wives, your sisters, and your children shop. Think about it: mad niggers everywhere you go but without the identifying skin colour that would have previously warned you when you thought all niggers were black. The scenario scares me; it should terrify the average citizen.

"But," you answer, "we have police to protect us from such predators." That is certainly true, but the very nature of crime and random violence precludes its prevention, and like it or not, it does not take a lot of creativity to avoid the police long enough to commit a crime. The role of the police is after all, apprehension. They catch us *after* we have committed whatever offense we have chosen to perpetrate, which means that no one is safe from someone harbouring a grudge that has festered for twenty or thirty years. I repeat: no one is safe. Examine the conventional wisdom: niggers are crazy. We do not care who we hurt in the process of getting what we want. If that is the case, then why persist in legitimizing a system that creates niggers in an assembly-line process, turning them out year after year like so many new models of automobiles with built-in engineering defects: accelerators jammed at full throttle with no steering?

Some primitive societies believe that knowing a person's name confers an advantage on the one knowing, and thus names are kept a secret. So it is with convicts. I know my name, even if society sees me as a nigger and even refers to me as such. If society agrees about the definition of a nigger, that distinction is society's alone. Most men and women do not see themselves in that role, no matter how often they hear the term applied to them. They retain their distinct, personal identities, even if they have to submerge them to survive, and society should be thankful that they preserve that degree of autonomy instead of acting according to the model urged on them.

Call me Ishmael[17] or what you will, I refuse to be anyone's nigger, because, whether society realizes it or not, its niggers are dangerous people when pushed, and I have more important things to do than ponder revenge. That is, unfortunately, not a universal sentiment behind the walls and fences communities have erected to contain their prisoners. Those men and women whom society has discarded—its niggers—will, like Frankenstein's monster, one day turn on their creator, not behind the walls where society will be able to ignore the consequences, but out there in the street. For those of you who have forgotten, Mary Shelley's novel (1818) was subtitled "A Modern Prometheus," but unlike the legend, the fire this time will consume rather than console.

17 Ishmael refers the wandering sailor immortalized in the classic 1851 novel *Moby Dick* by Herman Melville.

Chapter Nine

The Mark of Criminality

Rejections and Reversals, Disclosure and Distance: Stigma and the Ex-Prisoner

Melissa Munn

Prologue

There has never been a time when my life was not touched by the criminalization of a family member or friend. When I was a young girl I sat with my mother as she wrote a letter to her imprisoned younger brother. She typed her notes onto pink cue cards and taped them together accordion style—she wanted to make him laugh and, perhaps more importantly, remind him that he was not forgotten. When I was a pre-teen, Dad and I stopped at Canadian Tire to get some car parts before picking up his best friend at the Don Jail when he was released; on the way to the institution we picked up an extra submarine sandwich for him, thinking he would likely be hungry when he got out. Years later, I would accompany my own friends to court with the same matter-of-factness that I'd seen in my parents. People made decisions—some were good and some were not. It had not occurred to me that there was any particular stigma around contact with the criminal justice system—not until I arrived to study criminology at university. There, in the classroom, I was taught that my family, my friends, and I were deviant, or worse, pathological. We were either to be feared and ignored or treated, managed, and corrected. Ironically, my participation in post-secondary study meant that some of my family members thought that I was now to be avoided and they became nervous around me. I began to understand and experience stigma and its management. My work with prisoners and the paroled made me more acutely aware of the generalized stigma directed at criminalized individuals but, given my own life experience, I had difficulty reconciling the broad essentializations with the specifics of the individuals. This book chapter is part of my attempt to make sense of the ways that discriminatory discourses, intersecting with individual decisions, get played out interactionally.

> *The fact is now I'm a lifer and I'm different and I'm going to be treated different. And when people find out about it, they're going to treat me that way.* (Joel)

> *Prisoners are not welcomed back in the community per se. You are stigmatized. You know, I mean it's real. People don't like ex-convicts. It's not in your head. You're not wanted. You're not liked. You are something to talk about or be watched. So, how do you deal in the community when the community doesn't want you?* (Mr. Flowers)

Few identities[1] receive more mainstream media attention than that of the "criminal." Prime-time television is filled with police dramas, crime scene investigations, crime stories on the news, true-crime biographies, and series which profile a particular criminal and construct him as dangerous (Altheide 2002; Altheide and Devriese 2007; Cavender 2004). Canada even has its own reality TV game show (Redemption Inc.) which features "ten ex-cons [identified primarily by the crimes they have been convicted of] and one rich man" (who, as the title suggests, has the financial power to redeem them from their criminal ways). While the image of the convicted individual is "presented in a stylized and stereotypical fashion by the mass media" (Cohen 1972, 9), his own sense of self can often be quite different than this social identity. It is therefore not surprising that fear of stigmatization is one of the issues individuals anticipate upon returning to the community following a period of incarceration.

In this chapter we will explore ex-prisoners' acute awareness of the essentialization of their character and reflect upon their engagement with the contradictions (and confirmations) between this ascription and their self-conception. We then move on to consider how both symbolic and structural stigma (Hannem, this volume) affect the ex-prisoner in multiple ways. Finally, we conclude

1 Identity is used in this chapter to denote "one's sense of self, and one's feelings and ideas about oneself" (Scott and Marshall 2005).

with an examination of the range of stigma management strategies employed by these individuals.

Method and Sample

This chapter is based on research that employed a qualitative approach to examine the issue of stigma for ex-prisoners.[2] Men were contacted through personal networks and with the assistance of workers at the Lifeline In-Reach Program[3]. Ultimately, twenty men who had previously been incarcerated for long periods (defined as ten years or more)[4] and who had been out of prison for more than five years were interviewed for between 1.5 and 3 hours.[5] Length of time served is a critical variable in the design of this research since an individual sentenced to at least a decade in prison is assured to have a major disruption in their lives and this increases the likelihood that their stigmatized status will be known. The majority (sixteen) of the men in this sample were serving life sentences,[6] and the amount of time spent imprisoned ranged between ten years and over thirty, with the median being eighteen years. The minimum time since release was five years, but two of the men had been out for over twenty years at the time of their interview. Given the amount of time the men who participated in this research had spent in prison, it is not surprising that they were predominantly middle-aged:

---

2 This research is part of a larger Social Science and Humanities Research Council (SSHRC) funded project titled "Release and Reintegration After Prison: Negotiating Gender, Culture, and Identity" headed by Sylvie Frigon and Chris Bruckert of the University of Ottawa. The research explores the reintegration experiences of male and female prisoners and the experience of support people and partners of released prisoners.

3 On April 16, 2012, Correctional Service of Canada announced that the award-winning Lifeline program will no longer be funded. Lifeline employed released "lifers" to assist incarcerated men serving life sentences to adjust to prison life and assist in release planning,

4 The periods adopted for this project are those utilized by the state to define long-term incarceration and successful reintegration (Canada 2000, 1998, 1994, 1992). Ten years is also employed by the men themselves. For example, in many penitentiaries in Canada, prisoners have established 10+ groups to support those men and women serving ten or more years of incarceration.

5 While this study has attempted to put the neglected voices of the successful ex-prisoners on the record and thus expand the discussion of stigma, it is at the same time limited. Specifically, this study excluded those individuals who returned to prison for new criminal charges. Those men may have experienced and managed stigma in different ways. While several of the men in this study felt able to mitigate the stigmatic effects, those who returned to prison may not have been similarly able. Also, by chance, rather than design, none of the men in this study was labelled as dangerous or sex offenders, and this too may have mitigated their experience. Future research may want to explore the experience of stigma for those who return to prison and for those with other, concurrent, stigmatic designations.

6 In Canada, a life sentence means that an individual is given a minimum period of incarceration but no maximum.

twelve of the men were between 40 and 55, seven of the men were over 56, and only one was under 40 years of age.

During their interviews, the respondents were asked to contemplate stigma and its effects on their preparation for release, the period immediately after discharge, and in the years that followed. With only one exception, every man spoke of some experience during which they were aware of their "outsider" status.

"Spoiled" Identities

The individuals who participated in this research were acutely aware that following the act that led to their long period of incarceration, judgement was passed on both their actions and their character. Each man's public image is now "constituted from a small selection of facts which may be true of him, … inflated into a dramatic and newsworthy appearance and then used as a full picture of him" (Goffman 1963a, 71). Through "status degradation ceremonies" (Garfinkel 1956, 420) the individuals in this research were transformed from members of the general population to convicted persons; their public identities were spoiled (Goffman 1963a) and *new* attributes ascribed to them (Becker 1963). In the following quote, Luc spoke to his awareness of the stereotyping that occurs:

> *Some people see criminals as dirty individuals, dirty uneducated individuals. Very few people see [a] criminal as a normal human being with feelings that can be educated, can be polite, can be clean. We don't see them that way.*

As Hannem noted (Chapter Two, this volume), the effect of this process is to push this entire group of criminalized individuals to the margins of society and to frame them as morally bereft. Some men internalized these negative judgements and, as a result, became very cognizant of the stereotypes associated with their group. Indeed, the respondents often adopted the terms used to essentialize them and the following language emerged in their self-descriptions: "scumbag," "screwed-up kid," "manipulator," "petty criminal," "loner," "violent," and "rebel." By using these terms, the men assumed, or at least reiterated, a subject position consistent with dominant public and academic discourses concerning criminalized persons.

This internalization of blemished character is, however, not absolute as many attempt to incorporate other socially positive elements into their conception of self. For example, Ziggy struggled to reconcile having committed a homicide with his private identity as someone who "*never wanted to hurt anybody.*" These men battle the guilt they feel because of their crime and oscillate between feeling worthless and feeling "decent." As Joel said, "*I still feel guilt and also a certain sense of unworthiness and sometimes I resent society because no matter what I do, the world will not accept [me].*" In short, since the men previously considered themselves to be, and were considered by others to be, just "average" individuals, they often held the same beliefs about the deficiencies of the stigmatized other (Goffman 1963a)—a role that they now assume. They must wrestle with the ideas that they held (and could readily employ) to distance themselves from the criminal and their own conception of self. This struggle is intensified because, unlike other designations, their criminalization places a new master status upon them.

Master Status and Courtesy Stigma

Uggen et al. (2004) argued that once an individual is criminalized the label of *(ex)* "convict" becomes his or her primary and dominant identity marker, especially in interactions with acquaintances made after prison.[7] In both formal and informal day-to-day interactions, an individual may adopt "convict" as his or her master status (Lemert 1967). As Schur (1971) clarified,

> One major consequence of the processes through which deviant identity is imputed is the tendency of the deviator to become "caught up in" a deviant role, to find that it has become highly salient in his overall personal identity (or concept of self), that his behaviour is increasingly organized "around" the role, and the cultural expectations attached to the role have come to take precedence, or increased salience relative to other expectations, in the organization of his activities and general way of life. (69)

Maruna et al. (2004) have noted that the acts that bring about this master status among criminalized individuals may be attended to disproportionally. This is blatantly evident in the aforementioned television program, *Redemption Inc.*, when on multiple occasions each participant is shown standing behind prison bars with a subtitle that identifies their time served and the crime committed. Thus, according to the "negativity bias" principle (Baumeister, Bratlavsky, Finkenauer and Vohs 2001), a multitude of non-deviant acts may precede and follow one deviant act, but it is the single deviant event that indefinitely stigmatizes the

7 In this segregating and branding process, stigma is reaffirmed by the state and by others through disenfranchisement, denial of jobs, the loss of parental rights, etc. (Irwin 1970; Petersilia 2001; Travis 2002; Uggen et al. 2004). Some authors have argued that official state stigmatization should be used more extensively so that it will serve as both a general and a specific deterrent. For example, see the work of Funk (2004).

individual. Doc provided an illustration of his awareness of his master status: "*When I am out here, I'm a parolee—all the time. I'm not a citizen out here.*"

It was apparent from the interviews that the men's intimates were also affected by their master status and a sense of responsibility for this "courtesy stigma" (Goffman 1963a, 30) weighed upon some of the respondents. Dave provided a powerful example:

> *I brought a lot of shame to the family. When I was charged with murder and my brothers and sister were just kids then. They were told "Your brother is a murderer," "I'm not hanging around with you," or "My parents won't let me hang around with you"... they'd come home crying. What did my mother have to face when she went downtown? What did my father have to face?*

Although some of the men partially internalized the stereotyped notion of "criminal" and accepted responsibility for the impact of courtesy stigma on their intimates, they did not have to accept their stigmatization at all times and in all places. We turn now to consider the men's post-carceral experiences with stigma, which are fragmented and complex.

Release and Post-Release Experiences with Stigma

Clear and Dammer (2000) argued that the multiple implications of being convicted, "doing" time, and being released result in pains of re-entry for the criminalized individual since "the former inmate always faces the cold fact that no truly 'clean start' is possible. The change in status is from convict to former convict; the new status is nearly as stigmatizing as the old" (213). This idea is certainly supported by some of the interviewees, particularly with regard to structural stigma. That said, examples of non-stigmatizing experiences were more frequently noted in the narratives. The respondents often indicated that on many occasions their expectations of stigmatization did not materialize in reality.

Expectations and "Amazing Reversals"

Many of the men in this study stated that in the years since their release they had not felt personally stigmatized in the community based on their status as former prisoners.[8] Arguably this experience is partly related to their ability to hide the stigmatic attribute and therefore adopt a position that allowed them to be discreditable, rather than discredited. Marcus noted, "*The community was blind to me. There*

8 See also Irwin (1970) for a similar finding.

was no public knowledge of who I was... I walked through a whole crowd of people. You know, just a regular old white kid with short hair. Nobody even paid a second glance to me." Bobby echoed this sentiment and confirmed Goffman's (1963a) notion of hyper-awareness when he stated, "*No. No. No. I've never had a negative stigma coming from anywhere. Anytime, it's mostly been my anxiety, my anticipation.*"

Indeed, for several respondents, the anticipation and expectation of stigma surpassed any evidence of a negative reception in the community. Several of the men indicated that their anxiety made them fear they were physically marked. As Marcus explained:

> *I had no idea what to expect. For all I knew, I was going to have this big sign on my head, "Prisoner," "Convict." So I had a lot of stress about that and then I was also worried because I didn't know what I was going to do for employment.*

Marcus's concern about stigma jeopardizing his job chances may have some basis in fact since researchers have indicated that employability is an area in which the negative implications of stigma manifest (Clear and Dammer 2000; Funk 2004; Harding 2003; Irwin 1970; Petersilia 2001; Travis and Petersilia 2001). However it is also possible that his own "stigma consciousness" (Pinel 2004) made him anticipate stigma when none in fact emerged. Many men in this study were offered work despite their expectations that they would be unable to secure employment because of their criminal record and, in particular, for the types of crimes they had committed:

> *I went for an interview. They called me the next day at the halfway house. They said they liked me and ... "We want to do two things. We'll put you on the payroll and then we're going to do a criminal records check." [I said] "I got a criminal record." ... "We've hired people before with criminal records. Come on in, we'll talk about it." ... I go on in there ... I said "I'm presently on parole, Life parole, for murder." He said "What?" I said "You asked me. I'm telling you. You said you've hired people with criminal records before." [He said] "Yeah, but those were car thefts and purse-snatchers and stuff like that. Not murder" ... I assured him I would be an asset to the association. So, I left ... feeling dejected. ... Two days after that, they called me and they wanted me to come in for another interview. I went down there and the first thing they said to me was "Who here that works here knows that you had a criminal record?" I knew I had the job as soon as he said that.* (Jean)

Jean's story is consistent with a major finding from Pager's study, which concluded that "personal contact did go a long way in reducing the negative effects of a criminal record" (2007, 104).[9] In order to receive this type of treatment, the men had to be able to draw upon their ability to present "well" and leverage this skill as a type of capital. For example, Puzzle utilized his confidence and awareness of the stigma when he approached the boss of a company directly:

> *I told him this is who I am. This is where I've come from. I'm asking you ... I want a decent paying job.... I'm not here to cause you any grief.... "All I'm here to do," I said, "is try and get back in the community. I'll be a damn good worker."*

This research suggests that members of the public do not simply accept the dominant discourses regarding those who are criminalized. Rather, we see that when presented with an individual and an opportunity to make their own assessment, the "normal" will draw upon his/her own values and beliefs in order to make a decision on how to proceed—in short, they often reject existing stereotypes in favour of micro-level assessment. Indeed, it would appear that some individuals go beyond just rejecting the stereotype and engage in challenging the dominant discourses. For example, one interviewee told of having his employers defend him against a parole officer who didn't think the ex-prisoner was doing suitable work. According to Mr. Flowers, his employer contacted the parole board and told them, "*There is absolutely no way that we will let a parole board member, [or] the parole board, in any way censor our employees. Mr. Flowers works for us; he happens to be on parole. He is not a parolee that happens to be working for us.*"

Several of the men experienced such acceptance on the part of certain members of the community and felt "welcomed back"—one of them referred to this as "*amazing reverses of stigmatization*" (Gord). Bob provides an excellent example:

> *I went over to the bank and I said "I want to get a credit card." ... [this] lady sat me down and I was very nervous because I didn't want to reveal my past. She asked me my particular information and she checked my credit rating and ... she said "You don't have a credit rating." So I had to tell her where I was. And her comment to me was "Well banking is our business, that's your business." And I really appreciated it. I never forgot that comment. ... No stigmatization or anything like that. And I'll always remember that, how kind she was to me. And she got me a credit card.*

---

9 Pager's (2007) study also recognizes that the likelihood of being allowed to make a "personal presentation" is much greater for Caucasian applicants than for those who are black. Unfortunately, due to the racial homogeneity of the sample in this research, it is not possible to include race as a point of variance in this regard. It may be reasonable to assume that the men in this study did not provide an exception to the "white privilege" that dominates in Western society. Despite being asked about race, most of the men did not speak to this and so it would be irresponsible to speculate further.

This story also highlights another common dynamic—the interpretation of everyday or mundane acts as measures of great kindness. Arguably these actions, taken for granted by those who are not discredited, become seen as extensions of generosity and as extraordinary to marked and therefore "situation conscious" individuals (Goffman 1963a, 111). Specifically, the discreditable individual in the interaction may be hyper-aware of reactions and interactions. These acts may also be interpreted as exceptional because some of the men have internalized their unworthiness and thus are surprised when they encounter others who do not hold, or act upon, this discredited status.

Affirming Power: Stigma from the State

In a particularly clear illustration of structural stigma, individuals sentenced to serve long periods of incarceration are considered by the state to be "risky"—individuals from whom society needs the greatest protection. The incapacitation of the men may be the result of their criminal actions, but beyond this, further interaction is based not on the individual but on the actuarial norm of the supposed dangerous class to which they now belong. The state scrutinizes, treats, and manages the convicted men based on their risk assessment scales, as a result the men spoke of being treated as dossiers rather than as individuals.

Notably, when the men in this study did speak of stigma, the "normal" was often part of the criminal justice system. While the men may not always be "marked" or "detected" by the community, agents of the state were definitely aware of the men's past misdeeds and the imposition of structurally influenced stigma was evident. The respondents shared many different examples of the way state agents ensure that convicted individuals are aware of the "riskiness" ascribed to members of their out-group. Puzzle expressed his thoughts on this:

> *Lifers are looked at the worst. They're looked at worse than sexual offenders. Because the cop looks at a lifer as someone whose crossed the line and can never walk back. They don't think you can ever be rehabilitated.*

As Puzzle noted, this stigma from the state was especially directed to those who were serving life sentences and, as a result of the different regulatory requirements placed upon this group, agents of the state are positioned to enact the stigma with near impunity. Exemplifying the interplay between structural and interpersonal stigma were the stories of the men having to report to local police stations when visiting friends or family in other communities and receiving treatment based on the stigma of having been sentenced to life:

> *The only place that I felt stigmatized was when I went over to the Police Station ... 'cause they would play some games every once in a while. You'd go in [and] you're supposed to check in at the desk and they were very polite, courteous, until they found out you were a parolee. And then they'd say, "Go upstairs" and you'd go upstairs, and the guy would say "You don't come up here. You check in downstairs." So, it's just these little games they would play for themselves.* (Bob)

Not surprisingly, given that most of the men in this study were serving life sentences, their vulnerability to the state is evidenced by being the subjects of additional surveillance. Their stigmatized status ("lifer") qualifies them for perpetual surveillance and their privacy may be invaded at the will of state representatives, reaffirming the regulatory structures of sovereignty, discipline, and government under which each of these men live (Foucault, 1980/1991).[10] Moreover, this monitoring, often justified as risk management, becomes bound up with sending the message of undesirability and the "unfitness of these subjects to be 'in society'" (O'Malley 2001, 94). Jean offered an example of trying to engage in a commonplace activity (during his graduated release program) with his family, but having their experience jeopardized because of extensive police surveillance:

> *My first UTA [unescorted temporary absence] was a Christmas pass to London and I ... had to sign in a police station when I got there, and I had to sign in when I left. I walked in and they were nice and pleasant to me and my mother, and I handed them my parole papers and everything changed. It went from pleasant to friggin' nasty in seconds. They didn't want me in London.... He [the police officer] made me sit on a chair for about 45 minutes and they were calling all these cops in off the street and cops and detectives coming down from different floors and pointing at me .... [Later that day] around one o'clock in the morning, I hear pounding on the door of my mother's house so the door opens, [to] a cop [I said] "What do you want?" [He says] "Well, I was just checking to see if you were home, you know. You're not drinking" and he had his flashlight in my eyes. There was no privacy.... They were following me all over the place. They parked out in front of the house.*

Some of the ex-prisoners recounted their experiences of the "negativity bias" in which it is assumed that they will fail.[11] Gord noted that "*if 20 years down the line,*

10 Foucault (1980/1991) pointed out that "we need to see things not in terms of the replacement of sovereignty by a disciplinary society and subsequent replacement of a disciplinary society by a society of government; in reality one has a triangle, sovereignty-discipline-government which has as its primary target the population and as its essential mechanism the apparatus of security" (94).

11 More specifically, Baumeister et al. (2001) state that "when equal measures of good and bad are present, however, the psychological effect of bad ones outweigh those of the good ones" (323).

I happen to screw up, 'well, we've done told you he would.' You know, that's the way they are." In our study this assertion applied predominantly to state agents since, as we discussed earlier, often employers and the public were willing to rely on their own judgement, reject the risk discourse, and allow the individual to earn new credibility.

Corporeally Located Stigma: The Convict Body and the Aging Body

To this point, the discussion has focussed on the essentialization of the criminal identity and the individual's partial rejection of the stereotype. However, the men did express that two corporeally located stigmata did affect them in terms of experiencing discrimination in the community: being physically marked and being aged.

In spite of the increased popularity and more mainstream adoption of tattoos over the last decade, a number of the interviewees highlighted the significance of their tattoos as a means to mark them as convicts; the images are understood as stigmata, which brand them as outsiders (Stiles and Kaplan 1996). The respondents told of their prison-generated body art being a visible schema through which others read their (criminal) attributes and histories:

> *I got tattoos and a lot of people know that they are jail tattoos from just the way they look.*[12] *And I went to one [yard sale] and I could see the guy's checking me out. He comes over ... and he goes, "You've done time before, eh?" And I'm like ... "What do you mean?" ... [He says] "I can tell by your tattoos."* (Fred)

The corporeal dimension of marked/tattooed "convict bodies" (Demello 1993, 12) creates a greater imperative to self-regulate and focus on presentation more intensely. For example, Gowan recounted that he was hesitant to show his tattoos on the job site because of the potential for negative consequences:

> *I'm a good worker, and I don't need to be fired over tattoos, especially when the whole world's almost full of them now. And he [the boss] says "I'm not going to fire you." And I had my shirt off. The next day he told me not to come in.*

Still, the tattooing of the body is the result of the individual exercising some agency over his body in an otherwise highly controlled space of the prison and

12 The ability to make this distinction varies by the knowledge of the viewer. In some cases, the tattoos have obvious prison-related themes (e.g., cell bars) but, in other instances, it is the particular method used to create them which makes them distinguishable. In the latter, the viewer must either be knowledgeable about prisons or about the art form. For more of a discussion on this, see Demello (1993) or McDonough (2001).

this differentiates the tattoo from another form of discrimination that the men faced upon release—ageism.

Ageism has been defined as "a process of systematic stereotyping and discrimination against people because they are old"[13] (Butler 1995, 35). According to Palmore (1999), the stigma attached to the individual emerges from the elderly (as a group) being viewed as ill, impotent, ugly, mentally unfit or mentally ill, isolated, poor, or depressed. The ex-prisoner is not the only target of ageism, but for the men in this study who had spent a great deal of their lives behind bars, the ageism they encountered was complicated and compounded. These individuals return to the community, not as the boys or young men they were when they entered the federal correctional system, but as middle-aged or, in some cases, as senior citizens. They no longer profit from the value placed on youthfulness, nor do they have the experience to benefit from seniority in the workplace. While other individuals of their age were establishing work histories and social networks, these men were passing time in prison. Some viewed their inability to obtain employment as being the result of ageism rather than criminalization:

> *If there was any ... stigma, [it] was a lot more age related than anything else. There wasn't prisoner-related. There was age related. "What's this guy offering me? I need somebody's going to put doors on my wall.... Has he ever done that? No. Can I train him? He's kind of old, eh. He's small, and he's old. So—no, I don't want him."* (Luc)

With regard to age and the presence of jailhouse tattoos, we see that these signs of social information are "reflexive and embodied. That is [they are] conveyed by the very person it is about, and conveyed through bodily expression" (Goffman 1963a, 43). The individual can be discredited and discreditable since the mark's presence on the body can be alternately visible and concealed and as a result, the men adopted a variety of strategies (such as maintaining their physique and wearing long sleeves) to manage the possibility of being "outed."

Stigma Management

Goffman (1963a), Jussim et al. (2000), and Hebl et al. (2000) have noted that managing stigma requires the targeted individual to be vigilant in social interactions in order to prevent or minimize negative consequences. Given the very real consequences of stigma (return to prison, loss of work, impact

13 Palmore (1999) argued that the definition of ageism should be inclusive of all regardless of age group; thus, youth could be victims of ageism. However, in the interest of specificity, Butler's (1995) definition seems more appropriate.

on family, etc.) the men employed a variety of management techniques including: rejecting stigma, emphasizing alternate identities, utilizing the stereotype to advantage, concealing, disclosing, and creating social or physical distance.

Rejecting the Stigma

A number of the men in this study were adamant about their refusal to accept the stigmatized label that was attached to them. Barry provided an example of this defiance:

> *I feel that there are people who attempt to stigmatize me. Some who work in corrections who know who I am and know my track record—but I don't feel stigmatized because I don't allow it to occur.*

Goffman (1963a) noted that while rejecting the stigma may be a useful coping strategy, it can also create a disjuncture in the individual since, while they speak of declining the stigma, at some level they sometimes understand it to be earned. For example, Jean, when asked about experiencing stigma, referred to his crime first—thus, reifying the master status:

> *If they only knew ... I'm a murderer and all this stuff. (Did you worry about stigma in those first couple of years? Did you worry about people finding out?) I don't really care ... people got a problem with me, then that's their problem. I don't have a problem with me.... If somebody else is going to have a problem with me because of my criminal past, that's their problem—not mine.*

The bravado Jean voiced in the quote above may be the result of having spent many years in confinement with similarly stigmatized others, and this allows him to reject the stereotyped notion of the "type of person" who serves long periods in prison. Another strategy of rejecting the stereotype is to make a distinction between being a *criminal* and being a *lifer*. In their interviews, the men spoke of not necessarily having "criminal values" and felt that this set them apart from others who are criminalized:

> *I think most lifers are not of the criminal element.... They did something wrong which was a criminal act but they're not criminals. They didn't intentionally go out and hurt a bunch of people or break into a dozen homes to pay for their drug habits or anything like that. You know, they were "straight Johns" who were out in the community and something happened.* (Ziggy)

This attempt to distinguish themselves from other (ex-)prisoners may speak to a preservation of identity by discredited individuals and it distances them from the stereotype. However, as we see in the above quote, this tactic occurs at the expense of others who are also discriminated against.

Emphasizing Alternate Identities

Some men make conscious attempts to mitigate their master status by getting others to see them as fathers, husbands, workers, etc. This effort was sometimes a source of tension given that new and old associates wanted him to fulfill the expectations associated with his previous public identity.[14] Fred, speaking of returning to his childhood community and to those who knew him before and after his sentence, noted that people wanted him to be the "party guy" and resented him when he didn't conform to this:

> *When I first got there, I had people ... coming to my door ... like clockwork. Non-stop people at my door. "Come on, Let's go. Come on. Let's go" and I'm telling them "Hey, that's not my lifestyle anymore. I've got a family now and I'm a family person. ... I'm not that partying kid that was running around here 15, 20 years ago" ... they thought "Oh, well ... you think you're too good for us" and ... that was everywhere.*

Like Fred, the other interviewees offered various public identities that they felt equally, or more aptly, represent who they are. These presentations move them away from a position of exclusion to one in which they see themselves as deserving of social inclusion (see also Deane, Bracken, and Morrissette 2007).

While some research has examined the role of alternate identities in desistance from crime, most of this work positions these self-concepts as changed or new (see Giordano, Cernkovich, and Rudolph 2002; Laub and Sampson 2001; LeBel, Burnett, Maruna, and Bushway 2008). For example, Laub and Sampson wrote, "It seems that men who desisted changed their identity as well, and this in turn affected their outlook and sense of maturity and responsibility" (2001, 50). Accepting these alternate identities as *new* leaves the previous essentialized identities unchallenged and consequently confirms or reinforces them. Possibly the alternate subject positions *are* recently manifested (as in Fred's example above); however, it is also probable that the individual had not previously seen himself to be "other" in need of reformation. Despite the attempt

14 This desire to have the individual conform to the "deviant identity" can become a plight through which the individual returns to behaviour that is considered deviant by the mainstream, leading to what Jussim et al. (2000) called a self-fulfilling prophecy.

to strip the individual of previous identities and create a "role dispossession" (Goffman 1961, 14), we know that this divestment is not always complete and that a sense of the pre-mortification[15] self remains. Demonstrating the ability to maintain or create identities, the men provided examples of old and new personas and the most common of these were: "normal guy"/ "average Joe," worker, and good citizen.

"Normal Guy"/"Average Joe"

The quest for normalcy was a pre-occupation of the men and, despite their convictions, they often considered themselves to be average.[16] That the terms "average" and "normal" appear frequently in the transcripts draws our attention to the idea that the disciplinary rationality of governance manifests in the respondent's experiences. The men seek to evaluate themselves relationally to the general population and self-regulate in order to appear statistically "normal." After serving many years in prison, it is logical that the men would not necessarily strive to be exceptional but rather to be indistinguishable in the social body. For example, Marcus said: *"I'm just a regular member of society. I work. I pay my taxes. I make sure my family is safe at the end of the day. I look out for my neighbours and I don't infringe upon anybody's rights."* Doc also speaks to this: *"I'm not going to be the guy that breaks the mould.... I'm no more different or unique than anybody else."* One of the ways the men were able to convince others of their normalcy was by getting and keeping a job and this established, or reaffirmed, their identities as workers.

Worker

In most of the interviews, the men identified themselves as workers, and this identity was especially evident for those who were from working-class backgrounds. By positioning themselves as able to labour, the men normalized their position within a capitalist society and within conventional gender relations (see Callard 1998; McDowell and Court 1994). For members of the working class, this position is reinforced through social structures and, as Willis (1981) asserted:

> The point at which people live, not borrow, their class destiny is when what is given is re-formed, strengthened and applied to new purposes. Labour power is an important

15 According to Goffman (1961), a mortification of the self occurs when someone is subjected to life in a total institution. The mortification of the self involves the stripping away of previous identities by removing contact with previous life, stripping them of possessions, and requiring the "inmate" to show deference to authority, among other techniques.

16 This was especially evident in the two men who felt that they had been wrongfully convicted.

> pivot of all of this because it is the main mode of active connection with the world: the way *par excellence* of articulating the innermost self with the external reality. It is in fact the dialectic of the self to the self through the concrete world. (2)

Many of the men had laboured before and during their imprisonment and continued to see themselves as "*Joe Worker*" (Tom). As such, some felt that the focus on employment skills in prison programming was the result of the stigmatic assumption that they are unskilled. Doc said, "*[They were] almost assuming that a guy had never worked. Well I worked. I was 25 years old [when I went to prison]. That's young but I started working at age 16. So I already had some good experience.*" Drawing attention to one's identity as a worker can also be understood as affirming manliness since "the workplace is an area which men have established as being a significant site for the social construction of masculinity, including masculine identity" (Drummond 2007, 10).

As is evident in the following excerpt from Bob's interview, there is a corollary for some of those who were not currently working in the paid-labour force and felt this as a loss to their sense of self: "*I was really struggling with feelings of worthlessness—that I don't have an identity. I don't work.*" Puzzle also speaks to this belief: "*A large part of what I hold as my value, my own self-worth, is in working and doing a good job.*"[17] Assuming and reproducing a very traditional and conservative discourse, many indicated that their ability to work made them feel like a contributing member of society and, by extension, good citizens.

Good Citizen

In contrast to their desire to be seen as "normal," eight of the men also spoke of going beyond the requirements placed on them by society. For most, this need to exceed normative requirements took the form of doing volunteer work in their community, including sharing their stories in classrooms, coordinating sporting events, and putting in unpaid time at their work. Jean shared his story:

> *You see me at charitable events and working with handicapped people. I take them out and do stuff... with them.... I get respect not only from them but from their families, co-workers, and people in the community who see me working at these various events... I'm like a rock star here.*

In some cases their volunteerism, especially speech giving, can be linked to "redemption scripts" wherein the person can rewrite "a shameful past into a necessary prelude to a productive worthy life" (Maruna 2001, 87). In this process,

17 In this sample, there was only one man who did not speak to his identity as worker. Instead, F. G. recounts a lifetime of not working and of not using employment, or ability to labour, as an identifier.

the individual maintains some cohesion in their self-identity rather than amputating a particular element. They can be conceived of as "heroes of adjustment" (Goffman 1961a, 25) and this has the effect of reaffirming the rehabilitation discourse. However, not all the men embraced the idea of reformation and, instead, we see some using stigma to their advantage.

Utilizing Stigma to Advantage

Adopting a "hostile bravado" (Goffman 1963a, 17) allowed at least one of the men to utilize his stigmatized identity to advantage. Bobby is aware of the fear and sense of danger the term "lifer" conveys and has employed this identity in his interactions with co-workers:

> *I've used it as an asset. If guys give me a hard time, [I] say "look, don't screw me around. I've been in jail for a very long time and I'm not about to start playing games with you ... I'm a fucking lifer. Don't fuck with me."*

Fred also realized during his incarceration that he was subject to a dual stigmatization since he was both a lifer and an Aboriginal man. However, he understood that the structural stigma that accompanied the latter identity was being eroded by changes in the sociopolitical discourse. For example, the paternalistic *Indian Act* (1951), which created classes of Aboriginal people, allowed for their confinement on reserves and justified atrocities such as involuntary placement of children in residential schools (under the guise of education and not assimilation), is increasingly being recognized as a discriminatory piece of legislation. More specifically, Correctional Service of Canada (2007) has recognized the over-representation of Aboriginal people in federal prisons,[18] and the Parole Board of Canada has implemented elder-assisted hearings to acknowledge "the distinctive needs and characteristics presented by Aboriginal peoples" (Canada 2007). Fred speaks of utilizing this sensitivity to his advantage and recounts that he participated in Native Brotherhood activities and emphasized his heritage during his parole board hearing: "*When I went up for parole, it's like 'Oh, you're a Native offender and you're unique and ... so we'll give you the benefit of the doubt.*" This strategy, of course, can only be utilized in particular settings and with specific interactions and audiences. As a result, it was rarely employed by the interviewees and instead, the men most often attempt to ensure that their criminal pasts are not revealed.

---

18 According to this report, "Aboriginal peoples represent 2.8% of the Canadian population, but account for 18% of the federally incarcerated population" (Correctional Service of Canada 2007).

Concealing the Stigma

Concealment of a criminal past was the most often employed management strategy. Approaches ranged from merely allowing people to make assumptions of "normalcy," to actively strategizing to mask things that would identify the individual's criminal conviction. Interestingly, even those men who stated that they rejected the stigmatization of being a criminal expressed a need to hide their prison past in some social situations; they were perpetually aware of the stigma and while not always accepting of its basis, nonetheless, engaged with the consequences. For example, Jean and Barry, who both indicated that they were not bothered if individuals knew about their histories, spoke of their "passing" behaviour. Jean said, "*I never told anybody that I had a criminal record, what I was in for, or anything like that. I just acted like I was a normal guy out having a beer with some friends. I knew I had to.*" Negotiating identity can be complex and these men must have sufficient self-esteem to reject the firmly entrenched label that constitutes their social image while accepting that the latter impinges upon their sense of self.

The men also spoke of the need to conceal those matters that mark them as convicted people. Many of those who were tattooed described keeping the body art covered when around others—especially co-workers and employers. Other men feared that showing their convict body would lead to courtesy stigma for their intimates, and used concealment as a way of managing this potential. Gowan, for example, stated that his daughter was very grateful that he kept a long sleeve shirt with him to change into if he was attending her school events. Some of those who were "unmarked" by tattoos claimed this absence as a dis-identifier and used it to maintain their non-disclosure strategy: "*I was working with the senior staff and doing a lot of office work and I mixed well with them and of course, I don't have tattoos and everything*" (Joel).

This sense of being "unmarked" carried over in other ways as well. Some of the men spoke of being able to "pass" because people in the community had an image of what criminals, and more specifically murderers, looked like and they used these stereotypes advantageously to conceal their own criminalized status. Bob provided an example: "*I don't appear to be an ex-offender. Whatever that is! But that's the comment that's been made many, many times to me.... 'Nobody would know you'd ever spent a day in jail.'*" Dave, talking about a situation where it became known that an ex-prisoner was living in his building, provided a story of how stereotypes aided him in not being detected:

> *We had a couple that lived there and they were all up in arms about the fact that there were lifers living there, criminals living there. I never said a word. I'd meet them in the*

> *elevator and I'd say "Hi," you know, and talk and chat and all and everything. (And so they never knew that you were a lifer?) No.*

The men's lack of response in these situations created a condition in which their complacency reaffirmed the judgements made of "others." Bruckert (2002) made a similar finding in her work on erotic dancers and she points out that "the judgements of these 'insiders' which replicate the dominant discourses and position their moral self-identity against that of the deviant 'other,' powerfully legitimate dominant understandings" (130).

The men also recounted that they tried to emulate the behaviours of "normal people" in the community by mimicking their style of dress or avoiding particular forms of attire. This action is consistent with Goffman's (1963b) assertion that in public places, manner of dress is a means of demonstrating that one is similar and belongs. One man felt the pressure not to wear black leather because it would be indicative of his past association with a motorcycle club, while another spoke of taking great care to dress in "*beautiful civilian clothes*" (Dave).

Another concealment approach used was the creation of "back stories" to account for the time they were in prison. This strategy may require the co-operation of intimates and those who are "wise" to the situation[19] and can assist the person to "pass":

> *I made up a resume that was 18 years full of bullshit, but I had people to back it up. I had a buddy [who] owned a bike shop ... and I had it all lined up and if they called any of that, it would have all come out right.* (Tom)

However, this type of concealment becomes particularly complex when the men are trying to conceal their past from family. Several of the men hid their prison past from their young children who may be seen as "unsafe receptacles ... or of such tender nature as to be seriously damaged by the knowledge" (Goffman 1963a, 54). This task is particularly challenging for those respondents who remain on parole or who live with their children. Some of the men who chose to remain in the community where they had served their time indicated that this choice had implications for concealment as their children could be informed by others of their father's status:

> *And they went and told him, said "Oh your dad, yeah he was in jail." "My dad wasn't in jail." "Yeah, he killed somebody." ... I will never lie. And [when my son asked] I just*

19 "Wise" is a term used by Goffman (1963a) to denote those individuals who were not stigmatized by a given attribute but who were aware and sympathetic to the targets of the stigma.

> *said, "Yes I did." And he goes "Oh dad, that's ba-a-ad." And he couldn't get over it for a week.... 'cause he knows it's bad.* (Gowan)

Once the concealment fails, as in the case above, more negative traits can be attributed to the individual since the person is now not only a convict but may also be considered a manipulator or liar; because of this possible double-reaction, some of the former long-term prisoners chose to disclose their background.

Disclosing the Stigma

For several of the respondents, admitting the stigmatized attribute up front (full disclosure) or at the appropriate moment ("conditional disclosure") (Harding 2003, 79) was a technique used to manage stigma. Marcus provided a clear example of being aware of the potential for a double-reaction if he did not reveal his criminal past:

> *I told [the people at work] the first day ... one guy he says, "So, what have you been doing your whole life?" I said, "Well, I was in jail for ten years." He almost fell on the floor and he said, "Hey listen, don't tell anybody that." So I told him, "Either I'm honest with you now and you find out or I tell you something else and you find out later and you don't want to work with me."*

Doc, who primarily engaged in concealing behaviour, addressed the need to be up-front with intimates or potential intimates. Speaking of a new romantic interest, Doc said, "*This woman had no idea who she was ending up with. I told her everything ... Why would you tell somebody a story? ... Tell them the truth, you know, then sift through it.*"

Bobby recounted that he tried a variety of approaches and understood that sometimes his up-front disclosure meant that he wasn't called back for a second job interview. However, because of the men's hyper-awareness of situations, it may be impossible for the individual to interpret the event in a way that does not relate to stigma (Goffman 1963a). Such "stigma consciousness" places an awareness of the discredited attribute at the forefront of the individual's mind and thereby conditions their interpretation of encountered negativity (Pinel 2004). For example, individuals may not receive a call back for a job because there was a more suitable candidate, but this rejection becomes framed as the result of being an ex-prisoner.[20]

20 Notably, in this study, only one man used his stigmatized status as a reason for his current unemployment and so we see very little evidence of what Goffman referred to as "secondary gains" (1963a, 10).

Some of the respondents utilized full disclosure because they were trying to educate others, raise awareness, or prevent youth from engaging in criminal behaviour. However, for the men in this research, this identity does not always take on the qualities typically ascribed to "professional ex-s" (Brown 1991, 219), wherein they use their past experiences as a means to exit a previous deviant status (i.e., the drug addict becomes the ex-addict and addictions counsellor). For an individual convicted of homicide, no positive category of "ex-murderer" can be created or inhabited. The act that brought about their stigmatized status remains and while it can be tempered, it is never eradicated and, as such, sharing their stories in public has potential consequences. Some spoke of weighing the benefits of disclosing for the greater good versus concealing for their own personal gain. Rick told of appearing on a television show to debate a prison-related issue and his co-workers subsequently treating him like he was a "*coffee table book*" on prison. This type of reaction highlights a risk of this approach because, as Goffman (1963a) has noted, the individual can be forced into representing all like-stigmatized individuals.

In addition, these acts of tertiary deviance[21] (Kitsuse 1980) can force a confrontation with the essentialized identity and take an emotional toll on the men. Like members of the gay, lesbian, bisexual, and transgendered community, "coming out" requires the individual to confront his fear of losing his job, losing his friends, and being physically or verbally attacked (see for example, Day and Schoenrade 1997; Dindia 1998; Morris, Balsam, and Rothblum 2002): *I had done talks for five hours, three different classes ... a girl came up and just raked me over the coals. [She said] 'I think it's terrible what you're doing.'* (Joel)

While Joel made the decision to be public about his stigmatic attribute, when confronted by an individual who held firm to her opinion about people of his "out group," he exemplified how difficult this strategy can be to maintain. As a result, even "out" individuals may try to create a distance between themselves and similar others.

Creating Distance

The act of disclosure opens the individual to rejection and in some cases further trauma. In order to avoid this possibility and the exhausting nature of trying

21 Tertiary deviance is used "to refer to the deviant's confrontation, assessment, and rejection of the negative identity imbedded in secondary deviation, and the transformation of that identity into a positive and viable self-conception ... it is possible for the stigmatized, ridiculed and despised to confront their own complicity in the maintenance of their degraded status, to recover and accept the suppressed anger and rage as their own, to transform shame into guilt, guilt into moral indignation, and victim [I would add "perpetrator"] into activist" (Kitsuse 1980, 9).

to conceal stigma (Smart and Wegenr 2000), some of the men chose to maintain both spatial and social/emotional distance. In terms of physical distancing, this effort may include avoidance of particular places, which Goffman (1963a) referred to as "civil" or "out-of-bound" areas, where the chance of stigmatization may be greater, or the individual may also choose to remain in places where they are accepted. Some of the men talked about not returning to their pre-prison communities or to the areas in which their major crime occurred in order to manage the stigma geographically by creating distance between their current life and their past.

Creating social/emotional distance as a stigma management strategy refers to the practice of avoiding intimacy or closeness with others—even those who are similarly stigmatized. Several of the men noted they created social distance by isolating themselves and avoiding having a broad group of friends. This management strategy may be influenced by gender since Thompson and Whearty (2004) argued that men are more comfortable than women with having a limited social network and are less likely to seek replacements for friends who have been lost. This is an important consideration for men who have been incarcerated for long periods since long-term prisoners often sever ties with "external relationships to avoid the stress or 'hard time' produced by the attenuation process" (Flanagan 1981, 119). My research found that this may apply to pre-prison friends, who were rarely mentioned in the interviews.

Distancing may also be employed because "by declining or avoiding overtures of intimacy the individual can avoid the consequent obligation to divulge information" (Goffman 1963a, 99), and in so doing, the men evade judgement. Other men share that they avoid similar others (ex-prisoners) in an attempt to manage the stigma:

> *I tried to separate myself from them [former prisoners].... It was weird because everybody I would run into would call me Champ Champ Champ Champ. And then when I went home ... everybody would call me Fred ... then when I'd come back again ... people say "Hey Champ." And I'd say "Well, that's not me anymore ... just call me Fred."*

Discussion

Evident in this research is the complexity of the ways in which stigma is applied and then managed. The men in this study indicated that stigma was experienced in a multitude of ways and on a continuum ranging from no experience of stigma based on a criminal past to feeling discredited, rejected, and vulnerable because of it. The men demonstrated personal agency by employing management strategies that are varied, and at times, competing or incongruous. Disclosure and distancing sometimes intersect, and at times collide with attempts to conceal. The rejection of the stigmatized attributes by some individuals is in contrast with the way that others embrace them.

The men who participated in this study represent a unique subset of those convicted. The length of their prison sentences, and the crimes upon which they were based, ensure that the convicted men's lives become dramatically altered. The men in this study are not valorized[22] but are placed in positions where symbolic and structural stigma are easily applied and this requires them to make sense of their identities within the context of dominant discourses encountered in the media on an almost daily basis. They must negotiate the meanings attached to the stigma and find ways to mitigate the negative outcomes of this. As Bruckert (2002) has noted in her work on stigmatization:

> Different individual responses may not alter stigmatic designations in public and private discourses, but they transform the dynamic from the experience of shame or embarrassment to the negotiation of consequences. (133)

It is critical, however, that the exploration of stigma not rest solely with the ways in which stigma is experienced at the micro-level. Grounding the discussion in the experience of the men must only be a starting point for exploring the "truths" upon which the stigma is built. That is, it has been argued in this chapter that stigmatization of those criminalized is partly the result of dominant discourses that construct these individuals as dangerous and risky and which justify the application of structural stigma. A clear disjuncture exists between the actuarial level of risk[23] and that which is thought to exist; however, the dominant risk discourse limits strategies of resistance. Ultimately, this analysis confirms Hannem's (Chapter Two, this volume) assertions about the need to engage with stigma at both the level of the individual's experience and at the structural level so that its roots can be exposed and, to some extent, disentangled.

---

22 This valorization of the convicted person can be seen in Jamieson and Grounds (2002) study of members of the IRA who were imprisoned for long periods but who returned to their communities bearing an almost heroic status.

23 Government statistics indicate, for example, that 94 percent of those individuals released from prison on parole tend not to violate the terms of their conditional release (Public Safety Canada 2010).

Chapter Ten

Speaking Out

A Poem and a Conversation[1]

"Crazzy" Dave Dessler

Panner's Perspective

Just walk on by me, Not hearing what is said
Just totally ignore me, I might as well be dead,
I could sit here all day, well into the dark of nite,
It doesn't mean you'll see me, You don't have the insight.

I don't have a job,
Or anywhere to live,
I try not to be obnoxious,
And say thank you when people give.

I really don't want 2B here,
Begging in this way,
So a kind act or word,
Could really make my day.

1 Poetry by "Crazzy" Dave Dessler, originally printed in My Ottawa My Streets - Street Photography by Jean E. Boulay." Interview by Jean E. Boulay. Jean and Dave met while Dave was living on the streets in Ottawa. Reprinted by permission.

Not all of us are drunkards,
Or addicts or Insane in the head,
But I made this bed I lay in,
That's all that needs 2B said.

Conversation with Crazzy Dave (with Jean E. Boulay)

Jean: *How long have you been on the streets?*

Dave: *On and off, most of my life.*

Jean: *Have you ever spent an Ottawa winter outside before?*

Dave: *No, this is my first winter on the street.*

Jean: *Aren't you concerned about the weather? It gets pretty damn cold in this city.*

Dave: *No. I used to be a bike courier and worked in the winter. Compared to that, this should be a breeze.*

Jean: *What got you here?*

Dave: *You mean here, on this spot?*

Jean: *No, I mean how did you become homeless?*

Dave: *I was self-employed last year. Like I said, I was a bike courier. I paid my own taxes, paid into workmen's comp but not employment insurance. I did things backwards I guess. I had an accident on my bike during leisure time. Workmen's comp wouldn't cover me. I couldn't get pogie. So I'm here.*

Jean: *You said you were on and off the streets most of your life. How did that happen?*

Dave: *That's not relevant. I'm here and that's all that matters.*

Jean: *Yes, but something led you here. What kind of childhood did you have?*

Dave: *What? Are you asking me if I came from a broken home? Yes I did, but then again, so did many other people. I'm not pointing any fingers at any one thing. I believe there are some people that are pre-disposed to being criminals, to living the kind of life I've led.*

Jean: *Criminal? Have you been in jail?*

Dave: *Yes. I've done some pretty stupid things in the past. I chose a certain lifestyle for whatever reasons and yes, I've been in jail several times.*

Jean: *What are people like? How do they treat you as they walk through your living room?*

Dave: *Some people walk by and tell me to get a job. That's when I ask them if they have one to give me. I don't take any crap from them.*

Jean: *What's the worst thing besides "get a job" that people say to you?*

Dave: *When they berate the fact that I write and sell poetry. You know, the first five letters of ignore are the same as the first five of the word "ignorance." If you look up the definition of ignorance, the first thing it says is "lack of knowledge." Those people that laugh at me simply don't know. I don't believe in welfare. I won't apply for it.*

Jean: *Could you get it, given that you don't have a fixed address?*

Dave: *I could get some money from other social programs. I don't want it. Don't believe in it. I write poetry. Some people buy it; others don't but give a little to help out. Others just ignore me.*

Jena: *We're getting some looks as people walk by. Does that bother you?*

Dave: *No, most of them are just diamonds in the rough.*

Jean: *Wow! Diamonds in the rough! Where did you hear that term? My wife delivers an experiential program a few times a year and she uses it quite often. How do you know about such things?*

Dave: *Life. Everything I know I've learned by living life. Where I am today is where I am supposed to be. This is my destiny. I accept that.*

Jean: *Do you believe one can change one's destiny?*

Dave: *No. Our destinies are pre-determined.*

Jean: *Do you think it's possible to be on the wrong path? One that leads you away from your destiny?*

Dave: *Everything you do is the right path to reaching your destiny. Can you go off course? Yes, I believe you can. But going off course is part of the process.*

Jean: *Personally, I don't think you know it when you fulfill your destiny. It's like trying to answer the question "Which came first, the chicken or the egg?"*

Dave: *Oh, you'll know it.*

Jean: *How?*

Dave: *You'll just know it. Believe me.*

Jean: *Where do you see yourself twelve months from now? Is this it for you for the rest of your life?*

Dave: *Not sure about twelve months from now. I do know that my life will turn around by the time I'm fifty. Don't ask me how I know. I just do.*

Jean: *How old are you now?*

Dave: *Forty-four. This is karma at work.*

Jean: *How do you mean?*

Dave: *I've been an asshole most of my life. This is my payback. I'm here to make people happy.*

Jean: *How do you do that?*

Dave: *I make them smile. I give them the opportunity to do something that they'll feel good about, even if it's just having a conversation with them. Some people come to see me specifically to get advice. I help them out. I make them happy.*

A young lady walks by and Crazzy Dave says good morning and asks how she is. She smiles and responds that she is doing well and offers her own morning salutation.

Dave: *You see that? She smiled. And it wasn't one of those fake smiles. I can always tell which smiles are real and which are fake. That's how I make people happy because smiling is good for you. When you smile, you are happy, even if it's just for a second. You may not recognize that you are happy—but you are.*

Two older gentlemen walk by. One of them looks down at Crazzy Dave and makes that annoying disapproving sound. You know the one that sounds like "*tsk, tsk, tsk*." Dave and I continue to talk for a moment then he shouts out at the couple as they slowly walk away. "*What? You think I can't hear you? If you have something to say to me, why don't you just say it to my face?*" They keep on walking. I smile and continue with our session.

Jean: *If you were employed last year, why aren't you working today?*

Dave: *I can't. I could get a job as a cook if I didn't have Hep C. If I was to cut myself while working, they would have to stop everything and sanitize the place. I have arthritis everywhere in my body. I still have effects from the concussion I got when I had my accident. I lost three days of my life then. Don't know what I did during those three days.*

Jean: *What about fear? Aren't you afraid that other homeless people or street thugs might try to steal from you? What about the drug dealers?*

Dave: *We know who each other are. I've let it be known that I've been in and out of some of the worst prisons in Canada and that they don't want to fuck with me. You can't always be assertive. Sometimes you have to be passive, sometimes aggressive. I have no problem letting people know I'm not happy with them. Sometimes you have to grab someone by the throat and slap them on the side of the face, figuratively speaking of course. I won't let them drag me back there. I won't go back to prison, so that means not doing stupid things.*

A middle-aged couple walks by. The lady stops to examine some of Dave's cardboard poetry and smiles at him as she drops a two-dollar coin in his Rubbermaid container. "*Merry Christmas*" she says in her slight British accent. The man also smiles and tells us to enjoy the day. Dave reaches over and grabs the rubber money bin: "*I have to take out anything bigger than a dime.*"

Jean: *Why is that?*

Dave: *Sometimes some of the more desperate ones grab the container as they walk by and run like hell. As you can see, I'm not in a position to react quickly so I let them have it. They are obviously pretty desperate. The pennies I throw a few feet away. People can pick them up and use them to make a wish. You know—lucky pennies.*

An older lady walks by and sees a penny on the sidewalk near Dave. "*Maybe you should pick that up and make a wish,*" she says in a condescending tone. "*I put it there for you to do that,*" he replies. "*Have a good day, Ma'am!*"—"*Another diamond*" he says as he turns to continue our interview.

Dave: *I won't talk politics or religion.*

Jean: *Why not?*

Dave: *Because I don't want to offend anyone. My beliefs are my own and I wouldn't want to offend anyone who might be walking by and hear what I'm saying. That's just not right.*

At that moment, an attractive lady with stunning eyes stops while Dave is explaining his reasons for not discussing religion or politics. She's well dressed and quite good-looking. She stands close by and listens to our conversation. Then she reaches over and hands Dave something wrapped in a white paper napkin.

"*Hi, Dave, brought you a truffle*" she says, and then stands back. Dave and I continue our conversation while she waits, listening and watching us interact. Dave eats while we talk and when he's done she reaches down and takes the napkin. "*I'll get rid of that for you,*" she says, and walks away. "*I get all the good looking ones,*" Dave says.

Chapter Eleven

Concluding Thoughts

Academic Activism: A Call to Action

Stacey Hannem and Chris Bruckert

The situations and experiences presented in this book vary widely, however, the substantive themes are recurring: marginalized groups are profoundly affected by stigma at both the interpersonal and structural levels; individuals find themselves grappling with the effects of stereotype and stigma on their interactions with others and on their understandings of themselves; technologies of the self are employed to manage stigma and to resist the implications of its constraints, and even the most conscious social actors are not immune to the deeply embedded social constructs that condition our understanding of the world and lead to out-group divisions, prejudice and discrimination. In short, we are all affected by stigma as both subjects and perpetrators—indeed at times simultaneously.

Given the pervasive nature of our entanglements in social structure and culture, how can we, individually and collectively, resist stigma: resist the temptation to fall back on prevailing cultural stereotypes as shortcuts to interpreting the world around us; resist the temptation to (re)define ourselves or others solely as victims and therefore deny agency; resist the temptation of silence, or invisibility, or allowing stigma to justify the failure to engage in social life, or to fight injustice? In this concluding chapter, we briefly summarize the emerging themes of the book and start to unpack the role of academics, activists, and researchers in contesting and perpetuating stigma-normal distinctions. We discuss the difficulties inherent in mobilizing marginalized populations to challenge stigma and to engage in collaborative forms of resistance, and call on politically aware academics and researchers to act as the catalyst in moving toward social change and collective action.

Each chapter in this volume presents the stories and experiences of a different group who encounter interpersonal/symbolic forms of stigma in their everyday lives and interactions. Clearly the (re)actions of others form a significant part of the stigma experience and shape the ways that these individuals choose to engage in the social world. Although the basis of spoiled identity varies, these groups utilize many similar technologies of the self to manage stigma and to negotiate their spoiled identities. We have seen that what Goffman (1963a) referred to as "passing" still remains one of the most common means of dealing with the potential for stigma in interaction. While hiding a discreditable characteristic effectively protects one from others' negative reactions, clearly the failure to disclose key biographical information to acquaintances or friends can cause anxiety about the possibility of being "outed" and result in feelings of isolation and distance from others. It also opens up the possibility of being further discredited on the basis of their duplicity.

Another common tactic employed by marginalized persons as a means of protecting their identity is to attempt to separate themselves from existing stereotypes by reifying and supporting the dominant discourse while emphasizing their own difference. For example, we have seen how prisoners' family members support the use of ion drug scans in order to protect the security of the institution from others who would bring drugs in, although they all suggest that this security measure is not necessary for *them* and assert their own innocence (Hannem, Chapter Six). Similarly, we have seen how imprisoned women may rationalize their own self-injurious behaviour as a form of "coping," while simultaneously defining other women as "crazy" or "insane" for engaging in similar behaviours (Kilty, Chapter Seven). This strategy for normalizing and reclaiming individual identity has the effect of creating hierarchies among groups of marginalized persons in which individuals are defined (within their own group) as more or less stigmatized. Goffman refers briefly to this phenomenon as allowing the stigmatized individual to define himself as relatively "normal" with respect to others in his group who have more profoundly "spoiled" identities:

> The stigmatized individual exhibits a tendency to stratify his "own" according to the degree to which their stigma is apparent and obtrusive. He can then take up in regard to those who are more evidently stigmatized than himself the attitudes the normals take to him. Thus do the hard of hearing stoutly see themselves as anything but deaf persons, and those with defective vision, anything but blind. It is in his affiliation with, or separation from, his more evidently stigmatized fellows, that the individual's oscillation of identification is most sharply marked. (107)

This phenomenon underscores the pervasiveness of stigma as an operating category for human interaction; that is, we *all* act as stigmatizers and are positioned as stigmatized within specific social contexts. When stigma is based on stereotyped group characteristics, individual identity becomes subsumed and lost to the larger group identity. Marginalized persons find themselves desperate to make a distinction between their own identity and that of the group and to position themselves as normal, rational agents in a social context that portrays them as "risky" and damaged. Thus, the use of intra-group stigmatization and stratification is nominally functional for the discredited individual in protecting a sense of self and self-worth. Unfortunately, outsiders ("normals") who would label and stigmatize in accordance with the prevailing discourse are generally unmoved by pleas of innocence or difference and do not recognize the individual as a unique person (whose very existence should call into question the validity of existing stereotypes). These stereotypes and deviant labels reflect unequal power relations in society that enable those who exercise political and social authority to define those who are not like them as deviant. When those with limited economic, social, and cultural capital attempt to challenge the discourses, they most often go unheard and unheeded—they are and remain the deviant "other." The very stigmatic assumptions and stereotypes that define them as deviant delegitimize their claims and justify their silencing. In light of this tautological process it is not surprising that instead of having the desired effect of normalizing or redeeming the discredited individual in the eyes of others, intra-group stigmatization merely serves to reinforce existing stereotypes and perpetuate the marginalization of the group as a whole (Bruckert 2002).

The problem of intra-group stigmatization and stratification highlights the tension inherent in attempting to manage a spoiled identity at the individual level. Personal strategies of stigma avoidance and identity management fail to challenge the larger stigmatizing discourses and therefore tend to be counterproductive for the purposes of collective struggle. What we see are individuals attempting to negotiate structural level stigma in isolation, from a position of relative powerlessness, with few (if any) resources and little social capital. Clearly, the personal and lived aspects of stigma are foremost in their understanding and experience and call for immediate action to relieve the difficulties of marginality. However, this narrow and urgent vision obscures the larger picture of structural stigma and the marginality of their group as a whole, and often undermines the ability of marginalized persons to unite in a collective challenge to the discourses in which the injustices that they experience are rooted.

Marginalized persons are not the only ones who fall into this trap of defining stigma narrowly and waging isolated and personal battles against its symbolic and material realizations. Academics engaged in research and working with stigmatized populations are also all too often guilty of this type of shortsightedness. Due to the fragmented nature of academic research and specialization, researchers generally work with a single, carefully defined population and concern themselves with the issues that disadvantage and affect that group. Consequently the issue of stigma is usually understood and addressed in a fractured way that prioritizes the "normalization" or destigmatization of *that* group by challenging the applicability of dominant stereotypes. However, the stereotypes themselves are rarely the object of deconstruction—merely the question of their appropriateness for characterizing the population in question. For example, one of the authors has engaged in work on the subject of women working in strip clubs (Bruckert 2002). In her writing she was careful to normalize erotic dance as a form of labour and to challenge the notions that dancers are also "whores" and "druggies." While these are legitimate points that need to be raised, debunking the links between erotic dance and prostitution and drug use does not deconstruct the stigma associated with these stereotypes and risks creating a kind of hierarchy in which erotic dancers, who are understood as legitimate labourers, are positioned above those who engage in prostitution or individuals who use illicit substances. The author's awareness of the pitfalls and attempts to negotiate the tension proved insufficient—not least because, as a good feminist researcher, she was caught in another tension—commitment to honourably attending to the participants and acknowledging that they are the experts of their own lives precluded negating their truth.

It would appear that like the phenomenon of intra-group stigmatization, academics' singular approach to normalization may have the effect of reifying and strengthening stereotypes, binding them closer to stigmatized definitions. Thus, in our efforts to destigmatize and normalize the groups that we are engaged with, we find ourselves stigmatizing other populations and creating hierarchies of marginalized persons. Furthermore, it is also unclear that our attempts to separate the group at issue from the stigmatized stereotypes bound up with their collective identity have any redemptive power in the eyes of the larger society or within social institutions. For example, claiming that women who work in strip clubs are not prostitutes or drug addicts does not necessarily convince the general public that this is so, even if it comes from the educated voice of a university researcher. We see the need, therefore, to broaden our lens of inquiry to include not only individualized experiences of symbolic stigma but the implications of spoiled collective identity for marginalized groups.

When we begin to think about stigma as a collective experience, we are compelled to consider political action as a strategy for challenging stereotypes and resisting the marginality that accompanies a discredited identity. Recognizing that the personal is, in fact, political, we would argue that the scope of this political action must address the need for changes that go beyond relieving individual experiences of stigma and discrimination. The political action required is a form of collective resistance to stereotypes that would move beyond superficial, day-to-day strategies designed to mitigate symbolic stigma. Such collective resistance targets the deconstruction of discourses and stereotypes and emphasizes the elimination of collective stigmatization through the promotion of alternate knowledges and active protest of legal and social injustices. The type of political action that we envision would move beyond the barriers created by stigmatizing practices (and that we often reproduce through our solitary efforts to salvage a spoiled identity) to unite diverse groups of persons who share similar struggles. The populations described in this book, for example, may find allies among one another in their common experiences of stigma, marginality, and social injustice. These larger, united political movements against stigma would endeavour to erode existing stereotypes and to make the logic of stigma fall apart, rather than reproducing stigmatizing discourses in an effort to "normalize" a given population. Goffman, himself, recognized the need to acknowledge the similar situations and issues faced by diverse populations who are united in their experiences of stigma. He suggested that the most fruitful course of analysis would incorporate issues and concerns from multiple substantive perspectives:

> I have argued that stigmatized persons have enough of their situations in life in common to warrant classifying all these persons together for purposes of analysis... These commonalities can be organized on the basis of very few assumptions regarding human nature. What remains in each one of the traditional fields could then be re-examined for whatever is really special to it, thereby bringing analytical coherence to what is now purely historic and fortuitous unity. Knowing what fields like race relations, aging, and mental health share, one could then go on to see, analytically, how they differ... it would be clear that each is merely an area to which one should apply several perspectives, and that the development of any one of these coherent analytic perspectives is not likely to come from those who restrict their interest exclusively to one substantive area. (Goffman 1963a, 146–47)

We recognize, however that there are difficulties inherent in resisting arbitrary divisions between people and in combating our entanglements in stigmatizing structures. Creating alliances between groups of marginalized persons is a complex endeavour, particularly when the approach not only requires social actors to suspend their own immediate short-term interests but also to recognize the broader implications of their stigma management strategies. The notion that one's struggles to improve one's own life and circumstances may cause consequent harm to others is a difficult one. It may be equally challenging to convince persons to recognize and let go of the stereotypes and prejudices that they may hold against other stigmatized groups, regardless of their shared circumstances.

We conclude this book with a call to action. We believe that there is a role for academics and activists working with marginalized populations. By first unpacking stigma and rendering its insidious nature visible, we can then move beyond the individual deconstruction to start to address the underlying divisions within the social realm. It is imperative that we identify commonalities between disparate groups and initiate dialogue about shared concerns or experiences in order to build bridges and create alliances rooted in the ultimate goal of de-marginalization.

Finally, we must engage with broader society and contest the apparent utility of stigma-normal distinctions as operating categories for understanding and interpreting the world. As Huckelbury's writing suggests, this may involve acknowledging the potential for labels to become self-fulfilling prophesies that channel individuals into lives of perpetual marginality and deviance. The creation of indelibly stigmatized identities risks compelling deviance where none was previously present, as could occur if an Afghan man labelled as a terrorist began to identify with anti-Western sentiments and to support revolutionary (re) action. Conversely, in populations whose stigma is based on deviantized behaviours, the label may reduce the individual's opportunities and options to such an extent that he or she has little choice but to continue that behaviour, as when an ex-offender is unable to obtain gainful employment and resorts to continued criminal involvement. In this way, stigma and marginality are not only detrimental to those who live with these labels, but are also counterproductive in the larger sense of failing to protect society from the risk that they believe is posed by these "dangerous others" and perhaps inadvertently creating new risks.

In our quest to reduce exclusion and to deconstruct stigma, we believe that academics and activists have a vital role to play in presenting alternate discourses and challenging hegemonic presentations of marginalized persons in meaningful ways that will "speak the truth to power." The deconstruction of stigma categories must be undertaken with a careful awareness of the broader implications of our statements for marginalized groups, with an eye to ending the unintended perpetuation of stigma/normal distinctions. We hope that this volume has made some small steps in this direction and that it offers some insight into the everyday lived realities of individuals struggling with spoiled identities, recognizing that the lines that are drawn between the stigmatized and the normal are very thin, indeed:

The stigmatized and the normal are part of each other; if one can prove vulnerable, it must be expected that the other can, too. For in imputing identities to individuals, discreditable or not, the wider social setting and its inhabitants have in a way compromised themselves; they have set themselves up to be proven the fool. (Goffman 1963a, 135)

References

Adam, Barry D. 1998. "Theorizing Homophobia." *Sexualities* 1.4: 387–404.

Adler, Patricia, and Peter Adler. 2007. "The Demedicalization of Self-Injury: From Psychopathology to Sociological Deviance." *Journal of Contemporary Ethnography* 36.5: 537–70.

Ahmad, Muneer. 2002. "Homeland Insecurities: Racial Violence the Day After September 11." *Social Text* 20.3: 101–15.

Altheide, David L. 2002. *Creating Fear: News and the Construction of Crisis.* Hawthorne, NY: Aldine de Gruyter.

———, and Katie Devriese. 2007. "Perps in the News: A Research Note on Stigma." *Crime, Media, Culture* 3.3: 382–89.

American Psychological Association. 2000. *Diagnostic and Statistical Manual of Mental Disorders 4th Edition—text revision.* Washington, DC: American Psychiatric Association.

Anderson, Tammy L., and Frank Ripullo. 1996. "Social Setting, Stigma Management, and Recovering Drug Addicts." *Humanity and Society* 20.3: 25–43.

AVERT. 2010. *2007 Canada HIV Summary Statistics.* <http://www.avert.org/canada-hiv.htm> accessed August 1, 2010.

Aylesworth, Pat, and Erika MacPherson. 2008. *Pictures of Self-Harm* [Documentary]. Winnipeg, MB: Crossing Communities Art Project.

Bahdi, Reem. 2003. "No Exit: Racial Profiling and Canada's War against Terrorism." *Osgood Hall Law Journal* 4.3: 293–317.

Baker, Phyllis L. 2000. "I Didn't Know: Discoveries and Identity Transformation of Women Addicts in Treatment." *Journal of Drug Issues* 30.4: 863–80.

Bakker, Laura J., Barbara A. Morris, and Laura M. Janus. 1978. "Hidden Victims of Crime." *Social Work* 23.2: 143–48.

Barton, Judith A. 1988. *Courtesy Stigma and the Parents of Drug Abusing Adolescents.* PhD Dissertation. University of Colorado at Boulder.

Baumeister, Roy, Ellen Bratslavsky, Catrin Finkenauer, and Kathleen Vohs. 2001. "Emotion and Cognition: The Case of Automatic Vigilance." *Review of General Psychology* 5.4: 323–70.

Becker, Howard S. 1963/1973. *Outsiders: Studies in the Sociology of Deviance.* New York: Free Press.

Bell, Colleen. 2006. "Surveillance Strategies and Population at Risk: Biopolitical Governance in Canada's National Security Policy." *Security Dialogue* 37.2: 147–65.

Benoit, Cecilia, and Alison Millar. 2001. *Dispelling Myths and Understanding Realities: Working Conditions, Health Status, and Exiting Experiences of Sex Workers.* Victoria, BC: Prostitutes Empowerment, Education, and Resource Society (PEERS).

Berg, Bruce. 1998. *Qualitative Research Methods for the Social Sciences,* 3rd ed. London: Allyn and Bacon.

Blumer, Herbert. 1969. *Symbolic Interactionism: Perspective and Method.* Berkley, CA: University of California Press.

Boyd, Susan C. 1999. *Mothers and Illicit Drugs: Transcending the Myths.* Toronto: University of Toronto Press.

———. 2004. *From Witches to Crack Moms: Women, Drug Law and Policy.* Durham, NC: Carolina Academic Press.

Braithwaite, John. 1995. "Inequality and Republican Criminology." *Crime and Inequality.* John Hagan and Ruth D. Peterson, eds. Palo Alto, CA: Stanford University Press. 277–327.

Braman, Donald, and Jennifer Wood. 2003. "From One Generation to the Next: How Criminal Sanctions are Reshaping Family Life in Urban America." *Prisoners Once Removed: The Impact of Incarceration and Re-entry on Children, Families and Communities.* Jeremy Travis and Michelle Waul, eds. Washington, DC: Urban Institute Press. 157–88.

Branaman, Ann. 1997. "Goffman's Social Theory." *The Goffman Reader.* Charles Lemert and Ann Branaman, eds. Oxford: Blackwell Publishers. xlv–lxxxii.

Brown, J. David. 1991. "The Professional Ex-: An Alternative for Exiting the Deviant Career." *The Sociological Quarterly* 32.2: 219–30.

Brown, James. W. 2003. "Post-9/11 Discrimination against Arabs and Muslims." *Images that Injure: Pictorial Stereotypes in the Media.* Paul Martin Lester and Susan Dente Ross, eds. London: Praeger Publishers. 65–73.

Bruckert, Chris, 2000. *Stigmatized Labour: An ethnographic study of strip clubs in the 1990s.* Carleton University. Unpublished dissertation.

———. 2002. *Taking it Off, Putting it On: Women in the Strip Trade.* Toronto: Women's Press.

———, and Frederique Chabot. 2010. *Challenges: Ottawa-Area Sex Workers Speak Out.* Ottawa: POWER.

———, and Martin Dufresne. 2002. "Re-Configuring the Margins: Tracing the Regulatory Context of Ottawa Strip Clubs." *Canadian Journal of Law and Society* 7.1: 69–87.

———, and Sylvie Frigon. 2004. "Making a Spectacle of Herself: On Women's Bodies in Strip Clubs." *Atlantis* 28.1: 48–64.

———, and Stacey Hannem. Unpublished. "Rethinking the Prostitution Debates: Transcending Structural Stigma in Systemic Responses to Sex Work."

———, and Colette Parent. 2006. "Ottawa Area Erotic Dancers: A Labour Needs Assessment." How *to Respond to the Needs of Street Sex Workers in the Ottawa–Gatineau Region.* Ottawa: Status of Women Canada.

———, and Colette Parent. 2007. "La danse érotique comme métier à l'ère de la vente de soi." *Cahiers de recherche sociologique UQAM* 43: 97–108.

———, Collette Parent, and D. Poliot. 2006. *How to Respond to the Needs of Street Sex Workers in the Ottawa–Gatineau Region.* Ottawa: Status of Women Canada.

———, Collette Parent, and Pascale Robitaille. 2003. *Erotic Service/Erotic Dance Establishments: Two Types of Marginalized Labour.* Ottawa: Law Commission of Canada.

Burn, Shawn M. 2000. "Heterosexuals' Use of "Fag" and "Queer" to Deride One Another: A Contributor to Heterosexism and Stigma." *Journal of Homosexuality* 40.2: 1–11.

Busfield, Joan. 1986. *Managing Madness: Changing Ideas and Practice.* London: Hutchinson.

Butler, Judith. 1990. *Gender Trouble: Feminism and the Subversion of Identity.* London: Routledge.

Butler, Robert. 1995. "Ageism." *The Encyclopedia of Aging: A Comprehensive Resource in Gerontology and Geriatrics,* 2nd ed. George L. Maddox, ed. New York: Springer. 35.

Cahill, Spencer E. 1998. "Toward a Sociology of the Person." *Sociological Theory* 16.2: 131–48.

Cainkar, Louise. 2004. "The Impact of the September 11 Attacks and their Aftermath on Arab and Muslim Communities in the United States." *The Maze of Fear: Security and Migration After 9/11.* John Tirman, ed. New York: New York Press.

Callard, Felicity J. 1998. "The Body in Theory." *Environment and Planning D: Society and Space* 16: 387–400.

Campbell, Catherine, and Harriet Deacon. 2006. "Unraveling the Contexts of Stigma: From Internalisation to Resistance to Change." *Journal of Community and Applied Social Psychology* 16.5: 411–17.

Canada. 1992. "Problems Associated with Long-Term Incarceration." *Forum on Corrections Research* 4.2. Ottawa: Department of Justice.

———. 1994. *Long-term Federally Sentenced Women: Literature Review.* Ottawa: Correctional Service Canada.

———. 1998. *Implementing the Life Line Concept: Report of the Task Force on Long Term Offenders.* Ottawa: Correctional Service Canada.

———. 2000. *The Safe Return of Offenders to the Community.* Ottawa: Correctional Service Canada.

———. 2008. "From Confinement to Community: The National Parole Board and Aboriginal Offenders." <http://www.npb-cnlc.gc.ca/infocntr/fctc-eng.shtml> accessed June 20, 2008.

Canadian Criminal Code, L. R. 1985, ch. C-46.

Carlen, Pat. 2001. "Death and the Triumph of Governance? Lessons from the Scottish Women's Prison." *Punishment and Society* 3.4: 459–71.

Casey-Acevedo, Karen, and Tim Bakken. 2002. "Visiting Women in Prison: Who Visits and Who Cares?" *Journal of Offender Rehabilitation* 34.3: 67–83.

Castel, Robert. 1991. "From Dangerousness to Risk." *The Foucault Effect: Studies in Governmentality.* Graham Burchell, Colin Gordon, and Peter Miller, eds. London: Harvester Wheatsheaf. 281–98.

Castellani, Brian. 1999. "Michel Foucault and Symbolic Interactionism: The Making of a New Theory of Interaction." *Studies in Symbolic Interaction* 22: 247–72.

Cavender, Gray. 2004. "Media and Crime Policy: A Reconsideration of David Garland's *The Culture of Control.*" *Punishment and Society* 6.3: 335–48.

CBC. 2012. "Alleged Pickton Attack Survivor Won't Testify." April 10, 2012. <http://www.cbc.ca/news/canada/british-columbia/story/2012/04/10/bc-pickton-inquiry-sex-worker-witness.html> accessed April 28, 2012.

Choudhry, Sujit. 2001. "Protecting Equality in the Face of Terror: Ethnic and Racial Profiling and s. 15 of the *Charter*." *The Security of Freedom: Essays on Canada's Anti-Terrorism Bill.* Ronald J. Daniels, Patrick Macklem, and Kent Roach, eds. Toronto: University of Toronto Press. 367–82.

Chuang, Rueyling. 2004. "Theoretical Perspective: Fluidity and Complexity of Cultural and Ethnic Identity." *Communicating Ethnic and Cultural Identity*. Mary Fong and Rueyling Chuang, eds. Toronto: Rowman & Littlefield. 51–68.

City of Toronto, By-Law No. 574-2000, *A By-Law Respecting the Licensing, Regulating and Governing of Trades, Business and Occupations in the City of Toronto* (3 August 2000), schedule 1.

Clare, Anthony. 1976. *Psychiatry in Dissent: Controversial Issues in Thought and Practice.* London: Tavistock.

Clear, Todd R., and Harry R. Dammer. 2000. *The Offender in the Community.* Scarborough, ON: Thomson Learning.

Clear, Todd R., Dina R. Rose, and Judith A. Ryder. 2001. "Incarceration and the Community: The Problem of Removing and Returning Offenders." *Crime and Delinquency* 47.3: 335–51.

Coalition. 2012. "Open Letter: Non-participation in the Policy Forums/Study Commission" Addressed to the Missing Women Commission of Inquiry, April 10, 2012. <http://www.fns.bc.ca/pdf/OpenLetterstoMWCI_041012.pdf>.

Coffey, Amanda. 1999. *The Ethnographic Self: Fieldwork and the Representation of Identity.* Thousand Oaks, CA: Sage.

Cohen, Stanley. 1972. *Folk Devils and Moral Panics: The Creation of the Mods and the Rockers.* London: MacGibbon and Kee.

Collins, Randall. 1986. "The Passing of Intellectual Generations: Reflections on the Death of Erving Goffman." *Sociological Theory* 4.1: 106–13.

———. 2004. *Interaction Ritual Chains.* Princeton, NJ: Princeton University Press.

Conason, Joe. 2007. *It Can Happen Here: Authoritarian Peril in the Age of Bush.* New York: Thomas Dunne Books/St. Martin's Press.

Condry, Rachel. 2007. *Families Shamed: The Consequences of Crime for the Relatives of Serious Offenders.* Cullompton, UK: Willan Publishing.

Connell, Raewyn. 1992. "A Very Straight Gay: Masculinity, Homosexual Experience and the Dynamics of Gender." *American Sociological Review* 57.6: 735–51.

———. 2005. "Change Among the Gatekeepers: Men, Masculinities and Gender Equality in the Global Arena." *Signs: Journal of Women in Culture and Society* 30.3: 1801–26.

Connors, Robin. 1996. "Self-Injury in Trauma Survivors: Functions and Meanings." *American Journal of Orthopsychiatry* 66.2: 194–206.

Cookson, H. M. 1977. "A Survey of Self-Injury in a Closed Prison for Women." *British Journal of Criminology* 17.4: 332–47.

Cornell, Stephen E. 1988. *The Return of the Natives: American Indian Political Resurgence.* New York: Oxford University Press.

Correctional Service Canada. 2002a. *Commissioner's Directive 843: Prevention, Management, and Response to Suicide and Self-injuries.* Ottawa: CSC.

———. 2002b. *Security Classification of Offenders: Standard Operating Practices (700-14).* Ottawa: CSC.

———. 2004a. *Use of Non-Intrusive Search Tools: Guidelines 566-8-1.* Ottawa: CSC. <http://www.csc-scc.gc.ca/text/plcy/doc/566-8-1.pdf>.

———. 2004b. *Technical Requirements for Ion Mobility Spectrometry Devices: Guidelines 566-8-2.* Ottawa: CSC. <http://www.csc-scc.gc.ca/text/plcy/doc/566-8-2.pdf>.

Correctional Service Canada Review Panel. 2007. *A Roadmap to Strengthening Public Safety: Report of the Correctional Service of Canada Review Panel.* Ottawa: Minister of Public Works and Government Services Canada. <http://www.ps-sp.gc.ca/csc-scc/cscrpreport-eng.pdf>.

Corrigan, Patrick W., and Robert K. Lundin. 2001. *Don't Call Me Nuts! Coping With the Stigma of Mental Illness.* Chicago: Recovery Press.

Corrigan, Patrick W., Fred E. Markowitz, and Amy C. Watson. 2004. "Structural Levels of Mental illness Stigma and Discrimination." *Schizophrenia Bulletin* 30.3: 481–91.

Courtenay-Quirk, Cari, Richard J. Wolitski, Jeffery T. Parsons, and Cynthia A. Gomez. 2006. "Is HIV/AIDS Stigma Dividing the Gay Community? Perceptions of HIV-Positive Men Who Have Sex with Men." *AIDS Education and Prevention* 18.1: 56–67.

Cox, Simon. 2008. "Prisoners Get High on the Warders' Supply." *The First Post,* April 11, 2008. <http://www.thefirstpost.co.uk/27883,features,prisoners-get-high-on-the-warders-supply> accessed September 22, 2009.

Crawford, Robert. 1994. "The Boundaries of the Self and the Unhealthy Other: Reflections on Health, Culture and AIDS." *Social Science and Medicine* 38.1: 1347–65.

Crichlow, Wesley. 2004. *Buller Men and Batty Boys: Hidden Men in Toronto and Halifax Black Communities.* Toronto: University of Toronto Press.

Crocker, Jennifer, Brenda Major, and Claude Steele. 1998. "Social Stigma." *Handbook of Social Psychology*, 4th ed. Daniel T. Gilbert, Susan T. Fiske, and Gardner Lindzey, eds. Boston: McGraw-Hill. 504–53.

Cromwell, Jason. 1999. *Transmen and FTMs: Identities, Bodies, Genders and Sexualities.* Champaign, IL: University of Illinois Press.

Cruikshank, Barbara. 1996. "Revolutions Within: Self-Government and Self-Esteem." *Foucault and Political Reason*. Andrew Barry, Thomas Osborne, and Nikolas S. Rose, eds. Chicago: University of Chicago Press. 231–52.

Day, Nancy, and Patricia Schoenrade. 1997. "Staying in the Closet versus Coming Out: Relationships between Communication about Sexual Orientation and Work Attitudes." *Personnel Psychology* 50.1: 147–63.

Deane, Lawrence, Denis C. Bracken, and Larry Morrissette. 2007. "Desistance within an Urban Aboriginal Gang." *Probation Journal* 54.2: 125–41.

Demello, Margo. 1993. "The Convict Body: Tattooing among Male American Prisoners." *Anthropology Today* 9.6: 10–13.

Dindia, Kathryn. 1998. "Going Into and Coming Out of the Closet: The Dialectics of Stigma Disclosure." *Dialectical Approaches to Studying Personal Relationships*. Barbara M. Montgomery and Leslie A. Baxter, eds. Mahwah, NJ: Lawrence Erlbam. 83–108.

Dodds, Catherine. 2006. "HIV-Related Stigma in England: Experiences of Gay Men and Heterosexual African Migrants Living with HIV." *Journal of Community and Applied Social Psychology* 16.5: 472–80.

Donovan, Raymond. 1995. "The Plaguing of a Faggot, the Leperising of a Whore: Criminally Cultured AIDS Bodies and Carrier Laws." *Journal of Australian Studies* 43.1: 110–24.

Douglas, Mary. 1966. *Purity and Danger: An Analysis of the Concepts of Pollution and Taboo.* London: Routledge and Kegan Paul.

Drummond, Murray. 2007. "Age and Aging." *International Encyclopedia of Men and Masculinities.* Michael Flood, Judith Kegan Gardiner, Bob Pease, and Keith Pringle, eds. New York: Routledge. 10–13.

Durkheim, Emile. 1933 [1893]. *The Division of Labour in Society.* Trans. George Simpson. New York: Free Press.

Eliason, Mickey. 2001. "Bi-Negativity: The Stigma Facing Bisexual Men." *Journal of Bisexuality* 1.2/3: 137–54.

Epstein, Steven. 1996. *Impure Science: AIDS, Activism, and the Politics of Knowledge.* Berkeley, CA: University of California Press.

Faith, Karlene. 1993. *Unruly Women.* Vancouver: Press Gang Publishers.

Favazza, Armando R. 1996. *Bodies Under Siege: Self-Mutilation and Body Modification in Culture and Psychiatry.* Baltimore, MD: John Hopkins University Press.

Fiala, Irene Jung. 2003. "Anything New? The Racial Profiling of Terrorists." *Criminal Justice Studies* 16.1: 53–58.

Fillmore, Cathy, and Colleen Anne Dell. 2000. *Prairie Women, Violence, and Self-Harm.* Winnipeg, MB: The Elizabeth Fry Society of Manitoba.

Fishman, Laura T. 1990. *Women at the Wall: A Study of Prisoners' Wives Doing Time on the Outside.* New York: SUNY Press.

Flanagan, Timothy J. 1981. "Dealing with Long-Term Confinement: Adaptive Strategies and Perspectives among Life-Term Prisoners." *Criminal Justice and Behavior* 8.2: 201–22.

Flowers, Paul, Graham Hart, and Claire Marriott. 1999. "Constructing Sexual Health: Gay Men and 'Risk' in the Context of a Public Sex Environment." *Journal of Health Psychology* 4.4: 483–95.

Fong, Mary. 2004. "Multiple Dimensions of Identity." *Communicating Ethnic and Cultural Identity.* Mary Fong and Rueyling Chuang, eds. Toronto: Rowman & Littlefield. 19–34.

Foucault, Michel. 1977. *Discipline and Punish: The Birth of the Prison.* New York: Vintage.

———. 1978. *The History of Sexuality, Vol. 1.* New York: Pantheon Books.

———. 1980. *Power/Knowledge: Selected Interviews and Other Writings 1972–1977.* Colin Gordon, ed. New York: Pantheon Books.

———. 1982. "The Subject and Power," *Critical Inquiry* 8: 778–95.

———. 1985. *The Use of Pleasure: The History of Sexuality, Vol. 2.* Trans. Robert Hurley. New York: Random House.

———. 1986. *The Care of the Self: The History of Sexuality, Vol. 3.* New York: Vintage.

———. 1991. "Governmentality." *The Foucault Effect.* Graham Burchell, Colin Gordon, and Peter Miller, eds. Chicago: University of Chicago Press. 87–104.

———. 1999. *Abnormal: Lectures at the College de France 1974–1975.* Valerio Marchetti and Antonella Salomoni, eds. New York: Picador.

Fox, Ragan C. 2007. "Gays Grow Up: An Interpretive Study on Aging Metaphors and Queer Identity." *Journal of Homosexuality* 52.3/4: 33–61.

Funk, Patricia. 2004. "On the Effective Use of Stigma as a Crime-Deterrent." *European Economic Review* 48.4: 715–28.

Garfinkle, Harold. 1956. "Conditions of Successful Degradation Ceremonies." *American Journal of Sociology* 61: 420–24.

Gergen, Kenneth. 1991. *The Saturated Self: Dilemmas of Identity in Contemporary Life*, 2nd ed. New York: Basic Books.

Giddens, Anthony. 1991. *Modernity and Self-identity: Self and Society in the Late Modern Age*. Cambridge: Polity Press.

Giordano, Peggy C., Stephen A. Cernkovich, and Jennifer L. Rudolph. 2002. "Gender, Crime, and Desistance: Toward a Theory of Cognitive Transformation." *The American Journal of Sociology* 107.4: 990–1064.

Girshick, Lori B. 1996. *Soledad Women: Wives of Prisoners Speak Out*. Westport, CT: Praeger.

Goffman, Erving. 1959. *The Presentation of Self in Everyday Life*. New York: Anchor.

———. 1961. *Asylums*. New York: Anchor Books.

———. 1963a. *Stigma: Notes on the Management of Spoiled Identity*. Englewood Cliffs, NJ: Prentice-Hall.

———. 1963b. *Behavior in Public Places: Notes on the Social Organization of Gatherings*. New York: The Free Press.

———. 1967. *Interaction Ritual*. Garden City, NY: Doubleday.

Gray, David E. 2002. "'Everybody Just Freezes. Everybody Is Just Embarrassed': Felt and Enacted Stigma among Parents of Children with High Functioning Autism." *Sociology of Health and Illness* 24.6: 734–49.

Green, Jamison. 2005. "Part of the Package: Ideas of Masculinity among Male-Identified Transpeople." *Men and Masculinities* 7.3: 291–99.

Gutting, Gary. 2005. *Foucault: A Very Short Introduction*. Oxford: Oxford University Press.

Hacking, Ian. 2004. "Between Michel Foucault and Erving Goffman: Between Discourse in the Abstract and Face-to-Face Interaction." *Economy and Society* 33.3: 277–302.

Hadfield, Jo, Dora Brown, Louise Pembroke, and Mark Hayward. 2009. "Analysis of Accident and Emergency Doctors' Responses to Treating People who Self-Harm." *Qualitative Health Research* 19.6: 755–65.

Hall, Stuart. 1996. "Introduction: Who Needs Identity?" *Questions of Cultural Identity*. Stuart Hall and Paul du Gay, eds. Princeton, NJ: Princeton University Press. 1–17.

Hallgrimsdottir, Helga K., Rachel Phillips, Cecilia Benoit, and Kevin Walby. 2008. "Sporting Girls, Streetwalkers, and Inmates of Houses of Ill-Repute: Media Narratives and the Historical Mutability of Prostitution Stigmas." *Sociological Perspectives* 51.1: 119–38.

Haggerty, Kevin, and Ericson Richard. 2000. "The Surveillant Assemblage." *British Journal of Sociology* 51.4: 605–22.

Hannah-Moffat, Kelly. 2000. "Prisons that Empower: Neo-Liberal Governance in Canadian Women's Prisons." *British Journal of Criminology* 40: 510–31.

———. 2001. *Punishment in Disguise: Penal Governance in Canadian Women's Prisons*. Toronto: University of Toronto Press.

Hannem, Stacey N. 2008. *Marked by Association: Stigma, Marginalisation, Gender and the Families of Male Prisoners in Canada*. Doctoral Dissertation. Ottawa: Carleton University.

———. 2011. "Stigma, Marginality, Gender and the Families of Male Prisoners in Canada." *Critical Criminology in Canada: New Voices, New Directions*. A. Doyle and D. Moore, eds. Vancouver: University of British Columbia Press.

Harding, David J. 2003. "Jean Valjean's Dilemma: The Management of Ex-Convict Identity in the Search for Employment." *Deviant Behavior* 24.6: 571–95.

Hayman, Stephanie. 2006. *Imprisoning Our Sisters: The New Federal Women's Prisons in Canada.* Montreal: McGill-Queens University Press.

Healey, David. 2003. *Let Them Eat Prozac: The Unhealthy Relationship between the Pharmaceutical Industry and Depression.* New York: New York University Press.

Hebl, Michelle R., Jennifer Tickle, and Todd F. Heatherton. 2000. "Awkward Moments in Interactions between Nonstigmatized and Stigmatized Individuals." *The Social Psychology of Stigma.* Todd F. Heatherton, Robert E. Kleck, Michelle R. Hebl, and J. G. Hull, eds. New York: Guilford Press. 275–306.

Heney, Jan. 1990. Report on Self-Injurious Behaviour in the Kingston Prison for Women. Ottawa: Correctional Service Canada.

———, and Connie M. Kristiansen. 1997. "An Analysis of the Impact of Prison on Women Survivors of Childhood Sexual Abuse." *Women and Therapy* 20.4: 29–44.

Herek, Gregory. 1999. "AIDS and Stigma." *American Behavioral Scientist* 42.8: 1106–16.

———. 2004. "Beyond 'Homophobia': Thinking about Sexual Prejudice and Stigma in the Twenty-First Century." *Sexuality Research and Social Policy* 1.2: 6–24.

———, and John P. Capitanio. 1999. "AIDS, Stigma and Sexual Prejudice." *American Behavioral Scientist* 42.7: 1130–47.

House of Hope. 2003. *Families of Offenders Awareness Campaign.* Ottawa: House of Hope/Ministry of Public Safety and Emergency Preparedness.

Irwin, John. 1970. *The Felon.* Englewood Cliffs, NJ: Prentice-Hall.

Jamieson, Ruth, and Adrian Grounds. 2002. *No Sense of an Ending: The Effects of Long-Term Imprisonment amongst Republican Prisoners and their Families.* Republic of Ireland: Seesyu Press.

Janoff, Douglas. 2005. *Pink Blood: Homophobic Violence in Canada.* Toronto: University of Toronto Press.

Jeffrey, Leslie Ann, and Gayle MacDonald. 2006. *Sex Workers in the Maritimes Talk Back.* Vancouver: University of British Columbia Press.

Jeffreys, Sheila. 2000. "'Body Art' and Social Status: Cutting, Piercing, and Tattooing from a Feminist Perspective." *Feminism and Psychology* 10.4: 409–29.

Johnston, Denise. 1995. *Effects of Parental Incarceration.* Eagle Rock, CA: Centre for Children of Incarcerated Parents.

Jones, Anne. 1986. "Self-Mutilation in Prison: A Comparison of Mutilators and Nonmutilators." *Criminal Justice and Behaviour* 13.3: 286–96.

Jussim, Lee, Polly Palumbo, Celina Chatman, Stephanie Madon, and Alison Smith. 2000. "Stigma and Self-Fulfilling Prophecies." *The Social Psychology of Stigma.* Todd F. Heatherton, Robert E. Kleck, Michelle R. Hebl, and J. G. Hull, eds. New York: Guilford Press. 374–418.

Kampf, Antje. 2008. "A 'Little World of Your Own': Stigma, Gender and Narratives of Venereal Disease Contact Tracing." *Health* 12.2: 233–50.

Kanuha, Valli Kalei. 1999. "The Social Process of 'Passing' to Manage Stigma: Acts of Internalized Oppression or Acts of Resistance?" *Journal of Sociology and Social Welfare* 24.4: 27–46.

Kaufman, Joanne, and Cathryn Johnson. 2004. "Stigmatized Individuals and the Process of Identity." *The Sociological Quarterly* 45.4: 807–33.

Kaye, Kerwin. 2003. "Male Prostitution in the Twentieth Century: Pseudohomosexuals, Hoodlum Homosexuals, and Exploited Teens." *Journal of Homosexuality* 46.1/2: 1–77.

Kendall, Kathy. 2000. "Governing Female Prisons through the Psychological Sciences." *An Ideal Prison? Critical Essays on Women's Imprisonment in Canada*. Kelly Hannah-Moffat and Margaret Shaw, eds. Halifax: Fernwood Publishing. 82–93.

Kershaw, Anne, and Mary Lasovich. 1991. *Rock-a-bye Baby: A Death Behind Bars*. Toronto: Oxford University Press.

Kilty, Jennifer M. 2006. "Under the Barred Umbrella: Is there Room for a Women-Centred Self-Injury Policy in Canadian Corrections?" *Journal of Criminology and Public Policy* 5.1: 161–82.

———. 2008. *Resisting Confined Identities: Women's Strategies of Coping in Prison*. Doctoral Dissertation. Burnaby, BC: Simon Fraser University.

Kimmel, Michael S. 1997. "Masculinity as Homophobia: Fear, Shame and Silence in the Construction of Gender Identity." *Towards a New Psychology of Gender*. Mary M. Gergen and Sara N. Davis, eds. Westport: Praeger. 223–42.

Kinsman, Gary. 2000. "Constructing Gay Men and Lesbians as National Security Risks." *Whose National Security? Canadian State Surveillance and the Creation of Enemies*. Gary Kinsman, Dieter K. Buse, and Mercedes Steedman, eds. Toronto: Between the Lines. 143–53.

———, and Patrizia Gentile. 2010. *The Canadian War on Queers: National Security as Sexual Regulation*. Vancouver: University of British Columbia Press.

Kirby, Michael J. L., and Wilbert Joseph Keon. 2006. *Out of the Shadows at Last: Transforming Mental Health, Mental Illness and Addiction Services in Canada. Final report of the Standing Senate Committee on Social Affairs, Science and Technology*. Ottawa: Government of Canada.

Kissane, Rebecca Joyce. 2003. "What's Need Got to Do With It? Barriers to Use of Non-Profit Social Services." *Journal of Sociology and Social Welfare* 30.2: 127–48.

Kitsuse, John I. 1980. "Coming Out All Over: Deviants and the Politics of Social Problems." *Social Problems* 28.1: 1–13.

Kundnani, Arun. 2002. "An Unholy Alliance? Racism, Religion and Communalism." *Race and Class* 44.2: 71–80.

Kusow, Abdi M. 2004. "Contesting Stigma: On Goffman's Assumptions of Normative Order." *Symbolic Interaction* 27.2: 179–97.

Laub, John H., and Robert J. Sampson. 2001. "Understanding Desistance from Crime." *Crime and Justice* 28: 1–69.

LeBel, Thomas P., Ros Burnett, Shadd Maruna, and Shawn Bushway. 2008. "The 'Chicken and Egg' of Subjective and Social Factors in Desistance from Crime." *European Journal of Criminology* 5.2: 131–59.

Leinen, Stephen. 1993. *Gay Cops*. New Brunswick, NJ: Rutgers University Press.

Lemert, Edwin. 1951. *Social Pathology: A Systematic Approach to the Theory of Sociopathic Behavior*. New York: McGraw-Hill.

———. 1967. *Human Deviance, Social Problems, and Social Control*. Englewood Cliffs, NJ: Prentice-Hall.

Lerner, Melvin J. 1965. "Evaluation of Performance as a Function of Performer's Reward and Attractiveness." *Journal of Personality and Social Psychology* 1.4: 355–60.

———. 1970. "The Desire for Justice and Reactions to Victims." *Altruism and Helping Behaviour*. J. Macaulay and L. Berkowitz, eds. New York: Academic Press. 205–29.

———. 1980. *The Belief in a Just World: A Fundamental Delusion*. New York: Plenum.

Lewis, Jacqueline, Eleanor Maticka-Tyndale, Frances Shaver, and Heather Shramm. 2005. "Managing Risk and Safety on the Job: The Experiences of Canadian Sex Workers." *Journal of Psychology and Human Sexuality* 17.1/2: 147–68.

Lewis, Jacqueline, Eleanor Maticka-Tyndale, and Frances Shaver. 2006. *Safety, Security and the Well-Being of Sex Workers: A Report Submitted to the House of Commons Subcommittee on Solicitation Laws*. Windsor, ON: Sex Trade Advocacy and Research (STAR).

Liebling, Alison. 1994. "Suicides amongst Women Prisoners." *Howard Journal* 33.1: 1–9.

Link, Bruce G., and Jo C. Phelan. 2001. "Conceptualizing Stigma." *Annual Review of Sociology* 27: 363–85.

Linneman, Thomas. 2000. "Risk and Masculinity in Everyday Lives of Gay Men." *Gay Masculinities*. Peter Nardi, ed. London: Sage. 83–100.

Lloyd, Ann. 1995. *Doubly Deviant, Doubly Damned: Society's Treatment of Violent Women*. London: Penguin Books.

Lowman, John. 2000. "Violence and the Outlaw Status of (Street) Prostitution in Canada." *Violence against Women* 6.9: 987–1011.

Lyon, David. 2001. *Surveillance Society: Monitoring Everyday Life*. Philadelphia, PA: Open University Press.

Mahalingam, Ramaswami. 2003. "Essentialism, Culture, and Beliefs about Gender among the Arvanis of Tamil Nadu, India." *Sex Roles: A Journal of Research* 49.9/10: 489–96.

Maidment, Madonna R. 2006a. "Not All That Criminal: Getting Beyond the Pathologizing and Individualizing of Women's Crime." *Women and Therapy* 29.3/4: 35–56.

———. 2006b. *Doing Time on the Outside: Deconstructing the Benevolent Community*. Toronto: University of Toronto Press.

Marquart, James W., and Julian B. Roebuck. 1985. "Prison Guards and 'Snitches': Deviance within a Total Institution." *British Journal of Criminology* 25.3: 217–33.

Maruna, Shadd, Thomas P. Lebel, Nick Mitchell, and Michelle M. Naples. 2004. "Pygmalion in the Reintegration Process: Desistance from Crime through the Looking Glass." *Psychology, Crime and Law* 10.3: 271–81.

Marvasti, Amir, and Karyn McKinney. 2004. *Middle-Eastern Lives in America*. Lanham: Rowman & Littlefield Publishers.

Massage Therapy Act, S.O. 1991, C-27, amended to O. Reg. 474/99.

Mathiesen, Thomas. 2000. *Prison On Trial*. Winchester, UK: Waterside Press.

May, Hazel. 2000. "Murderers' Relatives: Managing Stigma, Negotiating Identity." *Journal of Contemporary Ethnography* 29.2: 198–221.

McDonough, Jodi. 2001. *Indelible Impressions: Tattoos and Tattooing in Context of Incarceration*. MA Thesis. Ottawa: University of Ottawa.

McDowell, Linda, and Gillian *Court. 1994.* "Performing Work: Bodily Representations in Merchant Banks." *Environment and Planning D: Society and Space* 12.6: 727–50.

Meyer, Ilan. 1995. "Minority Stress and Mental Health in Gay Men." *Journal of Health and Social Behavior* 36.1: 38–56.

Miller, Carol T., and Cheryl R. Kaiser. 2001. "A Theoretical Perspective on Coping with Stigma." *Journal of Social Issues* 57.1: 73–92.

Miller, Dusty. 1994. *Women Who Hurt Themselves.* New York: Basic Books.

Miller, Tracy. 2009. *Mapping the Global Muslim Population: A Report on the Size and Distribution of the World's Muslim Population.* <http://pewforum.org/newassets/images/reports/Muslimpopulation/Muslimpopulation.pdf> accessed October 8, 2009.

Morris, Jessica F., Kimberly Balsam, and Esther D. Rothblum. 2002. "Lesbian and Bisexual Mothers and Nonmothers: Demographics and the Coming-Out Process." *Journal of Family Psychology* 16.2: 144–56.

Mullaly, Bob. 2002. *Challenging Oppression: A Critical Social Work Approach.* Toronto: Oxford University Press.

NARCC, National Anti-Racism Council of Canada. 2007. *Racial Discrimination in Canada.* Toronto: NARCC

Nardi, Peter M. 1999. *Gay Men's Friendships: Invincible Communities.* Chicago: University of Chicago Press.

Nelson, Daniel N. 1994. "Introduction: After Authoritarianism." *After Authoritarianism: Democracy or Disorder?* Daniel Nelson, ed. Westport, CT: Greenwood Publishing. vii–x.

Noble, Jean Bobby. 2006. *Sons of the Movement: FTMs Risking Incoherence on a Post-Queer Cultural Landscape.* Toronto: Women's Press.

O'Malley, Pat. 2001. "Risk, Crime and Prudentialism Revisited." *Crime, Risk and Justice: The Politics of Crime Control in Liberal Democracies.* Kevin Stenson and Robert R. Sullivan, eds. Portland, OR: Willan Publishing. 89–103.

Ontario Municipal Act, S.O. 2001, c. 25.

Orbe, Mark P., and Tina M. Harris. 2001. *Interracial Communication: Theory into Practice.* Belmont, CA: Wadsworth/Thompson Learning.

Ottawa Police Services, *Community Safety Letter.* <http://www.ottawapolice.ca/en/CrimePrevention/CommunitySafetyLetter.aspx>.

Oyserman, Daphna, and Janet K. Swim. 2001. "Stigma: An Insider's View." *Journal of Social Issues* 57.1: 1–14.

Pager, Devah. 2007. *Marked: Race, Crime, and Finding Work in an Era of Mass Incarceration.* Chicago, IL: University of Chicago Press.

Palmore, Erdman B. 1999. *Ageism: Negative and Positive.* New York: Springer Publishing.

Parent, Collette, and Chris Bruckert. 2005. "Le travail du sexe dans les établissement érotiques: une forme de travail marginalisé." *Déviance et Société* 29.1: 33–53.

Parker, Richard, and Peter Aggleton. 2003. "HIV and AIDS Related Stigma and Discrimination: A Conceptual Framework and Implications for Action." *Social Science and Medicine* 57: 13–24.

Peters, Debra K., and Lillian M. Range. 1996. "Self-Blame and Self-Destruction in Women Sexually Abused as Children." *Journal of Child Sexual Abuse* 5.4: 19–33.

Petersilia Joan. 2001. "Prisoner Re-entry: Public Safety and Reintegration Challenges." *Prison Journal* 81.3: 360–75.

Pheterson, Gail. 1996. The Prostitution Prism. Amsterdam: Amsterdam Press.

Pickett, Brent L. 1996. "Foucault and the Politics of Resistance." *Polity* 28.4: 445–66.

Pinel, Elizabeth C. 2004. "You're Just Saying That Because I'm a Woman: Stigma Consciousness and Attributions to Discrimination." *Self and Identity* 3: 39–41.

Plummer, Kenneth. 1975. *Sexual Stigma: An Interactionist Account.* London: Routledge.

———. 1995. *Telling Sexual Stories: Power, Change and Social Worlds.* London: Routledge.

Pollack, Shoshana. 2006. "Therapeutic Programming as a Regulatory Practice in Women's Prisons." *Criminalizing Women*. Elizabeth Comack and Gillian Balfour, eds. Halifax: Fernwood Publishing. 236–49.

———, and Kathy Kendall. 2005. "Taming the Shrew: Mental Health Policy with Women in Canadian Federal Prisons." *Critical Criminology: An International Journal* 13.1: 71–87.

Polsky, Ned. 1967. *Hustlers, Beats and Others*. New Jersey: Aldine/Transaction Publishers.

Poon, Maurice K., and Peter T. Ho. 2008. "Negotiating Social Stigma among Gay Asian Men." *Sexualities* 11.1/2: 245–68.

Public Safety Canada. 2010. *Corrections and Conditional Release Statistical Overview Annual Report 2010*. Accessed online at http://www.publicsafety.gc.ca/res/cor/rep/2010-ccrso-eng.aspx#d8.

Ramirez, Deborah A., Jennifer Hoopes, and Tara Lai Quinland. 2003. "Defining Racial Profiling in a Post-September 11 World." *American Criminal Law* 40.3: 1195–1210.

Ramirez-Valles, Jesus, Stevenson Fergus, Carol Reisen, Paul Poppen, and Maria C. Zea. 2005. "Confronting Stigma: Community Involvement and Psychological Well-Being among HIV-Positive Latino Gay Men." *Hispanic Journal of Behavioral Sciences* 27.1: 101–19.

Ratner, Michael. 2005. "The Guantanamo Prisoners." *America's Disappeared: Secret Imprisonment, Detainees, and the War on Terror*. Rachel Meeropol, ed. New York: Seven Stories Press. 31–59.

Redman, Peter. 1997. "Invasion of the Monstrous Others: Heterosexual Masculinities, the 'AIDS Carrier' and the Horror Genre." *Border Patrols: Policing the Boundaries of Heterosexuality*. Deborah Steinberg, Debbie Epstein, and Richard Johnson, eds. London: Cassell. 98–117.

Reinharz, Shulamit. 1992. *Feminist Methods in Social Research*. New York: Oxford University Press.

Remis, R. 2008. *Epidemiology of HIV in Ontario: Update to 2008*. AIDS and Drug Prevention Community Investment Programs. Toronto Public Health. Toronto. November 25, 2008.

Ricordeau, Gwendola. 2008. *Les Détenus et leurs proches: Solidarités et sentiments à l'ombre des murs*. Paris: Éditions Autrements.

Riessman, Catherine K. 2000. "Stigma and Everyday Resistance Practices: Childless Women in South India." *Gender and Society* 14.1: 111–35.

Roach, Kent. 2003. *September 11: Consequences for Canada*. Montreal/Kingston: McGill-Queen's University Press.

Rocke, Michael. 1996. *Forbidden Friendships: Homosexuality and Male Culture in Renaissance Florence*. New York: Oxford University Press.

Rose, Nicolas. 1996. "The Death of the Social? Refiguring the Territory of Government." *Economy and Society* 25.3: 327–56.

Ross, Robert R., and Hugh B. McKay. 1979. *Self-Mutilation*. Lexington, MA: D.C. Health.

Said, Edward W. 1978. *Orientalism*. New York: Vintage.

Scheff, Thomas J. 2005. "Looking-Glass Self: Goffman as Symbolic Interactionist." *Symbolic Interaction* 28.2: 147–66.

Schilt, Kristen. 2006. "Just One of the Guys? How Transmen Make Gender Visible at Work." *Gender and Society* 20.4: 465–90.

Schneller, Donald P. 1975. "Prisoners' Families: A Study of Some Social and Psychological Effects of Incarceration on the Families of Negro Prisoners." *Criminology* 12.4: 402–12.

———. 1976. *The Prisoner's Family: A Study of the Effects of Imprisonment on the Families of Prisoners.* San Francisco, CA: R & E Research Associates.

Schur, Edwin M. 1971. *Labeling Deviant Behavior: Its Sociological Implications.* New York: Harper & Row.

———. 1980. *The Politics of Deviance: Stigma Contests and the Uses of Power.* Englewood Cliffs, NJ: Prentice-Hall.

Schwalbe, Michael, Sandra Godwin, Daphne Holden, Douglas Schrock, Shelay Thompson, and Michele Wolkomir. 2000. "Generic Processes in the Reproduction of Inequality: An Interactionist Analysis." *Social Forces* 79.2: 419–52.

Scott, James. 1990. "Behind the Official Story." *Domination and the Arts of Resistance: Hidden Transcripts.* James Scott, ed. New Haven, CT: Yale University Press.

Scott, John. 2003. "A Prostitute's Progress: Male Prostitution in Scientific Discourse." *Social Semiotics* 13.2: 179–99.

Sharp, Susan F. 2005. *Hidden Victims: The Effects of the Death Penalty on Families of the Accused.* New Brunswick, NJ: Rutgers University Press.

Shaver, Fran. 1985. "Prostitution: A Critical Analysis of Three Policy Approaches." *Canadian Public Policy* 11: 493–503.

———. 2012. "Legislative Approaches to Prostitution: A Critical Introduction." *Reading Sociology: Canadian Perspectives*, 2nd ed. Lorne Tepperman and Angela Kalyta, eds. Toronto: Oxford University Press.

Siegel, Karolynn, Howard Lune, and Ilan Meyer. 1998. "Stigma Management among Gay/Bisexual Men with HIV/AIDS." *Qualitative Sociology* 21.1: 3–24.

Sigelman, Carol K., Jennifer L. Howell, David P. Cornell, John D. Cutright, and Janine C. Dewey. 1991. "Courtesy Stigma: The Social Implication of Associating with a Gay Person." *Journal of Social Psychology* 131.1: 45–56.

Sim, Joe. 2005. "At the Centre of the New Professional Gaze: Women, Medicine and Confinement." *Women, Madness and the Law: A Feminist Reader.* Wendy Chan, Dorothy E. Chunn, and Robert Menzies, eds. London: Glasshouse Press. 211–26.

Smart, Laura, and Daniel M. Wegner. 2000. "The Hidden Costs of Hidden Stigma." *The Social Psychology of Stigma.* Todd F. Heatherton, Robert E. Kleck, Michelle R. Hebl, and Jay G. Hull, eds. New York: The Guilford Press. 220–42.

Smith, Dorothy. 1990. *Texts, Facts and Femininity.* London: Routledge.

Smith, Gabie, Kate Mysak, and Stephen Michael. 2008. "Sexual Double Standards and Sexually Transmitted Illnesses: Social Rejection and Stigmatization of Women." *Sex Roles: A Journal of Research* 58.5/6: 391–401.

Snow, David A. 2001. "Extending and Broadening Blumer's Conceptualization of Symbolic Interactionism." *Symbolic Interaction* 24.3: 367–77.

Stella. 2003. *The Art of Striptease.* Montreal: Stella.

Steyn, Johan. 2004. "Guantanamo Bay: The Legal Black Hole." *International and Comparative Law Quarterly* 53.1: 1–15.

Stiles, Beverly L., and Howard B. Kaplan. 1996. "Stigma, Deviance, and Negative Social Sanctions." *Social Science Quarterly* 77.3: 685–96.

Strong, Marilee. 1998. *A Bright Red Scream: Self-mutilation and the Language of Pain.* New York: Penguin Books.

Sykes, Gresham, and Matza, David. 1957. "Techniques of Neutralization: A Theory of Delinquency." *American Sociological Review* 22: 664–70.

Szasz, Thomas. 1961. *The Myth of Mental Illness: Foundations of a Theory of Personal Conduct.* London: Secker.

———. 1971. *The Manufacture of Madness: A Comparative Study of the Inquisition and the Mental Health Movement.* London: Routledge.

Tannenbaum, Frank. 1938. *Crime and the Community*. Boston: Ginn.

Task Force on Federally Sentenced Women. 1990. Creating Choices: Report of the Task Force on Federally Sentenced Women. Ottawa: Ministry of the Solicitor General.

Thompson, Edward H., and Patrick M. Whearty. 2004. "Older Men's Social Participation: The Importance of Masculinity Ideology." *The Journal of Men's Studies* 13.1: 5–24.

Thompson, Paul. 2004. *The Terror Timeline, Year by Year, Day by Day, Minute by Minute: A Comprehensive Chronicle of the Road to 9/11 and America's Response*. New York: Ragan Books/HarperCollins Publishers.

Travis, Jeremy. 2002. "Invisible Punishment: An Instrument of Social Exclusion." *Invisible Punishment: The Collateral Consequences of Mass Imprisonment.* Marc Mauer and Meda Chesney-Lind, eds. New York: New Press. 15–36.

———, Elizabeth Cincotta McBride, and Amy L. Solomon. 2003. *Families Left Behind: The Hidden Costs of Incarceration and Reentry.* Urban Institute: Justice Policy Center.

———, and Joan Petersilia. 2001. "Reentry Reconsidered: A New Look at an Old Question." *Crime and Delinquency* 47.3: 291–313.

Turell, Susan C., and Mary W. Armsworth. 2003. "A Log-Linear Analysis of Variables Associated with Self-Mutilation Behaviors of Women with Histories of Child Sexual Abuse." *Violence Against Women* 9.4: 487–512.

Uggen, Chris, Jeff Manza, and Angela Behrens. 2004. "Less than the Average Citizen: Stigma, Role Transition and the Civic Reintegration of Convicted Felons." *After Crime and Punishment: Pathways to Offender Reintegration.* Shadd Maruna and Russ Immarigeon, eds. Portland, OR: Willan Publishing. 261–93.

Ussher, Jane M. 1991. *Women's Madness: Misogyny or Mental Illness?* Amherst, MA: University of Massachusetts Press.

Valverde, Marianna. 1989. "Beyond Gender Dangers and Private Pleasures: Theory and Ethics in the Sex Debates." *Feminist Studies* 15.2: 237–54.

Van Brakel, Wim. 2006. "Measuring Health-Related Stigma: A Literature Review." *Psychology, Health, and Medicine* 11.3: 307–34.

van der Meulen, Emily, and Elya Maria Durisin. 2008. "Why Decriminalize? How Canada's Municipal and Federal Regulations Increase Sex Workers' Vulnerability." *Canadian Journal of Women and the Law* 20: 289–311.

Van Dijk, Teun A. 1993. "Principles of Critical Discourse Analysis." *Discourse and Society* 4.2: 249–83.

Vierucci, Luisa. 2003. "Prisoners of War or Protected Person qua Unlawful Combatants? The Judicial Safeguards to which Guantanamo Bay Detainees are Entitled." *Journal of International Criminal Justice* 1.2: 284–314.

Virginia Commission on Youth. 2002. *Children of Incarcerated Parents: To the Governor and the General Assembly of Virginia, Commission on Youth Document.* Richmond, VA.

Wacquant, Loic. 2007. *Urban Outcasts: A Comparative Sociology of Advanced Marginality.* Cambridge: Polity Press.

Walby, Kevin. 2009a. "Surveillance of Male-with-Male Public Sex in Ontario, 1983–1994." *Surveillance: Power, Problems and Politics.* Sean Hier and Josh Greenberg, eds. Vancouver: University of British Columbia Press. 46–58.

———. 2009b. "'He Asked Me If I Was Looking For Fags…' Ottawa's National Capital Commission Conservation Officers and the Policing of Eroticism in Public Parks." *Surveillance and Society* 6.4: 367–79

———. 2010. "Interviews as Encounters: Issues of Sexuality and Reflexivity When Men Interview Men about Commercial Same Sex Relations." *Qualitative Research* 10.6: 639–57.

Ward, James. 2008. *Sexualities, Work and Organizations: Stories by Gay Men and Women in the Workplace at the Beginning of the Twenty-First Century.* London: Routledge.

Weeks, Jeffrey. 1981. *Sex, Politics and Society: The Regulation of Sexuality since 1800.* London: Longman.

White, Ruth, and Robert Carr. 2005. "Homosexuality and HIV/AIDS Stigma in Jamaica." *Culture, Health and Society* 7.4: 347–59.

Whiteford, Linda M., and Lois Gonzalez. 1995. "Stigma: The Hidden Burden of Infertility." *Social Science and Medicine* 40.1: 27–36.

Wichmann, Cherami, Ralph Serin, and Jeffrey Abracen. 2002. *Women Offenders who Engage in Self-Harm: A Comparative Investigation.* Ottawa: Correctional Service of Canada.

Willis, Paul. 1981. *Learning to Labor: How Working Class Kids Get Working Class Jobs.* New York: Columbia University Press.

Withers, Lloyd. 2003. *A Strategic Approach and Policy Document to Address the Needs of Families of Offenders: Safety, Respect and Dignity for All.* Kingston: Canadian Families and Corrections Network.

Contributors

Chris Bruckert is an Associate Professor in the Department of Criminology at the University of Ottawa. Since receiving her PhD from Carleton University in 2000, she has devoted herself to researching various sectors of the Canadian adult sex industry (erotic dance, street level, in-call, and out-call) through the lens of feminist labour theory. She is committed to sex worker rights and endeavours to contribute to the movement as an academic activist.

Dave Dessler is a poet. He lives on a street corner in Ottawa. Dave is the co-author of a volume of poetry and photography entitled *Mindlessly Adrift: Street Poetry by "Crazy" Dave Dessler / My Ottawa Streets: Street Photography* by Jean E. Boulay.

Stacey Hannem is an Assistant Professor in the Department of Criminology at the Brantford Campus of Wilfrid Laurier University. She was formerly an instructor in the Department of Criminology at the University of Ottawa and held a SSHRC postdoctoral fellowship. She completed her PhD in sociology at Carleton University in 2008. Stacey has pursued research and published in the areas of reintegration for sexual offenders, restorative justice, and families affected by incarceration. She is currently the chair of the Canadian Criminal Justice Association's Policy Review Committee and serves on the editorial board of the *Journal of Prisoners on Prisons*.

Charles Huckelbury, Jr. was sentenced to life imprisonment (twenty-five year minimum) at the age of twenty-seven and has spent the last thirty-seven years in prison. Awarded second place in *Prison Life*'s fiction contest in 1995, he won the PEN first prize for fiction in 2001. A regular contributor to the *Journal of Prisoners on Prisons* since 1997, Charles joined the editorial board in 2001. He was one of four featured writers in Shawn Thompson's *Letters from Prison* (2001). His book of poetry, *Tales from the Purple Penguin* (2008) has received wonderful reviews.

Jennifer M. Kilty earned her PhD in criminology from Simon Fraser University in British Columbia. She joined the Department of Criminology at the University of Ottawa as an Assistant Professor in 2008 and also teaches in the Social Science of Health program. Professor Kilty's research interests include criminalized women, theorizing self-harming behaviour, the social construction of dangerous girls and women, transcarceration, penal abolition, and the criminalization of HIV/AIDS.

Nicholas Little is trained as a social worker. He holds two Bachelor degrees from McGill University (Montreal) and a Master's degree in Health, Community, and Development from the London School of Economics. After living in France, Nicholas moved to Ottawa where he worked as an HIV outreach worker in gay bathhouses, bars, and online chatrooms. Nicholas is a founding member of POWER (Prostitutes of Ottawa–Gatineau Work, Educate, and Resist), an organization of current and former sex workers and their allies advocating for recognition of sex workers' labour, Charter rights, and human rights. Nicholas now lives in the United Kingdom.

Melissa Munn received her PhD in Criminology from the University of Ottawa in 2009. She is the co-author (with Chris Bruckert) of *Falling Out of the Rabbit Hole: The Journey from Lengthy Imprisonment to Enduring 'Freedom'* (UBC Press). Melissa has been a prisoners' rights advocate for over two decades and researches in the areas of prisoner release, re-entry, and reintegration. She currently teaches in the sociology and women's studies departments at Okanagan College and in 2011 launched PenalPress.com, a virtual library of penal press materials.

Vajmeh Tabibi was born in Kabul, Afghanistan, and immigrated to Canada with her family in December 1990. She has worked with the Program Department of Correctional Service Canada and earned a Master's degree in Criminology in 2008. Since then, Ms. Tabibi has taught as a part-time instructor in the Department of Criminology at the University of Ottawa.

Kevin Walby is Assistant Professor of Sociology at the University of Victoria, Canada. He is co-editor of *Brokering Access: Power, Politics, and Freedom of Information Process in Canada* with M. Larsen (University of British Columbia Press, 2012) and *Emotions Matter: a Relational Approach to Emotions* with Alan Hunt and D. Spencer (University of Toronto Press, 2012). He is the Prisoners'

Struggles editor for the *Journal of Prisoners on Prisons*. He has many published articles including in *Social and Legal Studies*, *British Journal of Criminology* (with J. Piché), *Punishment and Society* (with J. Piché), and *Crime, Law and Social Change* (with R. Lippert). He is author of *Touching Encounters: Sex, Work, and Male-for-Male Internet Escorting* (University of Chicago Press, 2012).

Index